THE HAND & FLOWERS COOKBOOK
TOM KERRIDGE

PHOTOGRAPHY BY

CRISTIAN BARNETT

BLOOMSBURY ABSOLUTE

LONDON · OXFORD · NEW YORK · NEW DELHI · SYDNEY

Liam Gallagher ✓
@liamgallagher

Hand and Flowers, Marlow. Food of the Gods.
Tom Kerridge fantastic chap LG x

29/03/2015 16:16

To Bef and Acey

Bef, mate, I'm sorry that the three years you gave me at the
beginning took a little longer than expected, and no matter
what your dad says, the water is not that warm.
However, I couldn't think of a better person
to be swimming in it with!

GREENE KING
BURY ST EDMUNDS
The Hand & Flowers
Tel 01628 482277
Accommodation
The Hand & Flowers
INN
CASK MARQUE
GREENE KING

Contents

Introduction

For as long as I can remember, I've had a passion for pubs. I love the heart that they bring to a community, their laid-back vibe and their lack of pretension. I love the user-friendly style of food they offer and the extensive range of products in their well-stocked bars.

I can vividly recall me and my brother, when we were young, sitting in the back of Dad's car travelling to a pub near Whaddon in the Gloucestershire countryside. It was called the Four Mile House and we went there on more than one occasion. Dad would put us in the beer garden, get us a couple of Panda Pops and a packet of crisps, then head off into the bar. We would play for hours in the pub garden, happily kicking a football around until he was ready to go home.

When I was in my teens, I started to play rugby and joined Saintbridge former pupils' rugby club: and that's when I first encountered beer and ale. After training or a match, we'd all have a drink in the club bar. Everyone would sit around chatting about what had gone on in the past week, and what they'd got planned for the week ahead. Maybe we'd be playing cards or darts. Somehow, we had created a great energy in what was, essentially, just a bare room.

That social aspect of the rugby club – of getting together, regularly, with a core of mates – is available in spades in pubs. I discovered that fact when I was about 16 years old and started going out on a Friday and Saturday night with my mates (and my fake ID!) to try and get into pubs and nightclubs. Pretty standard teenage behaviour, I think, which meant that by the time I was a young man and formally allowed to buy alcohol, pubs had cemented their place in my heart.

That love of pubs was reinforced as I got older, when I began to pop into my local and get to know its regulars. Now, in retrospect, I think, 'Wow, I sat with the same people telling the same stories to each other, over and over again – every week!' But it was (and still is) lovely how people can create a buzz and atmosphere in a pub. It's also nice when you go into your local and don't get caught in a headlock by one of the regulars! Instead, you are welcomed in by a core group of drinkers. Those are the best pubs: buzzy and still a proper local. As a punter, you always feel lucky to stumble across them. They're great places and they're the pubs that succeed.

Given my affection for pubs, it's not surprising that when I was in a position to open my own business, I gravitated towards a pub-restaurant. My career as a chef prior to The Hand & Flowers was spent almost entirely in fine-dining, so I instinctively brought those traditions and standards with me, fusing them with what I loved most about pubs.

I was able to do that because pub food had undergone something of a revolution across the UK. In 2006, not long after The Hand & Flowers opened, we were lucky enough to win a Michelin star – at the same time as the Mason's Arms in Devon, which is owned by chef Mark Dodson. In doing so, we joined a cluster of pubs that had achieved that accolade. I was only 31 years old when I opened The Hand & Flowers and I'm sure it helped to make other young, would-be chef-proprietors realise they could do the same thing: create great food in tiny kitchens, with relatively low overheads.

Things have moved on even more now. People are still opening pub-restaurants very successfully, but pubs in local communities and on small high streets have done so well that they've pushed the British neighbourhood dining scene away from top-end fine-dining or French-style bistros. The pub dining scene broke that 'posh' barrier down; it made it possible for people to go out and eat simple food in lovely, unstuffy environments.

Now, disused shops, old containers and abandoned restaurant sites on the high street are being transformed into places where you can eat some of the most exciting food in the UK. Groundbreaking chef-proprietors on the gastropub scene – the likes of Andrew Pern, Steve Terry, Stephen Harris – showed the way for a new wave of young chefs saying: 'Well, I don't actually need a pub, I can just set up in this little shop.'

That trend helped to lead people back to eating locally. They can pop around the corner, have an amazing meal in a restaurant that has no tablecloths, get a drink at the bar from a tattooed guy with a beard, and watch a chef in a blue-and-white striped apron go about his business in an open kitchen. It's exactly what those of us operating out of pubs have been doing for the last couple of decades; we've been able to show what can be done from very little with a major amount of graft.

I'm very proud to be a part of the British food scene that kicked pub-dining into the limelight; to stand alongside The Star Inn at Harome in Yorkshire, and The Trouble House in Tetbury, Gloucestershire, among many others. Thanks to places like these, you presume that a meal in a pub is going to be good. If you go to any local pub, you expect to be able to get freshly grilled mackerel with a really nice salad, rather than the deep-fried breaded mushrooms and rubbish lasagne of the bad old days!

I know it's not all happy days in the sector, though. Many traditional pubs are closing, unable to balance the books. But they still present plenty of opportunity for good operators to transform those beautiful, characterful buildings, which have a heritage of serving food to the masses and perhaps giving someone a bed for the night, into something to be proud of.

Starry, starry nights

I've always been acutely aware of Michelin stars. In the kitchens I worked in, prior to opening The Hand & Flowers, everyone spoke about them. One of my first jobs, when I was about 18 or 19 and still studying at college, was at Calcot, a luxury hotel in Gloucestershire (actually, not far from The Trouble House), which had a star at the time. At Calcot, there was a level of expectation about what went on the plate and a working practice that was very different from college. It felt pressurised because of the star, and I remember the head chef walked around the place with an air of absolute intent. That put all the young chefs on edge, but if you're ambitious you have to enjoy and be willing to work with a bit of fear – with that feeling of being on the edge, of knowing that you're pushing things to the limit and that one slightly incorrect move can make things go drastically wrong.

A Michelin-starred kitchen is an adrenaline-fuelled and exciting place to be in because you are 'on the push', trying to concentrate on everything that needs to be done. It's a fine line between getting things right and everything crumbling around you. Making it into the Michelin Guide represents a standard reached, and recognition from both fellow chefs and customers that you've arrived.

On the flip side, however, the intimidation felt by some chefs around the Michelin Guide can make working in aspirational kitchens – and even eating in them – unenjoyable for some. It was very typical in the early 1990s, that scenario, but thankfully it's less common now. And I think the gastropub movement helped to break the tension.

The funny thing is, that little red book is hardly more than a guidebook with maps in – it simply tells you where the restaurant is, the type of dishes it serves and what its overall rating is. Michelin didn't create the angst around stars, everybody else (the restaurateurs, the chefs, the press, the customers) did. When I was starting out, we all thought that Michelin stars involved white tablecloths, three different types of amuse-bouche, a pre-starter, a starter, a main course, a pre-dessert, dessert, 11 different types of petits fours, pristine waiters. In reality, Michelin has only ever talked about the food on the plate. And if you just think about the food, not – at least in the first instance – the environment it's served in, then you become ingredient-led, simplified. You zero in on good cooking.

I'd worked that out by the time we opened The Hand & Flowers in 2005. And I'd realised that there was a huge opportunity to use cuts from well-looked-after cows that the top-end restaurants didn't want: after all, the tail, shins, brisket, cheeks come from the same animal as the fillets do, don't they? The same beast that's been cared for, properly, for 18 months. So we opened at The Hand & Flowers with rump steak and shins of beef on the menu, while the fillets went elsewhere.

Prior to opening the pub, I sent Michelin a letter enclosing my CV, saying who I was and that we were opening a restaurant in a pub. But as I had decided I wanted to ditch all the faff associated with fine-dining (amuse-bouche, tablecloths, pre-desserts etc.) I didn't have any expectation of quick recognition. I just wanted us to be about good produce, three courses, à la carte: choice.

It sounds as if I really have an issue with formal fine-dining. I don't! I love the idea of eating at a three-Michelin-starred restaurant once in a while, on special occasions. However, when it came to setting up The Hand & Flowers, I didn't want someone to eat with us once every two years – or worse still, only eat there once to tick it off the dining bucket list then never come back again. I wanted a restaurant that was accessible and friendly, which meant that a high standard of hospitality and professionalism were very important.

Every good restaurant will tell you the same. People should be made to feel welcome when they come through the door. Guests should have an understanding of the menu, have a nice time, enjoy their food, drink what they want, say thank you and leave. It's that simple. Customers should go away thinking, 'that was a lovely evening, thanks very much, see you again.'

Hopefully, our guests feel a buzz when they visit us. I've always hated the idea of quiet restaurants where people are too scared to talk to each other or have a laugh; where the only sound is of glassware or cutlery, or the noise of smartphones taking pictures so that everybody can over-analyse the food, even when they go home. What's wrong with having fun?

Something else bothered me too, when we launched The Hand & Flowers. I couldn't understand why so many chefs worked in restaurants that they didn't eat in. And I still don't get it. Chefs come from all sorts of backgrounds: you can have highly educated people working alongside others who've come from nothing, started washing up and decided they wanted to cook. But in the kitchen, they're all on a level playing field, irrespective of class, economic or cultural background. Our industry is all-embracing. No-one cares where you're from.

That's brilliant. But a lot of chefs find themselves cooking for a very specific group of diners, putting out food that they wouldn't actually eat themselves. I mean, how many chefs eat lobster and caviar at home? Every now and then it might happen because the restaurant is closed for two days and there's some left in the fridge, but no-one goes and buys a tin of caviar on their day off. To my mind, if you're a chef in a restaurant making food for a particular type of customer – one that's never going to be you – you're always second-guessing what that person wants to eat.

The Hand & Flowers was never going to be like that! If you cook food you want to eat then you put your heart and soul into it and *that* is conveyed to the customer. I'm sure it's one of the reasons we have done so well. But The Hand & Flowers wouldn't have opened in its current form or found its feet if my wife Beth and I hadn't gone to The Trouble House in Tetbury while we were visiting my mum. Michael Bedford was chef/proprietor at the time.

Beth and I had been married for five years at this stage. We'd met in the late 1990s on a night out with my flatmate who, together with Beth, worked for the incredible late, great abstract sculptor Sir Anthony Caro, and I was immediately struck by how amazing and dynamic she was. She had her own career, her own path to drive, and an amazing ability to be very headstrong in a competitive marketplace. She's a welder, she deals with molten bronze, she carves things out of stone; all pretty cool. There was never any way that Beth was going to live her life being just the wife of a chef.

And she immediately understood that being a chef is a way of life, because it's the same for artists. When we first moved in together, she never once moaned about the hours I worked. Once we'd taken the decision to set up on our own, she took a break from her art to get the business off the ground. She said she'd give me three years; it was more like eight.

The thing is, Beth has all the natural skills that make a great front-of-house manager. She has a gift for creating a warm and caring environment, which is at the heart of great hospitality. She describes it as wanting to give people a hug, of inviting them into our living room. And that became the reality when we were living upstairs at The Hand & Flowers in the early days.

That meal at The Trouble House showed us the way to go, and how we could translate both of our skill-sets into a business. It was a pivotal moment for us. The great thing about The Trouble House is, number one, it's a pub (on a main road); and number two, when we walked through the door the first thing we clocked was someone standing behind the bar in jeans, T-shirt and a blue-and-white butcher's apron who smiled and said 'hello' like they do in any other pub. It was warm and friendly, and there were a couple of locals at the bar having a drink.

The people serving the food, wearing trainers and jeans, were really lovely and they were also professional. The level of food was a perfect fusion of Gary Rhodes' simplicity and Pierre-Koffmann-like flavour. All the side dishes came out in little copper pots. I remember having red mullet soup to start, a braised beef dish as a main course – beef cheek, I think – and I'm fairly certain we had a soufflé for dessert. Every ounce of flavour was squeezed out of the ingredients in each dish. Beth and I were blown away.

At some point that evening we both went to the loo (not together, I might add); I walked through a small corridor that Michael had covered with framed press clippings, reviews and other bits and bobs, all telling the story of The Trouble House. I paused to take a quick look at them – there were loads – and one paragraph stuck out from the rest: Michael saying that when he was thinking about opening a business, he had stumbled across the idea of taking on a brewery-owned tenancy. Under these terms, the brewery owned the building, while he ran the business. In other words, he didn't have to shoulder things like rent or refurbishment costs entirely on his own.

I returned to the table, sat down, thought, 'that's pretty interesting.' Later, after Beth had seen the cuttings and come back to our table, it turned out she'd zoned in on exactly the same paragraph. This was it! 'Oh my god,' we said to one another, 'we can't easily raise £500,000, but we could take the same approach as Michael. *This* is how we get our restaurant!'

The next day, we were looking on the internet for pub tenancies and The Hand & Flowers stood out on the Greene King website. I said to Beth, 'That's the one. I know that's the one.' And when we went to see it, we saw instantly that it was small enough to be run by the two of us. The kitchen was tiny and the pub itself was manageable – compact enough on a quiet night to still feel cosy, but it would be packed with energy on a busy night. We decided that we would rather have a snug, busy, full place than one that rattled with empty space and lacked atmosphere.

I also knew exactly what kind of food I wanted to cook. My ambition was to focus on flavour-driven cooking, using techniques that would deliver real depth of flavour. And I knew I wanted to simplify dishes, so that the ingredients could speak for themselves. My logic was to make sure everything on the plate was perfect, simple in presentation; but that also means there's no place to hide. You can spot a mistake a mile off.

The truth is, I like simplicity, I like honesty of purpose. As a human being, I'm fairly straightforward, robust, solid, dependable, and my food is the same.

I may love directness and simplicity, but I also love to analyse people and I'm always busy trying to work out what they want to eat. When I travel somewhere new and eat something delicious, I want to know how it's made, where the ingredients are from and what the story is behind a dish. That desire to find out about and analyse things translates, in my cooking, into dishes that have underpinning layers; sometimes several of them. They're deceptively simple, if you want, and that's because cooking in a way that's a natural reflection of who I am has always been important to me.

I'd be lying if I said that getting a Michelin star had been totally erased from my mind when we opened, but it was way down on the list. Of course I wanted a star! But I'd made some stark choices about the kind of food I produced in the kitchen – and at that point I had no idea what the inspectors would think of it.

The results are in

The moment when you learn you've got your first star is very special. It was Daniel Clifford of the amazing Midsummer House in Cambridge who told me we'd won ours. He rang me on the night the 2006 guide was released, when I was winding down after service. When he discovered I hadn't seen the results online, he said: 'Well you better go and have a bloody look then' (or words to that effect). So I did.

I couldn't quite fathom that after only 10 months of being open, we'd won a star. It took a while to sink in. It was particularly unexpected because when Michelin had first inspected us (in an announced visit) I was ill in bed with blood poisoning, feeling horrible, on antibiotics and hallucinating really badly! Chris Mackett, who's now our development chef, was in the kitchen back then and had to carry the cooking without me.

Chris and I had worked together at Adlard's in Norwich (where I'd been able to retain its star), so we were singing from the same hymn sheet. But The Hand & Flowers had only been open about three weeks so we were still finding our feet. I'd been working pretty much 24 hours a day. Beth and I – and our two dogs – were living in a tiny room above the pub, and my best mate (who was running the bar at the time) was in another room. There was just enough space for an office. And controlled chaos downstairs!

The next time Michelin carried out an inspection, the inspector's car was broken into in our car park. It was an unannounced visit that time, but when Beth went out to help clear up the mess that had been left behind, she found Michelin-headed paper everywhere so the cat was out of the bag. After going into turbo-driven mop-up mode, she came into the kitchen and broke the news to me.

My thought process was along the lines of: 'This is the worst thing, the very worst thing, that could happen…' So I launched into damage limitation too, going out to say hello and 'I'm ever so sorry' to the inspector. I ended up having a very open conversation with him, about our business and how things were going at The Hand.

Two things that I said in that conversation have stuck in my mind. The first was something that popped out of my mouth almost accidentally: 'Long term, I'd like to be the Le Manoir of pubs.' I remember writing to Raymond Blanc when I was 18, and being told there was a two-year waiting list for the kitchen. Back in the early 1990s there were only a few restaurants with that kind of draw, where every young chef wanted to go. Le Manoir, La Tante Claire, the Waterside Inn, Le Gavroche. That was it. So I've always thought it would be lovely to be recognised as the equivalent in pubs. But when I said it that night, it felt very far away!

The other thing I distinctly remember was asking the inspector: 'What do you look for in a great restaurant?' and finding out that he benchmarked most meals – particularly at one-star level – on Gary Rhodes' style of food, which was always about what's been taken away from the plate, rather than what you're adding to it. That's because the more you complicate a dish, the more room for error there is. If you are going to put six things on the plate, all six things have to be perfect. The same principle obviously applies if you're only putting three things on the plate. So it reinforced what I was already thinking: to get the highest standard consistently, it's better to put three things on a plate not six things, every time.

I didn't hold back with the inspector in that chat. I was brutally honest about the difficulties we were facing at the time. Things were hard. We struggled for business at the beginning of every week. We had borrowed a lot of money to open The Hand & Flowers so we were permanently stressed about making ends meet.

You tell a few porky pies, don't you, when you believe in something and want it really badly? When we took the pub on, we'd told the bank we were borrowing money to do an extension on our house, then used it to take over the tenancy of The Hand & Flowers instead. With a tenancy, you don't own the lease but you do have to pay for the fixtures and fittings. Essentially, Beth and I were a management couple with a five-year tenancy and we had to show Greene King our books – but any profit, if we made it, was ours.

For our first kitchen, I bought everything from an auction. The fridges had no legs, so they were put on house bricks wrapped in tin foil. I had a six-ring burner and a Falcon Dominator with a gas grill; Beth and I learnt very quickly how to maintain it when it went wrong (so if you ever need a thermocouple changing on a gas solid top, we'll do it for you!). The oven door broke, so we used to put a 25-litre drum of veg oil in front to stop it falling open. Every time you cooked anything in the oven, you'd have to shift the oil drum.

I tiled the kitchen on my own, and I put up the shelves myself. I need to hold my hands up here and admit there was a time when the shelving fell down with all the restaurant crockery on it. We used to serve side dishes in little Le Creuset pots, but when the shelves collapsed, the pots got smashed. That's when I decided to buy some copper pots like the ones I'd seen at The Trouble House, so that when the shelves fell down again, the pots wouldn't break!

Marlow is a brilliant, beautiful town that is incredibly supportive of small businesses. We were lucky that very soon after we opened The Hand & Flowers, word began to spread in the town that this pub, where many locals had sunk their first pint, now had someone cooking good food in it.

After that, our reputation spread to Henley, Beaconsfield and all the surrounding areas, so by the time we won our Michelin star, Saturday nights were usually booked up from the Monday of each week; and the following Saturday would already be half-full. For a small independent business, that created a lovely little buzz. It was great.

Winning the star was a catalyst for national interest in us and we started getting even busier. The business was turning a profit, but costs got bigger too and our profit was immediately reinvested into the business. Because of this, we were always looking for ways to bring in extra funding and when a cottage next to The Hand & Flowers came up for sale, we grabbed the chance to buy it so we would have a couple of rooms to offer guests. The credit crunch hit just as we were deciding whether to go for a second cottage, but we made a decision that it was now or never. We made some compromises and had to deal with the fact that the bank pulled its funding at a crucial moment. It was tough, but when you run a business, you do what you have to in order to survive.

So we put a £10 set lunch on, and I did 48-hour shifts over the weekends in order to be able to make bread after Friday evening service, which Beth would then sell on a Saturday at a little stall in Marlow High Street. Even though we weren't making a single penny on the £10 lunch, we were full at lunchtimes and it generated a vibe. I thought: 'People are coming in, having a great time, spending a tenner. They'll go away thinking this is a great place and they'll come back.' And they did. And we survived.

Double bubble

Winning a second Michelin star in October 2011 was beyond the realms of anything I'd ever dreamt of. It was an incredible achievement for the whole team, driven by a collective passion for food and service, as well as a fantastic reward for having the belief in The Hand & Flowers.

For me, it was a tribute to people like Lourdes Dooley, who ran with an opportunity as a young front-of-house manager and delivered exceptional service with warmth and professionalism. And it was payback for myself, my then head chef Aaron Mulliss, and the whole team pushing to get things relentlessly correct, every single time. The sheer bloody mindedness of never, ever accepting 'that will do'.

I didn't know how to cook two-star food. I just cooked. The Hand & Flowers is the only two-Michelin-starred kitchen I've ever worked in. I can't tell you what goes into achieving that level of food apart from consistency, drive, character and teamwork. Those things all have to sit together, I think.

The moment when we learnt about our second star was captured on video by Michelin. It was a huge moment when I opened the letter and read it aloud to the team. Everyone was over the moon; there were tears. The only thing that wasn't perfect was the fact that Beth was in hospital at the time, following an operation. Obviously, the first thing I did was to ring her, and she responded with whoops of joy.

In the next few hours, and days, we got phone calls and letters from all sorts of people: chefs, people who'd eaten with us, others in the hospitality industry, it was incredible. Naturally, we celebrated a bit! We went over to O'Donoghue's pub (now The Butcher's Tap) after finishing service nice and early. It stayed open late for us and Daniel Clifford drove over all the way from Cambridge to join us.

Then, out of the blue, there was a weird backlash. We went through 18 months of what seemed like a bit of old-school snobbery; of people not understanding how a place without tablecloths and a table that Beth had built from scaffolding boards could achieve two Michelin stars. We got comments about not being like other two-Michelin-starred places, such as The Ledbury and Le Manoir. Well, no, we're not. We're The Hand & Flowers. Some restaurant critics who reviewed us didn't like us. And it meant that in the first six months after being awarded the stars, I had to grow a thick skin, quickly; the same went for the team.

But eventually all that died down, as more and more people began to understand our food and why we were the way we were. In the Michelin guide, The Hand & Flowers entry doesn't have the hotel icon or knife and fork – it's a pint pot, and that's important. We are a pub. Now, in 2020, if you look in the Michelin guide, there are many amazing pubs listed with stars.

The top of the food scene has changed so much and although it might make me a little uncomfortable to say it, I think that The Hand & Flowers getting that second star was a bit of a turning point. There are so many of the country's best chefs cooking outside of posh, table-clothed environments now, putting out shins of beef or oxtail and the like; not using expensive cuts of meat, but treating produce with love and respect. And that's got to be good for the industry and diners, hasn't it? More and more chefs cooking with heart and soul in accessible restaurants.

However, eating out in places that have well-sourced produce isn't necessarily going to be super-cheap. There is always going to be a certain price level because quality produce is expensive and the staff that serve you are professionals who have been working in the industry for a long, long time. They treat hospitality as a career and they care for their guests. They try desperately hard to make a difference. That's why an incredible meal costs what it does.

Today at The Hand

I can't believe The Hand & Flowers has been open for 15 years. I won't lie, at times it's felt like a lifetime! But, mostly, the years seem to have disappeared super-quickly. What I can say, hand on heart, is that the whole process of running our own business has been a hundred times harder than Beth and I ever thought it was going to be. It's one of the most difficult things you can do and I take my hat off to anyone who has a go.

The hospitality industry, particularly restaurants, makes extreme demands on you. There are lunches and dinners to put out; if you do rooms, it's breakfast, lunches and dinners. And you work weekends; when everyone else is relaxing and having a nice time, that's when you are at your busiest. Even today I never feel complacent, either as a chef or with the business in its wider sense. Beth and I both know that we need to keep investing in our business and diversifying it because that will create a safety net.

So things are unrelenting, all-encompassing, all-absorbing. But I find hospitality is also the most wonderful, incredible, fantastic, stunningly brilliant industry to be in! You meet amazing people and you get to do very cool things. You can travel the world. All you have to do is work hard. It doesn't matter what background you are from or what education you've had, if you possess an enthusiasm and a willingness to learn, the ability and drive to push yourself to be better, stronger, faster and quicker than everyone else, you will succeed.

Beth and I made the decision to open The Hand & Flowers because we had confidence in my cooking – based on good produce – and in our vision of a warm welcome for our customers. Our work ethic has been grabbed by every single member of staff who has ever come through The Hand & Flowers door and it's the team who have allowed it to grow; they've harnessed its energy and achieved a level of success that none of us could ever have imagined at the start.

At first, Beth and I thought The Hand & Flowers would simply be a nice place for me to cook good food, and give Beth the freedom to make her art in an uncompromised way. That's all we wanted. Beth's now won the Global Art Award for Sculpture! Her huge, 16-foot marble *Dhow Sail* is positioned in front of the Dubai Opera House. She has her own studio and continues to create new work, free from external pressure or constraints (some of her pieces actually end up being showcased in our restaurants).

I've won amazing, unexpected recognition for my cooking and we've got six other businesses including lovely, big, gorgeous hotel-restaurants in London's West End and the centre of Manchester. We also have a brilliant foundation on which to bring up our little man, Acey. And it's all built on this tiny little pub in Marlow, west of London.

The recipes in this book reflect the journey we have been on since 2005. Some dishes are on the menu now (such as smoked haddock omelette and the crème brûlée), some have come and gone, and others will no doubt make a return. That's been the interesting thing about doing this; reacquainting myself with some of those earliest recipes and finding that they could easily sit on the menu now. The process has been fascinating. The recipes chart the past 15 years at The Hand & Flowers, they show how we have driven dishes forward, pushed flavour forward. And I've no doubt the next 15 years will see us doing exactly the same.

Whatever happens now, it's in the hands of our super-talented team, still driven by me and Beth. Is there more to come from The Hand & Flowers? Maybe. What I'm certain of is that there's a lot still to come from the people who bring it to life each and every day. And that's really the next journey.

Twenty-four hours

at The Hand & Flowers

My wife Beth and I lived above the pub when it first opened, and so it literally did start off as 'twenty-four hours' for us. We always felt that if we were paying rent for a pub that's open 365 days of the year, we had to try and maximise every little bit of energy – and opportunity to trade – from it. From the early-morning deliveries by our fish and fruit and veg suppliers to the last customers departing and the team cleaning down after service, it doesn't feel like The Hand & Flowers ever actually goes to sleep, especially now that we also offer a bed for the night to room guests. It's like a generator – a tiny, magical building that's constantly whirring and buzzing.

Midnight The last customers have left, the senior team are filling out their end-of-service reports and the bar staff are cleaning down.

5am Fresh produce starts arriving.

8.45am The deliveries are unpacked and checked against stock.

10am Breakfast is in full flow for our room guests.

10.30am The dough for our soda bread is prepared.

10.45am Final stages of mise-en-place.

11am Team briefing, prior to service.

12.30pm Lunch service is underway.

3pm Bedrooms are checked before the new room guests arrive.

5.15pm Staff tea.

8pm Dinner service is in full swing.

11.10pm The kitchen starts its clean down.

Midnight The ovens are off, the kitchen is clean, ready for tomorrow.

STARTERS

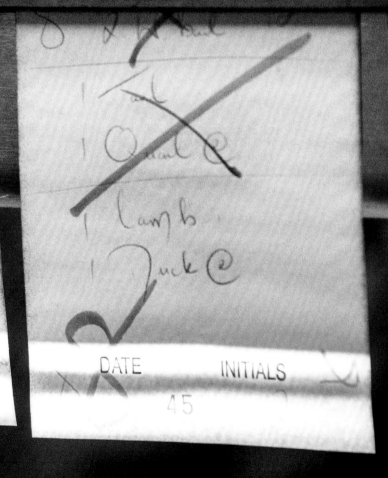

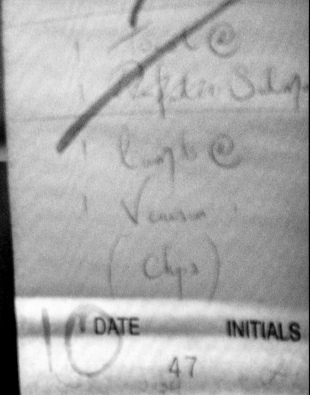

From the first moment we started planning the launch of The Hand & Flowers, I knew we were going to be offering a three-course, à la carte menu: starters, mains, desserts. Nothing complicated, nothing too over the top.

After years of honing my craft in other chefs' kitchens, I'd learnt that the perfect starter menu often included a terrine, a soup, a hot starter and a smoked (or cured) fish. I was confident that if we included these four options at The Hand & Flowers, they'd do well.

Starters come from a kitchen's larder section, in larger kitchens. My own time as a chef has pretty much always been spent around the larder or sauce sections, and I love the process of larder work. There's always lots to get set up and ready for lunch, as well as constantly preparing for something further down the road. There are processes that might take a week or so, such as cooking, pressing and piecing together the different elements of a terrine. You've always got to be thinking ahead; that's how a professional kitchen works and I love the challenge of it.

The sauce section is where the mains get sent out from. It's true that chefs are normally handling the most expensive ingredients at that point and you can't afford to mess up, but everything starts in the larder. If you push all the starters out at the same time, then that's going to have a knock-on effect on the sauce section and its team will struggle to deliver all their dishes simultaneously. You must never be slow, but you have to be well-paced and well-organised as well as fast. When you are on the larder section, you dictate the pace of the kitchen. You're running the show.

As a larder-based chef, you can create the pretty dishes that form a diner's first impression of a place. If you like, you're throwing a ball up in the air for the sauce section, and then hitting it out of the park; setting the scene for something amazing. It's a wonderful responsibility. You have to start strong!

Oak-smoked salmon

with raw salmon parfait, pine emulsion & beer cracker

I absolutely love pub classics, and a simple dish of smoked salmon with brown bread has got to be up there with some of the most popular starters. That was the inspiration for this dish, which is relatively new on our menu. But, of course, we always want to give dishes a Hand & Flowers twist, so this particular version of the timeless pub staple has not just one style of salmon, but two: a brined, smoked and confit salmon fillet; and delicate discs of salmon parfait.

The salmon itself is lightly cured and then gently cold-smoked before it is briefly confited in smoked oil so it is just cooked. It's served with smoked salmon parfait, made from the fish trim and single cream and blended in a Pacojet machine to get it nice and smooth. The parfait is topped with a layer of apple tartare and a spoonful of burnt lemon purée, and the taster is then sandwiched between two nasturtium leaves, which give it a peppery kick. For a bit of luxury, it's topped with a spoonful of caviar.

The brown bread is a cracker made with leftover sourdough and beer, which complements the fish beautifully. It has a great texture and the most incredible flavour: nutty, beery and distinctly sourdough. Wonderful.

You get a very simple but beautifully executed dish which, at its heart, is a play on smoked salmon and brown bread.

Brined salmon

1kg salmon fillet (skin on)
1 litre cold water
100g table salt
5g liquid smoke flavour

Check the salmon fillet for any pin bones. In a large bowl, whisk the water, salt and smoke flavour together to make a brine.

Place the salmon fillet in a vacuum-pack bag along with the brine and seal. Leave to brine in the fridge for 25 minutes.

Remove the salmon from the brine and place on a wire rack to air-dry.

Oak-smoked salmon

100g smoking wood chips
1kg brined fillet of salmon (see above)

Place a lidded deep-sided metal tray over a medium heat, add the wood chips and heat until smoking.

Using a cook's blowtorch, ignite the smoking chips and immediately extinguish by covering with a second tray to starve the fire of oxygen.

Remove the tray lid and lay the wire rack holding the salmon in the tray. Cover with the lid again and smoke for 10 minutes, making sure the smoke isn't too hot, of course.

Once smoked, remove the salmon fillet from the wire rack, place in a vacuum-pack bag and seal. Keep in the fridge until ready to serve.

Salmon parfait discs

200g raw salmon fillet, diced
150ml single cream
10g glycerine
10g sea salt
Finely grated zest of ½ lemon
75ml smoked rapeseed oil

Put all of the ingredients into a Thermomix and blitz until smooth.

Spoon into a Pacojet beaker and freeze for 24 hours, then churn.

Line a baking sheet with a silicone mat. Spread the salmon parfait evenly on the prepared baking sheet to a 3mm depth and place back in the freezer.

Once solid, cut the salmon parfait into 10 discs, each 4cm in diameter. Wrap in cling film and store in the freezer until needed.

Burnt lemon purée

8 lemons
130g caster sugar
100g muscovado sugar
130ml water
290ml Sleeping Lemons beer
  (from the Wild Beer Company)
30ml lemon juice
7g salt
5g charcoal powder

Heat up a plancha or non-stick heavy-based frying pan. Add the lemons and colour, turning as necessary, until soft and evenly charred all over; this will take about 15 minutes.

Meanwhile, put the sugars, water, beer, lemon juice and salt into a heavy-based saucepan, heat slowly to dissolve the sugars and bring to a simmer. Take off the heat.

Once the lemons are soft, transfer them to a high-powered jug blender (Vitamix). Blend until smooth, gradually pouring in enough of the hot lemon syrup to give a thick purée consistency. Add the charcoal powder and blitz to combine.

Pass the lemon purée through a fine chinois into a bowl. Cover the surface closely with cling film to prevent a skin from forming and refrigerate until needed.

Frosted malts

100g caster sugar
25ml water
50g chocolate malts

Put the sugar and water into a heavy-based saucepan, heat to dissolve the sugar and bring to the boil. Cook until the sugar syrup reaches 150°C (use a digital probe to check the temperature).

Over a medium heat, stir in the malts and agitate to crystallise the sugar on them. Once a white crust forms on the malts, remove from the heat and pour the mixture onto a silicone mat. Leave to cool.

Pine oil

300ml vegetable oil
50g pine needles
200g parsley leaves

Heat the oil in a Thermomix to 70°C and add the pine needles and parsley leaves. Blend for 1 minute at 70°C, then pass through a fine chinois into a bowl and leave to cool.

Pine emulsion

65g free-range liquid egg yolk
4g salt
300ml pine oil (see above)

Put the egg yolk and salt into a high-powered food processor (Robot Coupe) and briefly blend on a slow speed to combine.

Slowly add the pine oil, blending until fully emulsified. Transfer to a piping bag fitted with a 1cm plain nozzle and keep in the fridge until ready to serve.

Smoked oil mayonnaise

1 medium free-range egg yolk
1 tbsp Dijon mustard
1 tsp white wine vinegar
200ml smoked rapeseed oil
Juice of ½ lemon
Sea salt and freshly ground pepper

Put the egg yolk, mustard and white wine vinegar into a bowl and whisk to combine.

Slowly add the smoked oil, whisking constantly, until you have a thick, shiny mayonnaise.

Add the lemon juice and season with salt and pepper to taste. Transfer to a container, cover and keep in the fridge until needed.

Beer glaze

125ml Rebellion ale
50g malt extract

Pour the ale into a saucepan, add the malt extract and bring to the boil, stirring. Reduce to a glaze.

Beer crackers

400g sourdough, torn into pieces
800ml ale
Vegetable oil for deep-frying
Sea salt and freshly ground pepper

Line 3 baking sheets with silicone mats. Put the sourdough and beer into a jug blender and blend to a thick, smooth paste.

Spread out on the prepared baking sheets to a 4mm thickness. Place in a steam oven at 100°C with 100% humidity and cook for 1 hour.

Transfer the silicone mats to the dehydrator set at 70°C and leave to dry overnight until dry and brittle. Break into individual crackers.

When ready to serve, heat the oil in a deep-fryer to 180°C. Deep-fry the sourdough crackers, one or two at a time, for about 1 minute until golden brown and crisp. Drain on kitchen paper and season with salt and pepper.

To finish the salmon & serve

600ml smoked rapeseed oil
3 Granny Smith apples, peeled and cut into 3mm dice
10g shallots, cut into 3mm dice
10g cornichons, cut into 3mm dice
10g lilliput capers, drained
10g frosted malts (see opposite)
1 tsp chopped parsley
1 tsp chopped chives
About 3–4 tbsp smoked oil mayonnaise (see opposite)
20 nasturtium leaves, cut into 3cm discs
50g oscietra caviar
50ml beer glaze (see opposite)
5g pine needles, finely chopped
50g burnt lemon purée (see page 33)
Flaky sea salt

Heat up a plancha or non-stick heavy-based frying pan and oil lightly. Cut the smoked salmon fillet into 80–90g portions. Lay the salmon fillets skin side down on the plancha or in the pan and cook for a few minutes to crisp the skin.

At the same time, heat the smoked oil in a deep-sided tray to 40°C.

Add the salmon fillet portions, skin side up, ensuring the oil comes just below the skin, and confit for about 5 minutes until it reaches a core temperature of 40°C (check the temperature with a digital probe).

Meanwhile, assemble the parfait discs. Put the diced apples into a bowl with the shallots, cornichons, capers, frosted malts, parsley and chives. Toss together, then mix in enough smoked mayonnaise to bind the apple tartare.

Lay a nasturtium leaf disc on each serving plate and cover with a disc of salmon parfait. Spread a layer of apple tartare on the parfait, then cover with a thin layer of burnt lemon purée. Top with another disc of nasturtium and finish with a quenelle of caviar.

Lift the confit salmon out of the oil and drain on kitchen paper. Brush with the beer glaze then top with the finely chopped pine needles and a little salt. Place a salmon portion on each plate, alongside the parfait and pipe a little mound of pine emulsion onto each plate. Serve at once, with the beer cracker.

Moules marinière

with warm stout foam & treacle bread

This is a Hand & Flowers classic, which has been on the menu since the beginning. Everyone loves it. Made from humble ingredients and big on flavour, it's rustic in style and relatively inexpensive.

The classic French way to cook mussels is to steam them with white wine. I love the idea of that, but for our version I started thinking about the amazing shellfish we're lucky enough to get our hands on in the UK and Ireland. Here, people enjoy their pint of prawns with beer and brown bread, or order a Guinness to go with their Irish oysters. You get an incredible bitterness from stout, which works so well with shellfish and their phenomenal taste of the sea.

So, this dish starts off like a classic moules, but is topped with the stouty bitterness of Guinness foam. When you put your spoon through it, it's like you're drinking the head of a Guinness with its astounding, silky texture. The ultimate pint of stout, but with mussels!

Treacle bread

450g wholemeal flour
170g 'T45' plain flour, plus extra
   for dusting
20g fresh yeast
250ml tepid water
2 tbsp honey
2 tbsp black treacle
3 tsp salt
Spray oil

Put both flours into a mixer fitted with the dough hook. In a separate bowl, dissolve the yeast in the tepid water. Add to the flour mix with the honey, treacle and salt. Mix on a slow speed to combine. Continue to work until you have a smooth, firm dough.

Remove the dough hook from the mixer and cover the bowl with a damp, clean tea towel. Leave to rise in a warm place for about 45 minutes until doubled in size.

Once risen, turn the dough out onto a lightly floured surface and knock back, then divide into 50g balls. Shape and roll to fit into silicone mini loaf moulds.

Spray a sheet of cling film with one spray of oil, then lay it, oiled side down, over the tray of dough. Leave to prove in a warm place for 25–30 minutes until the dough is risen and filling the loaf moulds.

Preheat the steam oven to 250°C/Fan 240°C/Gas 10 with 60% humidity. Bake the loaves in the oven for 4 minutes, then lower the setting to 180°C/Fan 160°C/Gas 4. Bake for a further 4 minutes or until the loaves are brown and sound hollow when tapped on the base. Turn out onto a wire rack and leave to cool.

Guinness foam

140ml Guinness
30g unsalted butter
30g plain flour
360ml double cream
Sea salt and freshly ground pepper

Warm the Guinness in a small pan.

Melt the butter in a saucepan over a medium-low heat, stir in the flour and cook, stirring, for 2–3 minutes to form a roux. Gradually add the Guinness, whisking as you do so, then whisk in the cream.

Simmer gently for 20 minutes, stirring from time to time. Season with salt and pepper to taste and pass through a chinois into a jug.

Pour the liquid into a 1-litre ISI gun and screw the lid on with a nozzle attached. Charge with two ISI gas cartridges and shake well. Keep warm in a bain-marie until needed.

Moules marinière

1kg medium-large fresh mussels
in shells, de-bearded and cleaned
250ml white wine

Check the mussels, discarding any that do not close when tapped sharply on your work surface.

Place a heavy-based saucepan (that has a tight-fitting lid) over a medium-high heat. Add the mussels, along with the wine, and put the lid on. Cook for 4–5 minutes until the shells open; discard any that remain closed.

Tip the mussels into a colander set over a bowl to catch the wine and mussel juices. Leave until cool enough to handle then remove the mussels from their shells and place them in a bowl.

Set a chinois lined with 3 layers of muslin over the bowl of mussels and pour the wine and mussel stock through onto the mussels; this will keep them moist.

To assemble & serve

100g shallot, peeled and
cut into 5mm dice
100g carrot, peeled and
cut into 5mm dice
100g celeriac, peeled and
cut into 5mm dice
4 drops of truffle oil
5 tbsp hollandaise sauce
(see page 403)
3 tbsp chopped curly parsley
Lemon juice, to taste

Preheat the oven to 205°C/Fan 185°C/Gas 6–7. Warm the mini loaves through in the oven for 4 minutes.

Meanwhile, drain the mussels, saving the stock. Put the stock, shallot, carrot, celeriac, truffle oil and hollandaise sauce into a saucepan. Bring to the boil and reduce until the stock starts to emulsify. Fold in the mussels and gently warm through. Stir in the chopped parsley and lemon juice to taste.

Divide the mussels, veg and liquor between warmed serving dishes. Top with the Guinness foam. Serve immediately, with the warm treacle bread, on napkin-lined plates.

Cured Cornish mackerel

with apple pancake, avruga caviar & dill oil

Mackerel is abundant in British waters – a big tick – and it's got a super-fresh taste. Being part of the tuna family means the flesh, both raw and cooked, also has an incredible texture. On top of that, it doesn't cost a lot and it's good for you because it is rich in omega-3 oil.

This recipe is a kind of play on an escabeche, with its warm Mediterranean flavours and Scandinavian dill riff in the cure. We've got a bit of lime, lemon and grapefruit in there, and acidity and sweetness in the apple pancake. You could say there's a sweet and sour signature to the dish. For a bit of indulgence, we've added avruga caviar, too.

All the ingredients sit brilliantly together: the flavours really tie in. That said, you can vary the fish – it works well with cured salmon, for instance.

Dill oil

1 large bunch of dill
*300ml non-scented oil (sunflower
    or rapeseed)*

Roughly chop the dill and place in a
high-powered jug blender (Vitamix).
Pour on the oil and blitz thoroughly.

Line a chinois with three sheets of
muslin and set over a bowl. Pour the
blended oil into the muslin-lined
chinois and leave to slowly pass in
the fridge. (You will have more dill
oil than you need; refrigerate any
you're not using straight away.)

Compressed apple

1 Granny Smith apple
35ml dill oil (see left)

Peel the apple and cut off the cheeks
to leave the core.

Place the apple cheeks in a vacuum-
pack bag with the dill oil, vacuum-
seal and compress for 24 hours.

Apple purée

2 Bramley apples
150ml water
50g caster sugar
7g Sosa Antioxidant Gel Powder
Juice of ½ lemon

Peel, halve, core and slice the
Bramley apples. Put the water, sugar,
antioxidant and lemon juice into a
small saucepan and bring to the boil.
Add the sliced apples and cook for
about 15 minutes until soft.

Transfer the mixture to a jug blender
and purée until smooth. Pass
through a sieve into a bowl, cover
and keep in the fridge until you are
ready to serve.

Cured mackerel

2 mackerel, 400g each, filleted
   and v-pin-boned
75g table salt
¼ tsp coriander seeds, toasted
¼ tsp fennel seeds
50g caster sugar
Finely grated zest of ¼ lemon
Finely grated zest of ¼ lime
Finely grated zest of ¼ orange
Finely grated zest of ¼ grapefruit

Check over the mackerel for any tiny pin bones, then set aside.

For the cure, put the salt and spices into a spice grinder and blitz until the seeds are broken down, then tip into a bowl. Add the sugar and stir to mix, then add the citrus zests and mix again to combine.

Spread half the cure mix out on a tray. Lay the mackerel fillets skin side down on the tray and sprinkle on the remaining cure. Leave to cure at room temperature for 8–10 minutes.

Rinse the cure off the mackerel under cold running water and pat dry with kitchen paper then lay the mackerel on a metal tray and set aside, ready to finish and serve.

Scotch apple pancake

75g self-raising flour
2g baking powder
2g cream of tartar
1 medium free-range egg
75ml whole milk
25g ricotta cheese
80g peeled, cored and grated
   Granny Smith apple
30g dried apple slices, diced
5g chopped dill
Finely grated zest of ½ lemon
2g table salt
1g cracked black pepper
A splash of vegetable oil
10g unsalted butter, diced

Put the flour, baking powder and cream of tartar into a bowl, stir to mix and make a well in the centre.

In a separate bowl, whisk the egg, milk, ricotta, grated apple and dried apple together, then pour into the well in the dry mixture. Add the chopped dill, lemon zest, salt and pepper and whisk to combine. Cover and set aside.

When you are ready to serve, heat the oil in a non-stick frying pan. When hot, add the butter and heat until melted and foaming.

Drop 4 separate tablespoonfuls of the batter into the pan, spacing them well apart. Fry for 3 minutes on each side until the Scotch pancakes are golden and cooked through. Remove from the pan and keep hot.

To assemble & serve

1 tbsp vegetable oil
4 heaped tsp thick crème fraîche
   (well drained)
4 tsp avruga caviar
4 small sprigs of dill

Take the compressed apple out of the bag and cut into 5mm dice, place in a bowl and mix in enough of the apple purée to bind.

Brush the mackerel fillets with the oil and blowtorch all over until charred and just cooked. Lay a mackerel fillet on each warmed serving plate with a Scotch apple pancake alongside.

Spoon a neat rocher of crème fraîche onto each plate next to the pancake. Make a small indent in the crème fraîche and add a little dill oil.

Quenelle the apple and place on the pancake, then add 1 tsp caviar and finish with a sprig of dill.

Red mullet bouillabaisse

with fennel jam, aïoli & herb cracker

Bouillabaisse is a classic French soup, which has stood the test of time. The combination of flavourful Mediterranean fish varieties and herbs makes a beautiful soup, but also a phenomenal sauce, which is where this particular recipe lies. Jamie May, our head chef at The Hand & Flowers, learnt about the dish while he was working for culinary genius Anthony Demetre at Arbutus in London.

At the core of this recipe is an incredibly intense stock, made from white fish bones, red mullet, chopped vegetables, herbs and spices, Pernod and dry Martini. But while a typical bouillabaisse includes fennel, we've translated that to a fennel jam, which sits under a roasted piece of red mullet fillet. Loving my Bramley apples as I do, we ran some through the jam as well, to counterbalance the sweetness and acidity levels. Confit red pepper and a drizzle of orange oil make the dish zing.

The dish is finished with a beautiful herb cracker, which is rolled and baked (a bit like Lebanese lavash dough), then brushed with garlic oil. Finally, there is the saffron-infused aïoli. So, taken as a whole, the recipe takes a classic bouillabaisse to another level.

Of course, the real secret to this recipe is to use very fresh red mullet. If it isn't in season, or our fish supplier doesn't feel it's top notch, we use grey mullet or pan-seared scallops instead – we find they work just as well. So much of the way that we work at The Hand & Flowers shows up in this dish. We create a fantastic dish, but the protein can be a movable feast – easily adapted to include an ingredient when it is at its best.

Fennel jam

150g trimmed fennel, finely sliced
50g peeled onion, finely sliced
15g peeled and cored Bramley apple,
*   finely sliced*
100ml apple juice
15g soft dark brown sugar
2g fennel seeds
1 tbsp white wine vinegar
15g peeled and cored Granny Smith
*   apple, finely diced*

Put the fennel, onion, Bramley apple, apple juice, sugar, fennel seeds and wine vinegar into a heavy-based saucepan and bring to the boil. Lower the heat and simmer slowly for 1–1½ hours until the mixture is reduced and thickened to a sticky, jam-like consistency. Remove from the heat and set aside.

Warm the fennel jam and stir in the diced Granny Smith apple just before serving.

Bouillabaisse

1kg white fish bones, cleaned
*   and chopped*
100g red mullet (fresh or frozen
*   and thawed), chopped*
50ml vegetable oil
1 onion, peeled and roughly chopped
1 large carrot, peeled and roughly
*   chopped*
¼ head of celery, roughly chopped
½ garlic bulb, cloves separated,
*   peeled and crushed*
5g fennel seeds
2g white peppercorns
1 star anise
5g sea salt
25g tomato purée
400g tin plum tomatoes
1 tbsp brandy
1 tbsp Pernod
1 tbsp dry Martini
3 litres cold water
A small pinch of saffron strands
Pared zest of ½ orange
Pared zest of ½ lemon
75g unsalted butter, diced

Preheat the oven to 205°C/Fan 185°C/Gas 6–7. Put the fish bones and chopped fish into a roasting tray and drizzle with half of the oil. Roast in the oven for 35–40 minutes, turning halfway through cooking.

Heat the remaining oil in a large heavy-based saucepan and add the onion, carrot, celery and garlic. Cook gently for 15 minutes until softened and golden; don't let them brown.

Add the fennel seeds, peppercorns, star anise, salt, tomato purée and tinned tomatoes and cook for a further 3 minutes. Add the brandy, Pernod and Martini, stirring and scraping to deglaze. Take off the heat.

Add the roasted bones to the pan and then deglaze the roasting tin with a splash of water, stirring and scraping up the sediment; add this to the pan.

Pour in the water, add the saffron and bring to the boil, then skim. Lower the heat and simmer for 20 minutes, skimming occasionally.

Pass the bouillabaisse through a mouli to extract all the liquor and flavour, then pass the stock through a chinois lined with 3 layers of muslin into a clean pan.

Add the citrus zests to the pan, bring to a simmer and reduce down until you have roughly 500ml stock. Remove and discard the zests.

Whisk in the diced butter and reduce the bouillabaisse stock by half. Pour into a container; chill until needed.

Red pepper discs

3 large Romano red peppers
2 tsp vegetable oil
Sea salt

Preheat the oven to 240°C/Fan 220°C/Gas 9. Drizzle the peppers with the oil and sprinkle with salt. Lay on a baking sheet. Place in the oven for 10–12 minutes until the skin starts to blister, then remove from the oven and allow to cool.

Peel the skin from the peppers, then cut each pepper along one side and open up, to form a rectangle. Cut off the top and remove the seeds, then cut out 12 discs using a 3.5cm cutter. Set aside until ready to serve.

Orange oil

100ml freshly squeezed orange juice
50ml cold-pressed rapeseed oil

Put the orange juice and oil into a pan and bring to the boil. Allow the liquid to reduce until the bubbles start to get bigger and slow down (about 5 minutes), then remove from the heat. Pour into a bowl and whisk to emulsify. (You will have more orange oil than you need; refrigerate any you're not using straight away.)

Herb crackers

40g wholemeal flour
35g strong white bread flour,
*   plus extra for dusting*
5g wheatgerm
2g salt
40ml warm water
8g fresh yeast
A small handful of dill leaves
A small handful of tarragon leaves
A small handful of flat-leaf
*   parsley leaves*
A small handful of edible flowers

Put the flours, wheatgerm and salt into a mixer fitted with a dough hook, make a well in the middle and add the water and yeast. Mix to combine and continue to work the dough for 8 minutes until smooth and elastic.

Remove the dough hook, cover the bowl with cling film and leave to prove for about 1 hour until doubled in volume.

Once risen, turn the dough out onto a lightly floured surface, knock back and then divide into 10 small balls.

Roll each ball through a pasta machine until the sheet of dough is thin enough for you to see your fingers through it.

Preheat the oven to 200°C/Fan 180°C/Gas 6 and line 2 large baking sheets with baking parchment.

To build the herb crackers, brush one sheet of dough lightly with water and lay the herbs and edible flowers decoratively on top, then lay a second sheet of dough on top. Pass through the pasta machine again, then cut into 8cm squares.

Bake in the oven for 14 minutes until golden and brittle. Transfer the herb crackers to a wire rack to cool.

Garlic oil

100ml vegetable oil
6 garlic cloves, peeled and grated
Sea salt and freshly ground pepper

Warm the oil in a small pan and add the garlic. Leave to infuse over a very low heat for 30 minutes.

Strain the oil through a fine chinois to remove the garlic. Season with salt and pepper. (You will have more garlic oil than you need; refrigerate any you're not using straight away.)

Aïoli

A good pinch of saffron strands
12ml white wine vinegar
100g dry mashed cooked potato,
*   passed through a fine sieve*
1 medium free-range egg yolk
15g Dijon mustard
15g peeled garlic, finely grated
1 tsp lemon juice
1 tsp salt
100ml vegetable oil

Pre-soak the saffron in the wine vinegar for about 30 minutes.

Put the mash, egg yolk, mustard, garlic, lemon juice, saffron-infused vinegar and salt into a blender and blend together.

With the blender on a medium speed, slowly drizzle in the oil to emulsify and create a thick, shiny aïoli. Pass through a fine chinois, then transfer to a piping bag, ready for serving.

To cook the red mullet

2 red mullet fillets, 150g each,
*   pin-boned and halved*
50ml extra-virgin olive oil
*   (we use Leblanc)*
4 small pinches of sea salt

Lay the red mullet on a baking tray and drizzle with the olive oil.

When ready to serve, preheat the oven to 205°C/Fan 185°C/Gas 6–7. Season the fish fillets with the salt. Place in the oven for 4–5 minutes until just cooked. Leave to rest for 30 seconds after cooking.

To assemble & serve

Vegetable oil to drizzle
4 small pinches of fennel pollen
8 picked tops of bronze fennel
Sea salt and freshly ground pepper

While the red mullet is cooking, warm through the fennel jam and stir in the apple.

Lay the red pepper discs on a tray, drizzle with a little oil, season with salt and pepper and warm through under the salamander or grill. Bring the bouillabaisse up to a simmer over a medium heat, stirring.

Place a large spoonful of fennel jam in each warmed serving bowl, then arrange 3 red pepper discs in each bowl. Season the rested red mullet fillets with the fennel pollen then place on the pepper discs. Pour on the bouillabaisse, drizzle the orange oil around the edge and garnish with a bronze fennel top.

Brush the herb cracker with the garlic oil and serve alongside the bouillabaisse, together with the aïoli topped with a sprig of bronze fennel.

Parsley & lovage soup

with smoked eel, apple, ham hock & blue cheese tortellini

SERVES 6

This soup is inspired by a trip Beth and I took to Paris many years ago, when we discovered an incredible little rock 'n' roll bistro with a tiny kitchen called Le Chateaubriand, which is now quite famous. The food was exceptional. The parsley soup was the standout dish from our whole weekend and knocked the socks off all the other dishes we had eaten at far posher, three-Michelin-starred places. It was beautiful – vividly green, simple and packed full of flavour. So, of course, I had to come up with my own version!

I had the idea of making an infused stock to cook the parsley in, and of using lovage, which is amazingly leafy and has a beautiful curry-like flavour. To lock in the flavour of the herbs, I blanch and freeze them both first. That soup in Paris had deliciously sweet orange confit and it counterbalanced the mild bitterness of parsley perfectly, so I was inspired to include that element too.

But I wanted to give my soup even more layers of flavour. I add pickled garlic for a cut of acidity, croûtons for crunch, smoked eel for a rich, smoky luxury, and a ham hock and blue cheese tortellini. Everything marries brilliantly in an unforgettable way, I like to think.

PARSLEY & LOVAGE SOUP

Parsley nage

Vegetable oil for cooking
70g Spanish onion, peeled and sliced
70g celery, finely sliced
1 large garlic clove, peeled and sliced
1 litre water
50g parsley stalks

Heat a splash of vegetable oil in a saucepan over a medium-low heat. Add the onion, celery and garlic and sweat until softened. Pour in the water and bring to the boil.

Add the parsley stalks and remove from the heat. Cover the pan with cling film and place in a blast chiller (or in a bowl of iced water) to cool quickly and retain the freshness of the stalks.

Once cooled, pass through a chinois, pressing the vegetables with the back of a ladle to extract all the liquid. Keep the parsley nage in the fridge until needed (or freeze in a vacuum-pack bag).

Parsley oil

300ml vegetable oil
250g parsley leaves

Heat the oil in a Thermomix to 70°C and add the parsley leaves. Blend for 1 minute at 70°C, then pass the oil through a fine chinois into a bowl and leave to cool. (You will have more parsley oil than you need; refrigerate any you're not using straight away.)

Pickled garlic cloves

1 garlic bulb, separated into cloves
* and peeled*
100ml pickling liquor (see page 404)

Place the garlic cloves in a small saucepan, pour on enough water to cover and bring to the boil. Drain the garlic and immerse in a bowl of iced water to refresh. Repeat this process twice more to lose the raw garlic flavour, using fresh water.

After the final blanch and refresh, drain the garlic and allow to cool.

Transfer the garlic to a vacuum-pack bag and pour in the pickle mix. Seal the bag and place in the fridge.

Diced orange confit

1 orange
50ml olive oil

Using a small, sharp knife, cut the rind off the orange in rectangular pieces. Square off any uneven edges, as this will help achieve perfect dice. Remove most of the white pith, leaving just a thin layer. Cut into 5mm perfect dice.

Bring a small pan of water to the boil. Add the orange zest dice and boil for 1 minute. Drain and refresh in iced water. Repeat the process twice more, using fresh boiled water.

Once cooled, transfer the blanched orange zest to a pan and pour on the oil. Cook gently over a very low heat for 30 minutes. Leave to cool, then place in the fridge until needed.

Remove from the fridge around 20 minutes before serving, to bring up to room temperature.

Parsley & lovage soup

200g bunch of lovage, leaves picked
350g bunch of flat-leaf parsley,
    leaves picked
Vegetable oil for cooking
170g Spanish onion, peeled and
    finely sliced
140g potato, peeled and finely sliced
Parsley nage (see opposite)
Sea salt and freshly ground pepper

Add the lovage to a pan of boiling salted water and blanch for about 1 minute until wilted. Drain and immerse in a bowl of iced water to refresh. Drain the leaves and squeeze out excess water. Weigh 40g, place in a vacuum-pack bag and freeze.

Blanch the parsley in the boiling salted water for about 1 minute until soft, then drain and refresh in iced water. Drain the leaves and squeeze out excess water. Weigh 40g, place in a vacuum-pack bag and freeze.

Heat a splash of oil in a saucepan over a medium-low heat and add the onion. Sweat gently, without colouring, until softened.

Add the sliced potato and 200ml of the parsley nage. Bring to the boil, lower the heat and simmer for about 10 minutes until the potatoes are fully cooked. Add the remaining nage and bring to the boil.

Take the parsley and lovage out of the vacuum-pack bags and place them in a high-powered jug blender (Vitamix). Pour in the hot soup base. Purée the soup until smooth – it will be green and vibrant – then season with salt and pepper to taste.

Immediately pass the soup through a chinois into a bowl containing clean ice packs and place in the blast chiller (or over a larger bowl of ice) to cool quickly.

Once cold, remove the ice packs, scraping off any excess soup, so as not to waste any. Keep the soup in the fridge until needed.

Croûtons

¼ wholemeal cereal loaf (we use
    NPAV2 Delice de France), frozen
50ml vegetable oil
Sea salt

About 20 minutes before you wish to bake the croûtons, take the bread out of the freezer to allow it to partially defrost.

Preheat the oven to 205°C/Fan 185°C/Gas 6–7 and line a baking tray with baking parchment. Cut the crusts off the bread, keeping the edges straight. Dice into small cubes, toss in the oil and season with salt.

Place the seasoned bread on the lined baking tray and bake in the oven for 15 minutes until crisp and golden. Remove from the oven and tip onto a tray lined with a clean J-cloth to cool.

Ham hock & blue cheese tortellini

225ml whole milk
15g unsalted butter
15g plain flour
60g blue Stilton, crumbled
75g flaked, cooked smoked ham hock
6 large thin square sheets of fresh
 pasta or wonton wrappers (we
 use Happy Boy wonton wrappers)
Semolina, for dusting
Sea salt and freshly ground pepper

Warm the milk in a small saucepan. Melt the butter in a separate pan, then whisk in the flour. Cook, stirring, for 3 minutes to cook out the raw taste of the flour.

Gradually ladle in the warm milk, whisking as you do so. Once all of the milk has been incorporated, simmer gently for 20 minutes, stirring occasionally.

Remove from the heat and stir the crumbled Stilton into the sauce. When the cheese is fully melted, stir in the flaked ham until evenly distributed. Season with salt and pepper to taste. Cover the surface with a piece of baking parchment to stop a skin from forming and allow to cool.

Once cooled, spoon the tortellini filling into a piping bag and snip off the end. Sprinkle a small tray with a fine layer of semolina.

Lay the 6 sheets of pasta or wonton wrappers on a lightly floured surface and pipe a neat mound (about 1 tsp) of filling in the centre of each.

Lightly brush the pasta around the filling with water, then cut out rounds, using a 6–7cm round cutter. Fold half of the pasta or wrapper over to enclose the filling, forming a half-moon shape; make sure you squeeze out any air bubbles and keep the ball of filling in a defined shape.

Bring the two corners together to form the tortellini and press them tightly together to seal.

Place the tortellini on the semolina-dusted tray and refrigerate until ready to cook and serve.

To prepare the smoked eel

1 smoked eel, about 800g

Lay the smoked eel on a large board and cut off the head with a large, sharp knife. Using a small knife, release the skin from the meat at the head end, then peel away the skin all the way back to the tail end.

Next, to fillet the eel, starting at the head, run a filleting knife along the backbone all the way to the tail. Turn the eel over and repeat the process for the second fillet.

Lay the eel fillets, bloodline up, on the board. Using the back of a knife, carefully clean away the excess fat that masks the beautiful colour of the eel. Once clean, flip the eel over and remove the rib cage at the head end.

Next portion the fillets into 10cm lengths, then cut into 1cm dice; you will need 5 eel squares per portion. Put the eel pieces in a container, cover and place in the fridge until ready to serve.

To assemble & serve

1 Bramley apple, peeled
and cut into 1cm dice
12 borage flowers
12 borage cress shoots

Gently warm the parsley and lovage soup in a saucepan and gently heat the eel under the salamander or grill.

Meanwhile, add the tortellini to a pan of boiling salted water, return to a simmer and poach for 3 minutes. Drain carefully.

In the bottom of each warmed serving bowl, place 1 tsp orange confit, 3 slices of pickled garlic, 5 cubes of apple, 5 cubes of warm eel and a poached tortellini. Lightly aerate the soup with a high-powered hand blender (Bamix) and pour into each bowl around the tortellini.

Add a handful of the croûtons to each bowl and drizzle with parsley oil. Finish with a couple of borage flowers and shoots of borage cress.

Sardines & tomato on toast

SERVES 4

When I was a kid, my mum used to give us tinned sardines on toast. Safe to say, I wasn't a big fan. It was the last thing in the world I wanted to eat! But when I became a chef and came across juicy, fresh sardines – simply chargrilled – I was wowed by their incredible flavour. In time, once I had opened my own restaurant, I got pulled back to the idea of sardines on toast.

I got to thinking about when I was a young chef in London in the 1990s, working for Gary Rhodes and Stephen Bull. Back then, everyone was introducing European influences into their food, such as pestos and tapenades. They were bringing simple, honest ingredients together and making them sing! My own song to sardines is a nod to Provençal-style cooking: flavourful tomatoes, black olives, basil, lush oily fish and a chunk of beautiful bread.

You just need to get hold of the best, most fantastically fresh, Cornish sardines. It's easy to underline their natural, zingy taste by curing and pickling, because being such an oily fish, sardines respond really well to these techniques. They also take extra oil brilliantly, so olive oil, plus a brush of perfect tapenade, straight from the south of France, increase the depth of flavour.

It's an upgrade of a wonderful, rustic French dish, and everything about it is just perfect. I love it!

Cured sardines

6 sardines, scaled, filleted
and pin-boned
30g table salt
30g caster sugar
200ml pickling liquor (see page 404)
200ml extra-virgin olive oil
(we use Leblanc)

Check over the sardines for any tiny pin bones, then set aside.

For the cure, stir the salt and sugar together. Sprinkle half of the cure mix evenly in a deep-sided tray and lay the sardines skin side down on top. Sprinkle the remaining cure mix over the sardines. Cover the tray with cling film and place in the fridge to cure for 2 hours.

Rinse the cure off the sardines under cold running water. Pat dry with kitchen paper.

Place the sardines in a vacuum-pack bag with the pickling liquor and vacuum-seal the bag. Place in the fridge to pickle for 6 hours.

Open the bag and tip the sardines into a colander to drain, then pat dry again.

Now put the sardines into a clean vacuum-pack bag with the olive oil. Vacuum-seal the bag and keep the sardines in the fridge until needed.

Just before serving, remove and drain the sardine fillets. Trim to neaten.

Tapenade

120g black olives, pitted
2 garlic cloves, peeled and grated
6g salted anchovy fillets (we use
Ortiz)
20g Parmesan, freshly grated
20g capers in brine, drained
140ml extra-virgin olive oil (Leblanc)

Place all the ingredients in a high-powered food processor (Robot Coupe) and purée until you have a smooth tapenade. Spoon into a container, seal and keep in the fridge until needed.

Remove the tapenade from the fridge about 20 minutes before serving, to bring it back to room temperature.

Dried tomato discs

2 firm, but ripe plum tomatoes
½ tsp salt

Cut the tomatoes lengthways into thin slices and lay them on a baking sheet lined with a silicone mat. Season the tomatoes with the salt.

Dry the tomatoes in the oven at 90°C/Fan 80°C/lowest Gas (with zero humidity) or in a dehydrator on the dried fruit setting for 3 hours. Carefully turn the discs over and continue to dry for a further 1 hour.

Once dry and brittle, store the dried tomato slices in an airtight container interleaved with sheets of baking parchment, with silica gel crystals in the bottom of the container to maintain a dry atmosphere.

Tomato petals & concasse

10 ripe plum tomatoes on the vine
½ tsp salt
1 tbsp olive oil

Using a paring knife, score a cross on the top of each tomato and remove the core. Immerse the tomatoes in a pan of boiling water and blanch for 20 seconds or so. Drain and refresh in iced water; drain again.

Peel the skin from the tomatoes, then quarter them lengthways and remove the seeds. Lay 12 tomato petals on a baking sheet lined with a silicone mat; set the rest aside.

Season these tomato petals with the salt and drizzle with the olive oil. Semi-dry in the oven at 90°C/ Fan 80°C/lowest Gas (with zero humidity) or in a dehydrator on the dried fruit setting for 2 hours.

Lay the remaining tomato petals between two J-cloths on a tray to soak up the excess moisture then place on a board. Square off the edges and dice the tomatoes into perfect concasse. Place in the fridge until needed.

Deep-fried basil leaves

Vegetable oil for deep-frying
12 small basil leaves
Sea salt

Heat the oil in a deep-fryer to 140°C. Add the basil leaves and deep-fry for about 20 seconds until they stop bubbling and turn translucent. Remove the leaves with a slotted spoon, drain on kitchen paper and season with salt.

To serve

1 wholemeal cereal loaf
  (baguette shaped)
40g small capers in brine, drained
40g banana shallots, peeled and
  finely diced
2 tbsp finely chopped flat-leaf parsley
4 tbsp extra-virgin olive oil (Leblanc)
2 tbsp red wine sauce (see page 402)
Sea salt and freshly ground pepper

Slice the loaf lengthways to get 4 even slices, 5mm thick, discarding the crusts. Place the slices on a tray and toast both sides evenly under a salamander or grill.

Meanwhile, in a bowl, mix the tomato concasse, capers, shallots, chopped parsley and extra-virgin olive oil together. Lightly season with salt and pepper and set aside.

When the toast is ready, spread the presentation side of each slice with 1 tbsp tapenade and cover with the tomato concasse. Arrange 3 cured sardine fillets on each slice and lay a semi-dried tomato slice and a deep-fried basil leaf on each fillet. Finish with a dried tomato disc.

Put a small spoonful of tapenade on each serving plate to stop the toast from sliding around. Carefully position the toast on the plates and drizzle the plate with a little red wine sauce. Serve at once.

Salt cod Scotch egg

with red pepper sauce & picante chorizo

This dish arose out of old-fashioned practicality. I needed to use some cod trimmings from a main course dish. The Hand & Flowers is a business: I always ask, what can we do with the trimmings? So, we decided to make a salt cod mix, like a brandade. Then, as we made that, the idea of a Scotch egg popped up. Boom! The creative touch-fire had been lit and we headed off towards Spain.

What started out as a simple Scotch egg has now been elevated into something very special. It's simply three things on a plate, or in our case, in a bowl – warm red pepper sauce, a Scotch egg (a quail's egg, wrapped in a salt cod brandade, coated in panko breadcrumbs and deep-fried), and a beautifully grilled piece of chorizo resting on top. They're all huge flavours that pack a punch. We poach the salt cod in olive oil, as that makes a big difference and gives the dish a proper sophistication.

Red peppers, saffron (what could be more Spanish than that), vinegar and sugar reduction: they're all there in the sauce and we melt in a bit of butter at the end to give a glossy shine, a bit like montéeing a French classic sauce.

But the real secret of the dish is to ensure the peeled quail's eggs are all the same weight once wrapped in the brandade. That way they will cook to perfection.

This salt cod Scotch egg has stood the test of time and appears on all of our restaurant menus: from The Hand & Flowers to The Coach to Kerridge's Bar & Grill in London, and to the Bull & Bear in Manchester. It's a great dish, and one that we're very proud of.

Salt cod

600g skinless cod fillet, pin-boned
60g flaky sea salt
60g caster sugar
2g saffron strands
4 tsp Pernod
70ml white wine
700ml olive oil

Dice the cod into 2cm pieces. In a large bowl, mix the salt, sugar, saffron, Pernod and white wine together to form a paste. Add the cod and turn to coat in the mixture. Cover the bowl with cling film and place in the fridge for 24 hours.

Tip the cod into a colander and rinse off the salt under cold running water for about 5 minutes. Drain well and pat dry with kitchen paper.

Preheat the oven to 160°C/Fan 140°C/Gas 3. Place the cod in a single layer in a small baking tray and cover with the olive oil. Cover the tray with foil and cook in the oven for 25 minutes. Remove and set aside to cool.

Once cooled, drain the cod from the oil.

Brandade

600g large potatoes
480g cooked salt cod (see left), flaked into large pieces
2 garlic cloves, peeled and grated
Sea salt and freshly ground pepper

Preheat the oven to 200°C/Fan 180°C/Gas 6. Bake the potatoes in the oven for about 1 hour until soft.

When cool enough to handle, halve the baked potatoes and scoop out the flesh from the skins. Pass the potato through a potato ricer or mouli. Weigh out 200g for the brandade and place in a bowl (freeze any leftovers).

Add the salt cod and grated garlic to the potato and mix thoroughly. Check the seasoning, adding pepper to taste, and salt if required. Allow to cool, then refrigerate.

Red pepper sauce

2 tbsp olive oil
4 banana shallots, peeled and sliced
6 red peppers, deseeded and sliced
2 red chillies, sliced (seeds retained)
1 tsp saffron strands
200ml white wine
100ml white wine vinegar
100g caster sugar
100g unsalted butter, in pieces
Sea salt and freshly ground pepper

Heat the olive oil in a wide pan and add the shallots, red peppers and chillies. Sweat gently for about 10 minutes until soft, then sprinkle in the saffron and cook gently for 20–25 minutes.

Add the white wine, wine vinegar and sugar and let bubble to reduce down until almost all the liquid has evaporated.

Transfer the pepper sauce to a blender and blitz until smooth. Add the butter and blend to combine; this will give the sauce a shine. Season with salt and pepper to taste. Pass the sauce through a sieve into a bowl and allow to cool.

Scotch eggs

8 quail's eggs
200g brandade (see opposite)
50g plain flour, for dusting
3 medium free-range eggs, beaten
100g panko breadcrumbs
Vegetable oil for deep-frying
6 slices of chorizo picante
   (we use Brindisa)
Flaky sea salt

Add the quail's eggs to a pan of boiling water and cook for 2 minutes and 10 seconds to soft-boil. Lift the eggs out and immerse them in a bowl of iced water to cool quickly. When cold, peel the shells – be careful not to break the eggs.

Divide the brandade into 8 portions and weigh the quail's eggs. The total weight of the quail's egg plus its brandade coating should be 90g, so adjust the portion of brandade accordingly. Shape the brandade around the quail's eggs and carefully roll each into a ball.

Roll each ball in flour to dust all over, then dip into the beaten eggs and finally into the breadcrumbs to coat fully. Gently roll each ball in your hands to ensure it is perfectly round.

Heat the oil in a deep-fryer to 180°C. Deep-fry the Scotch eggs in batches, being careful not to overcrowd the fryer basket, for 4 minutes until golden. Drain on kitchen paper and sprinkle with a little flaky salt.

To assemble & serve

8 slices of chorizo picante
   (we use Brindisa)
Flaky sea salt

While the Scotch eggs are frying, place the chorizo slices on a grill tray and heat under the grill for 1 minute. Remove from the grill and turn the chorizo over before laying a slice on top of each Scotch egg.

Place a large spoonful of warm pepper sauce in the middle of each warmed serving bowl.

Carefully place a chorizo-topped Scotch egg on the pool of sauce and sprinkle with a little flaky salt. Serve at once.

Smoked eel & beetroot royale

with apple & black truffle potato

SERVES 8

I love the romance of smokeries: the idea of catching something wonderful to eat, then putting that raw produce through an ancient preserving process and adding another layer of taste. Smoking ingredients is something we do really well in the UK; and the people who do it are passionate about their trade, like chefs. I adore that. Eel is a great fish for delicate smoking. It absorbs the nuances of the smoke beautifully. And the earthiness of beetroot goes incredibly well with it.

This dish builds layer upon layer of flavour. It begins with a beetroot royale – a lightly poached set egg custard made from double cream, whole milk and eggs, and flavoured with beetroot purée. This is topped with slices of black truffle potato and a piece of lightly grilled, beautifully smoked eel. A garnish of pickled beetroot gives the dish greater complexity and a little sharpness to cut through the custard's creaminess. To finish, there's a scattering of deep-fried crispy capers, delicate frisée, Granny Smith batons, a little extra virgin olive oil and a sprinkling of salt.

It's a dish that takes me right back to my formative years. The way we cook the beetroot royale – in a bain-marie – reaches back to when I was a young chef in London, learning to create vegetable royales at the Capital hotel. Of course, we've updated the royale's overall flavour and presentation. The result is a dish full of classic flavours that sit nicely together, and the rich beetroot pickle tops it off. Not only is it visually stunning, it tastes great.

To prepare the smoked eel

1 smoked eel, 800g

Lay the smoked eel on a large board and cut off the head with a large, sharp knife. Using a small knife, release the skin from the meat at the head end, then peel away the skin all the way back to the tail end.

Next, to fillet the eel, starting at the head, run a filleting knife along the backbone all the way to the tail. Turn the eel over and repeat the process for the second fillet.

Trim the sides of the eel. Using the back of a knife, carefully clean away the excess fat. Once clean, flip the eel over and remove the rib cage at the head end.

Using a sharp serrated knife, cut the eel into 8 equal portions. Square off the edges to neaten, then place on a tray, cover and keep in the fridge until needed.

Beetroot pickle

125g redcurrant jelly
125g red wine vinegar
2 cloves
35g Dijon mustard
100g cooked beetroot, peeled

Put the redcurrant jelly, wine vinegar and cloves into a small pan, bring to the boil and reduce to a thick glaze. Transfer to a bowl, remove the cloves, then whisk in the mustard. Leave to cool.

Cut the beetroot into 5mm dice and stir it into the cooled glaze. Cover and set aside until ready to serve.

Beetroot purée

500g cooked beetroot, peeled
80g unsalted butter
50g redcurrant jelly
20ml red wine vinegar
250ml red wine
Sea salt and cayenne pepper

Finely slice the cooked beetroot and place in a heavy-based pan with the butter, redcurrant jelly, wine vinegar and red wine. Bring to the boil and reduce until the liquor has almost totally evaporated.

Transfer to a jug blender and blitz until smooth. Pass the beetroot purée through a fine chinois into a bowl and season with salt and cayenne pepper to taste.

Cover and place in the fridge until ready to make the beetroot royale.

Beetroot royale

350g beetroot purée (see opposite)
300ml double cream
100ml whole milk
2 medium free-range eggs
6 medium free-range egg yolks

Put the beetroot purée, cream and milk into a bowl and stir to combine. In a separate bowl, beat the eggs and extra yolks together until smooth.

Fold the beetroot mixture and beaten eggs together, trying not to aerate the mix. Pass through a fine chinois into a bowl or jug. Place in the fridge to rest for 30 minutes or so, to release any air bubbles.

Preheat the oven to 120°C/Fan 100°C/Gas ½. Line a large roasting tray (that will hold the serving bowls) with a clean tea towel; this will prevent the bowls sliding about. Give the mixture a little stir with a spatula, then skim off any air bubbles from the surface with a small ladle.

Stand the serving bowls in the tray, spacing them apart to ensure even cooking. Pour in the beetroot mix, dividing it equally between the bowls. Carefully wrap each bowl with foil, to prevent a skin from forming on the surface of the royales.

Pour enough warm water into the tray to come halfway up the sides of the bowls. Place in the oven and cook for 10 minutes then rotate the bowls to ensure even cooking and return to the oven for another 10 minutes.

Remove the bowls from the oven and set aside in a warm place to rest until ready to serve.

Black truffle new potatoes

2 medium black truffle potatoes (we use Shetland Black), washed
50ml extra-virgin rapeseed oil

Cut the potatoes into neat 5mm thick slices. Add them to a pan of boiling salted water, return to a simmer and poach for 3–4 minutes until *al dente* (retaining a little bite rather than soft).

Drain the potato slices, spread them out on a tray and drizzle with the extra virgin rapeseed oil. Keep warm, ready to serve.

Crispy deep-fried capers

2 tbsp small capers in brine, drained
Vegetable oil for deep-frying

Put the capers into a small sieve or chinois. Heat the oil in a deep-fryer to 180°C.

Carefully lower the capers into the hot oil and fry for up to 1 minute until they stop bubbling. Remove and drain on kitchen paper. Leave to cool and crisp up.

To assemble & serve

A large handful of frisée, picked into fine sprigs, refreshed in iced water
1 Granny Smith apple, cut into thin batons
Sea salt
Extra-virgin olive oil (we use Leblanc), to dress

Gently warm the smoked eel portions under the salamander or grill.

Lay the sliced black truffle potatoes on top of the beetroot royales and place a portion of smoked eel in the centre.

Finish with the pickled beetroot, frisée, crispy capers and apple batons. Season lightly with salt, dress with a little extra-virgin olive oil and serve.

Smoked haddock omelette

A delicate, beautiful omelette is one of those pure dishes that makes you realise great food does not have to be about hundreds of ingredients on a plate. It's about allowing a simple product to sing. I learnt that lesson back in the day when I worked for Gary Rhodes and we used to do a lobster omelette which showcased the chef's technique rather than putting a load of fancy things on the plate.

This smoked haddock omelette, which has been on The Hand & Flowers menu pretty much since we opened, started off as a lobster one. But I took a sharp, commercial learning curve early on. Starting out, of course, we had no accolades and were relatively unknown, so there was no reason for customers to spend what, at the time, was the equivalent of £30 or £35 on an omelette, even if it had lobster in it!

I still loved the idea of an omelette, so we tried an omelette Arnold Bennett (a fluffy open omelette created at The Savoy in the 1920s for the novelist, playwright and critic). Most people didn't know who Arnold Bennett was, so we just called it 'smoked haddock omelette with Parmesan' and after a first couple of bumpy weeks it became one of our most popular dishes.

There is no reason why this dish should ever change. I can't improve it. The flavour profile of the humble omelette is heightened with gently poached smoked haddock, a brilliant glaze made from hollandaise sauce and a béchamel sauce flavoured with the fish poaching liquor. So, even the glaze has got that lovely smoked taste, which really drives the flavour.

Actually, this omelette is probably my favourite dish on the menu. I am very pleased to say the lobster version has reappeared at Kerridge's Bar & Grill in London some 14 or 15 years down the line, and has gone on to become one of our most Instagrammed dishes. Thank you Gary Rhodes…

Poached smoked haddock

*1 side of smoked haddock, 600g,
   skin and pin bones removed*
600ml whole milk

Check the smoked haddock for any
tiny pin bones. Bring the milk to
the boil in a wide-based saucepan.
Carefully lay the smoked haddock
in the pan, ensuring it is covered
by the milk. Place a lid on the pan,
turn off the heat and leave the fish
to poach in the residual heat for
about 10 minutes.

Once the haddock is cooked, remove
it from the milk and gently flake the
fish into a tray lined with greaseproof
paper. Cover the tray with cling film
and place in the fridge until ready
to serve.

Pass the milk through a fine chinois
into a clean saucepan and keep to
one side.

Smoked fish béchamel

*250ml smoked haddock poaching
   liquor (see left)*
15g unsalted butter
15g plain flour
Sea salt and freshly ground pepper

Bring the smoked haddock poaching
liquor to a gentle simmer.

In a separate pan over a medium-low
heat, melt the butter. Stir in the flour
to make a roux and cook, stirring,
for 2 minutes. Gradually ladle in the
warm poaching liquor, stirring as
you do so to keep the sauce smooth.
Cook gently over a very low heat for
20 minutes.

Pass the sauce through a fine chinois
and cover the surface with a piece
of baking parchment or cling film
to prevent a skin forming. Set aside
until needed. (You won't need all of
the fish béchamel but you can freeze
the rest.)

Omelette glaze

*4 tbsp warm smoked haddock
   béchamel (see left)*
*4 tbsp hollandaise sauce
   (see page 403)*
4 medium free-range egg yolks
Sea salt and freshly ground pepper

Gently warm the béchamel in a
saucepan then pour into a bowl and
whisk in the hollandaise and egg
yolks. Season with salt and pepper to
taste and pass through a chinois into
a warm jug or bowl. Keep warm to
stop the glaze from splitting.

To assemble & cook the omelette

12 medium free-range eggs
4 tbsp unsalted butter
100g aged Parmesan, finely grated
Sea salt and freshly ground pepper

Crack the eggs into a jug blender and blend briefly to combine. Pass through a chinois into a measuring jug. Place 4 individual omelette pans (we use Staub) over a low heat.

Take the smoked haddock from the fridge, remove the cling film and lay on a grill tray. Warm under the salamander or grill.

To each omelette pan, add 1 tbsp butter and heat until melted and foaming. Pour the blended egg into the pans, dividing it equally. Using a spatula, gently move the egg around in the pans until they start to firm up. Remove from the heat; you want the eggs to be slightly loose, as they will continue to cook off the heat.

Season the omelettes with salt and pepper and sprinkle the grated Parmesan over their surfaces. Divide the flaked smoked haddock between the omelettes, then spoon on the glaze to cover the fish and extend to the edge of the pans. If the glaze spills over the side of the pan, wipe it away, as this will burn on the side when blowtorching.

To finish, wave a cook's blowtorch over the surface of the omelettes to caramelise the glaze. Allow the glaze to become quite dark, as the bitterness will balance out the richness of all the other ingredients.

Bread

When Beth and I first opened The Hand & Flowers and were living above the pub, the first job I would do when I came downstairs in the morning was bake bread. It never felt like a chore for me: the making and baking of bread is just lovely. I'd do as many white rolls as we needed for lunch, and maybe enough for dinner – sometimes it was two batches, other days just one lot was enough.

For me, bread is a sign of generosity, a metaphorical warm hug for our lovely diners. Often, it's the first piece of food that you'll serve your guests; it gives a taste of what's to come and sets the tone for the meal ahead. Serving bread also helps the kitchen team, since it gives them crucial time to prepare each guest's first course.

As The Hand & Flowers became a bit more established, we started making loaves of brown soda bread each morning, as well as the white rolls. Soda bread is easy to make, as there is no yeast involved and the dough doesn't need to be proved – it's just knocked together. I use a recipe that I've had for years and years.

These days we also buy in sourdough, because this kind of bread takes 48 hours to prove and we simply haven't got the space to prep it. I know our soda bread is probably the best you can get, while the sourdough is even better than we can make ourselves at the restaurant.

Bread is more than just something to start a meal with, though. Back in 2008, when the global recession hit, there was a period when we were really struggling financially. There's a little alleyway in the centre of Marlow High Street and we asked the guys in the shop, which was a Threshers at the time, if we could 'borrow' it every Saturday morning.

We set up a little market stall and I would get up on a Friday morning, go into work, do a full day at The Hand and then, as soon as we had cleaned down on the Friday night (around midnight), I'd set up the two KitchenAids and a Kenwood mixer and make around 100 loaves of bread.

It took all night; the chefs would start coming in around about 7.30am and they'd find the loaves of bread waiting there. Beth would set up in the little alleyway and sell it from our stall – and that would cover her and my wages for the week.

I'm sure this story isn't dissimilar to what many other people with small businesses go through. Sometimes, it's what you have to do to make a new venture work: go the extra mile. Having the bread-stall sideline was something that defined our business at that moment, and it helped it to survive at a tough time. The bread was all right as well…

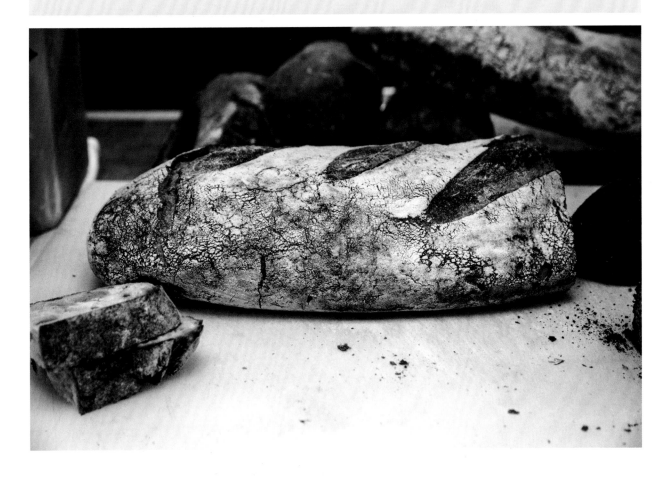

Chicken liver parfait

with bitter orange chutney & toasted brioche

SERVES 8

Chicken liver parfait is one of those things that you can eat anywhere and everywhere. It's a pub classic. Easy to make – although quite difficult to make technically well – it's relatively inexpensive, goes a long way, and people love it.

I remember eating chicken liver parfait at Marco Pierre White's three-Michelin-starred restaurant in Knightsbridge when I was in my late teens. It was beautifully presented – the jelly had set like glass and the parfait was served on top, with toasted brioche on the side. Stunning.

This recipe relies on a Pacojet, a food processor that transforms frozen ingredients into ready-to-eat ice creams and sorbets. It was the only thing that fitted onto the shelves in our tiny kitchen when we started, so I decided it was the one 'big' bit of kit that we would buy. It took around 18 months of tinkering to develop this dish, the parfait evolving from a simple slab of terrine to something that tasted incredible, with a texture that's rich and smooth, just like ice cream.

Presentation is always hugely important to us, and I adore the boards we had made specifically for this dish – for serving our brioche. Alongside the brioche is a generous dollop of bitter orange Seville chutney, which I've made since the mid 1990s when I was working at Stephen Bull's restaurant in St Martin's Lane, London. We use Seville oranges because they have a wonderful bitterness and the flavour profile that comes from them is just fantastic.

I absolutely love the simple elegance of this starter. And while it may be one of the most stripped-back dishes in our repertoire, it delivers on so many flavour fronts.

Chicken liver parfait

300g chicken livers, trimmed of
sinew and soaked in milk
overnight to remove bitterness
200g foie gras, diced
2g salt
4g saltpetre
80ml red wine
30g onion, peeled and finely sliced
1 small garlic clove, peeled
and grated
100g unsalted butter, softened
30ml glycerine

Drain the chicken livers and place them in a bowl with the foie gras, salt and saltpetre.

Mix together then tip into a vacuum-pack bag and vacuum at full pressure. Immerse in a water-bath at 50°C and cook for 1 hour.

Turn up the heat to 64°C and cook for a further 30 minutes.

Meanwhile, put the red wine and sliced onion into a small saucepan over a medium heat and cook until the onion is softened and the liquor has evaporated.

Open the vacuum-pack bag and tip the cooked chicken livers into a high-powered jug blender (Vitamix). Add the onion reduction, garlic, butter and glycerine. Blend until smooth, then pass through a fine chinois.

Pour into a Pacojet beaker and freeze for 24 hours. Churn before serving.

Bitter orange chutney

Finely grated zest and juice of
4 Seville oranges (if in season)
or use regular oranges
85ml red wine vinegar
50ml balsamic vinegar
225g caster sugar
1½ red onions, peeled and
finely diced
2 Bramley apples, peeled and diced
15g yellow mustard seeds

Put the orange juice and zest, wine vinegar, balsamic vinegar and sugar into a saucepan and bring to the boil. Add the diced onions and apples along with the mustard seeds.

Cook gently for about 45–50 minutes, stirring occasionally, until the mixture is reduced to a thick, rich chutney. Transfer to a bowl and set aside to cool.

Jellied poultry stock base

1 turkey drumstick, meat removed from the bone and cut into 2cm dice, bone chopped (ask your butcher to do this)
1½ tbsp vegetable oil
2 banana shallots, peeled and sliced
3 celery sticks, sliced
½ red pepper, deseeded and sliced
75ml runny honey
75ml soy sauce
2.5 litres chicken stock (see page 400)

Preheat the oven to 205°C/Fan 185°C/Gas 6–7. Lay the diced turkey and bone in a roasting dish and drizzle with 1 tbsp oil. Toss the meat, bone and oil together and roast in the oven for 25 minutes.

Put a large saucepan over a medium-high heat and add the remaining ½ tbsp oil. When hot, add the sliced shallots, celery and red pepper. Sauté until softened and fully caramelised. Remove the pan from the heat.

Tip the roasted turkey meat and bone from the tray into the pan with the vegetables.

Pour the honey into the roasting tin and place over a medium heat. Heat until the honey caramelises, then add the soy, stirring and scraping with a spatula to deglaze. If you need a little more liquid to deglaze, add a splash of the chicken stock. Add the honey and soy to the saucepan with the meat, bone and vegetables.

Pour on the chicken stock, bring to the boil and skim off any impurities from the surface with a ladle. Simmer for 2 hours, skimming regularly. Pour the stock through a fine chinois into a bowl, then through a chinois lined with 3 layers of muslin into another bowl or jug.

Allow the stock base to cool and set, then refrigerate until needed.

Poultry jelly

250ml jellied poultry stock base (see left)
2 sheets of bronze leaf gelatine
40ml vin jaune
Sea salt

Remove any fats from the surface of the set poultry stock with a spoon.

Soak the leaf gelatine sheets in a shallow dish of cold water to soften for 5–10 minutes.

Pour the stock into a saucepan, bring to a gentle simmer, then take off the heat. Squeeze out the excess water from the gelatine then add to the hot stock, stirring until fully melted.

Pass the stock through a chinois into a container, stir in the vin jaune and season with salt to taste. Cover and place in the fridge to set.

When ready to serve, transfer the jelly to a bowl and whisk until it has broken down to a smooth piping constancy. To remove any excess air bubbles, place the jelly in a vacuum-pack bag and compress on full pressure. As the air is excluded, the jelly will darken and become clear.

Open the vacuum-pack bag and put the jelly into a piping bag fitted with a 5mm plain nozzle.

Brioche

480g 'T45' plain flour, plus extra
    for dusting
2 tsp salt
85ml tepid whole milk
15g fresh yeast
30g caster sugar
6 medium free-range eggs, beaten
    (or 285g beaten egg)
400g unsalted butter, diced
    and slightly softened
Spray oil, for oiling

Put the flour and salt into a mixer fitted with the dough hook and mix briefly. Pour the warm milk into a jug, crumble in the yeast, add the sugar and stir to dissolve the yeast.

Add the yeast liquid to the mixer with the beaten eggs and mix on a low speed for 4 minutes; the dough will be very firm, tacky and pale yellow in colour.

Keeping the mixer on a low speed, add the soft butter pieces, one by one, at 3–4 second intervals, so each piece is incorporated into the dough before the next is added – you may find this takes a while.

Once the butter is fully incorporated, scrape the dough into a floured bowl and cover with cling film. Place in the fridge to rise slowly overnight.

The next day, take the dough out of the fridge, tip it onto a lightly floured surface and knock back. Roll into a smooth ball, then roll into a cylinder, the same length as a 1kg loaf tin.

Oil the loaf tin with one spray of oil, then lay the rolled dough in the tin and cover with cling film. Leave to prove in a warm place for about 1 hour until doubled in size.

Preheat the oven to 240°C/Fan 220°C/Gas 9. Bake the brioche in the oven for 10 minutes, then lower the setting to 200°C/Fan 180°C/Gas 6. Bake for a further 20 minutes or until a fine skewer, inserted into the middle, comes out clean.

Leave in the tin for 5 minutes then tip out onto a wire rack and leave to cool completely.

Once cooled, cut the brioche into 1cm thick slices, ready for toasting.

To assemble & serve

Flaky sea salt

Churn the frozen chicken liver parfait. Spoon the bitter orange chutney into small ramekins.

When the parfait is ready, using a large hot spoon, shape a large rocher for each serving and place on individual plates. Pipe the poultry jelly neatly and tightly around the base of each parfait. Sprinkle the top of each parfait with a little salt.

Toast the brioche until golden on both sides. Serve the parfait at once, with the warm brioche and bitter orange chutney on the side.

Goose egg 'ambassadrice'

with foie gras, bitter leaves & truffle brioche

—— SERVES 4 ——

This dish is like the best fried egg ever, with layers of astounding flavours and textures. Dean Timpson, one of our local suppliers, is its inspiration. He used to be head chef at the Compleat Angler in Marlow, just a stone's throw from The Hand & Flowers. These days, he's got a smallholding in High Wycombe where he keeps geese, among other things.

One day, Dean brought us some of his goose eggs. We fried them up and they were absolutely lovely. That made us think about the other delicious things that come from geese, like foie gras, and we built this sumptuous dish from there.

The dish includes really punchy, bitter leaves to wake up the taste buds; a rich, velvety sherry beurre blanc; a shallot dressing with truffle oil, which gives acidity and depth; and crispy pork puffs (dehydrated pork skin) which crunch and rattle satisfyingly around the mouth.

It all adds up to the most wonderful, balanced, sophisticated mouthful of fried egg you could ever imagine! It had to have a name to match, so Dean's goose egg ended up being called goose egg 'ambassadrice' – something fit for an ambassador… big and over the top.

Truffle brioche

10g dried trompette mushrooms,
   chopped
250g 'T45' plain flour, plus extra
   for dusting
1 tsp salt
40ml tepid whole milk
7g fresh yeast
15g caster sugar
3 medium free-range eggs
200g unsalted butter, diced and
   slightly softened
20ml Alba white truffle oil
30ml beaten egg yolks or liquid
   egg yolk, for glazing

Soak the dried mushrooms in warm water to cover for about 20 minutes, then drain and chop them; set aside.

Put the flour and salt into a mixer fitted with the dough hook and mix briefly.

Pour the warm milk into a jug, crumble in the yeast, add the sugar and stir until the yeast is dissolved.

Add the yeast liquid to the mixer with the beaten eggs and mix on a low speed for 3 minutes; the dough will be very firm, tacky and pale yellow in colour. In a separate bowl, mix the softened butter with the chopped mushrooms and truffle oil.

Keeping the mixer on a low speed, add the soft butter, mushroom and truffle oil mixture, a little at a time, at 3–4 second intervals, so each addition is incorporated into the dough before the next is added.

Scrape the dough into a floured bowl and cover with cling film. Place in the fridge to rise slowly overnight.

Take the dough out of the fridge, tip it onto a lightly floured surface and knock back. Divide the dough into 50g pieces and shape into balls.

Place the brioche dough balls in lined timbale moulds, brush with the egg glaze and leave to prove for about 45 minutes until doubled in size.

Preheat the oven to 240°C/Fan 220°C/Gas 9. Bake the brioche in the oven for 4 minutes, then lower the oven setting to 200°C/Fan 180°C/Gas 4. Bake for a further 4 minutes, or until a skewer inserted into the centre of one comes out clean.

Leave to cool in the tins for a few minutes then tip out onto a wire rack and leave to cool. Freeze any brioche that you are not serving immediately. The brioche are best eaten while still slightly warm. *Makes about 14*

Truffle shallot dressing

4 banana shallots, peeled and
    finely diced
70ml olive oil
5g truffle oil
Sea salt and freshly ground pepper

In a bowl, mix the diced shallots with the olive and truffle oils. Season with salt and pepper and set aside.

Sherry butter sauce

100ml warm beurre blanc
    (see page 403)
25ml dry sherry

Simply flavour the warm butter sauce with the sherry; keep warm.

Crispy pork puffs

50g Sosa Airbag Granet dehydrated
    pork skin, broken into very
    small pieces
Vegetable oil for deep-frying
Sea salt

Heat the oil in a deep-fryer to 190°C. Add the pork skin pieces and fry for about 40 seconds. Remove from the oil with a slotted spoon, drain on kitchen paper and season with salt.

To assemble & serve

100ml butter emulsion (see page 403)
2 chicory hearts, halved and turned
20 small girolles
4 slices of frozen rouge foie gras
30ml vegetable oil
4 free-range goose eggs
20g chives, chopped
A large handful of bitter leaves,
    such as frisée and red chicory
1 small black truffle, about 30g
Sea salt and freshly ground pepper

Heat the butter emulsion in a wide pan. Add the chicory and girolles and poach for about 2 minutes until just cooked, with a slight raw edge to the chicory, then take off the heat.

Meanwhile, heat a plancha or non-stick heavy-based frying pan over a high heat. Lay the frozen foie gras slices on the hot plancha or frying pan for about 40 seconds until cooked one-third of the way up. Flip the slices over and cook for another 30 seconds.

At the same time, heat 4 individual cast-iron dishes (we use Staub) over a medium-low heat and add a splash of oil to each.

Crack a goose egg into each dish and fry gently. Just before the eggs set, lay the foie gras slices in the dishes, to one side of the yolks and continue to cook until the egg white is set.

Briefly place the dish under the salamander or grill to warm the yolk through. Season the egg with salt and pepper to taste.

Sauce the dish with the truffle shallot dressing, then the sherry butter sauce. Sprinkle the chopped chives on top of the foie gras. Add the poached girolles and chicory and garnish with the bitter leaves.

Finish with a sprinkling of crispy pork puffs and a grating of black truffle. Serve at once, with the warm truffle brioche.

Gala pie

with Matson sauce

SERVES 6

I love those food products – like gala pie (pork pie with an egg) – that people usually think are somehow inferior. And I get a real buzz from using the finest ingredients I can get my hands on and transforming them into something fantastic for the restaurant.

This particular gala pie is a hymn to my childhood growing up near Matson, a council estate in Gloucester. The sauce is a tribute to the chippie around the corner from where I used to live, Matson Chip Shop (sadly no longer there). It's a thick, brown, vegetable curry purée with dried fruit to give it sweetness, and it's got my heart and soul in it! Which is why I've now got a (very important) Matson sauce (aka a super-posh 'chip-shop curry sauce') featuring prominently alongside my gala pie.

I encourage the front-of-house team to tell diners that Matson is an estate in Gloucester. I'm sure that conjures up a country pile for many, but I'm tickled by the fact that it's actually a salute to my humble beginnings. I think of Matson every time I serve the sauce. It makes me smile because I love Matson and I love Gloucester, and I'm so proud of growing up where I did.

Pork pie filling

A little vegetable oil for cooking
1 onion, finely diced
225g pork shoulder, diced
60g pork cheek oyster, diced
100g lardo, diced
1 small garlic clove, peeled
  and grated
½ tsp chopped sage
½ tsp thyme leaves
½ tsp salt
A pinch of cracked black pepper
2 splashes of Worcestershire sauce
1 medium free-range egg, beaten
30g fresh white breadcrumbs

Chill the mincer attachment for your mixer in the fridge for a minimum of 4 hours.

Heat a little oil in a pan over a medium heat, add the onion and cook until soft. Remove from the heat and set aside to cool.

When the mincer is thoroughly chilled, fit a 5mm die plate. Mix the diced pork shoulder, cheek and lardo together and press through the mincer into a large bowl.

Add the cooled onion, garlic, sage, thyme, salt, pepper, Worcestershire sauce, beaten egg and breadcrumbs. Mix to combine and work the mixture thoroughly with your hands (wearing disposable gloves).

To test the seasoning, heat a little oil in a small frying pan and fry a small nugget of the mixture, then taste and adjust the seasoning of the main mixture accordingly.

Cover the bowl and chill the mixture in the fridge for 1 hour.

Matson sauce

10g unsalted butter
1 large onion, peeled and finely sliced
1 garlic clove, peeled and grated
1½ tbsp mild curry powder
1 star anise
150ml chicken stock (see page 400)
1½ tbsp raisins
1½ tbsp malt vinegar
1 tbsp cornflour, mixed to a paste
  with 1 tbsp water
Juice of 1 lemon
Sea salt and freshly ground pepper

Heat the butter in a heavy-based saucepan over a medium-low heat. Add the onion and cook until softened. Add the garlic and spices and cook for a further 5 minutes to release their flavour.

Pour in the stock, bring to the boil, then add the raisins and vinegar. Reduce the liquor by half – you should have an equal volume of liquid to onion. Whisk in the cornflour paste and cook, stirring, for a few minutes, then remove the star anise.

Transfer the sauce to a blender and blitz to a smooth purée. Add the lemon juice and season with salt and pepper to taste. Pass through a fine chinois into a jug, cover and refrigerate until ready to serve.

Boiled quail's eggs

6 quail's eggs

Add the quail's eggs to a pan of boiling water and cook for 2 minutes and 10 seconds to soft-boil.

Lift out and immerse in a bowl of iced water to cool quickly. When cold, peel the shells – be careful not to break the eggs.

Place the eggs on a small tray lined with a clean cloth in the fridge to dry and chill for 30 minutes.

To build the pie filling

Pork pie filling (see page 89)
6 soft-boiled quail's eggs (see
page 89)
10g coriander leaves, chopped
12 large spinach leaves
200g caul fat, soaked in cold
water for 30 minutes

Divide the pork pie filling into
6 portions and weigh the quail's eggs.
The total weight of the quail's egg
plus its pork mix coating should be
60g, so adjust the portion of pork
mix accordingly.

Flatten a portion of pork mix in the
palm of your hand to the thickness of
a £1 coin, place the quail's egg in the
middle and mould the mix around
the egg filling, as you would a Scotch
egg. Repeat to coat the rest of the
quail's eggs. Sprinkle the gala pork pie
balls with the chopped coriander and
place back on the tray in the fridge.

Lay the spinach leaves on a steamer
tray and steam for 1 minute, then
cool quickly in the blast chiller
(or over a bowl of iced water).

Lay 2 spinach leaves, overlapping, on
a sheet of cling film and place a gala
pork pie ball in the middle. Bring the
spinach up around the ball to enclose
it, pulling the cling film up around
the spinach leaf to form a tight seal,
leaving no gaps. Repeat to wrap the
other gala pie balls in spinach.

Now lay a single sheet of caul fat on
a clean board. Remove the cling film
from one spinach-wrapped ball. Place
the ball in the middle of the caul and
wrap the caul around it, trimming off
the excess to ensure it is only a single
layer. Repeat to wrap the other
spinach balls in caul. Place in the
fridge to dry and set the caul fat.

Egg glaze

3 medium free-range egg yolks
5g dextrose
2 tsp whole milk

Whisk the egg yolks and dextrose
together to combine, then stir in the
milk. Leave the glaze to rest for an
hour before use.

Pastry

250g 'T45' plain flour, plus extra
for rolling
50g polenta
½ tsp bicarbonate of soda
½ tsp salt
75g lard, diced
95ml water

Put the flour, polenta, bicarbonate
of soda and salt into a mixer fitted
with the paddle attachment.

Heat the lard and water in a
saucepan to melt the lard and bring
to the boil. Pour into the mixer and
work to a smooth dough.

Once the pastry comes together,
remove from the bowl and divide
into 7 equal portions. Use straight
away, while the pastry is still warm.

To shape the gala pies

Roll out one piece of warm pastry on a lightly floured surface to a large thin disc. Place a caul-wrapped gala pie ball in the middle and quickly wrap in the pastry to make a perfect round ball, pressing out any creases. Repeat to shape the rest of the pies.

Wrap the remaining ball of pastry in cling film (this will be used to make the chimneys on top of the pies); keep it warm. Allow the pastry around the pies to cool and set.

Once the pastry is set, thinly roll out the remaining ball of dough on a lightly floured surface to a 2mm thickness. Cut 6 strips, 2 x 1cm.

Brush a small area on top of a pie with a little egg wash. Press a small tube (the width of a pen) into the top of the pie. Wrap the pastry strip around the base of the tube joining with the pie, trimming off any excess pastry. Carefully pull the tube from the pie.

Keep the pies in the fridge until ready to bake and serve.

To bake the pies & serve

1 tbsp black mustard seeds
1 tbsp picked thyme leaves
1 tsp sea salt

Preheat the oven to 205°C/Fan 185°C/Gas 5–6. Take the pies from the fridge and brush them evenly with the egg glaze. Sprinkle with the mustard seeds, thyme and salt.

Place each pie on a small square of non-stick baking parchment paper and place on a baking tray.

Bake the gala pies in the oven for 6 minutes, then rotate them to ensure even cooking and bake for another 6 minutes until golden and the filling is cooked through.

Remove the pies from the oven and leave to rest for 3 minutes.

Meanwhile, warm the Matson sauce and place 1 tbsp in the centre of each warmed serving bowl. Position a pie directly on the middle of the sauce; this will spread the sauce beneath to a perfectly round pool. Serve at once.

Potted artichoke

with trompettes, burnt rosemary butter & rye cracker

SERVES 8

This particular flavour combination suits the autumn and winter seasons. It goes back to when vegetarian food was just starting to come to the forefront on restaurant menus and we were looking at dishes that could be made to appeal to vegetarians. One of the beauties of Jerusalem artichokes is that they are quite fragrant and light, and those qualities work really nicely with truffle. We serve the potted artichoke with a delicious rye cracker to give the dish a lovely texture and crunch.

If you're a fully-fledged member of the carnivore society, like me, you might think, 'right, the artichokes and truffle looks lovely in a bowl, drizzled as they are in butter emulsion, but let's put a sheet of very fine lardo over it and then pop the bowl under a little heat so it melts'! If you do that, you get an enticing, shiny, translucent piece of lardo giving a wonderful porky, salty fattiness that tastes incredible with the artichokes and truffle. You could serve the dish without it for vegetarians (leaving out the bacon and pork sauce, too) but the lardo makes it very special.

The garnish of chervil signs the dish off with a delicate hint of aniseed – a touch of freshness to contrast with the fat. In fact, chervil and artichoke is a classic French flavour combination. And, actually, you can substitute chervil root for the Jerusalem artichokes in the recipe as their flavours are quite similar.

Jerusalem artichokes

800g Jerusalem artichokes
Juice of 1½ lemons (approximately)
125g beurre noisette (see page 403)
1 garlic clove, peeled and sliced
3 sprigs of thyme
75ml double cream
5ml black truffle oil
Sea salt

Peel and dice the artichokes, adding them to a bowl of cold water with the juice of 1 lemon added as you do so, to prevent discoloration.

Drain the artichokes and place in a vacuum-pack bag. Add the beurre noisette, garlic and thyme. Vacuum-seal under full pressure then cook in a water-bath at 88°C for 30 minutes until the artichokes are tender.

Open the bag, drain off and reserve the beurre noisette. Set aside half of the cooked artichokes. Put the rest of the artichokes into a saucepan, pour on the cream to cover and bring to the boil. Lower the heat and simmer for 5–10 minutes, until soft.

Tip the artichokes in cream into a blender and purée until smooth. Add the truffle oil, and salt and lemon juice to taste. Pass through a sieve into a bowl, cover the surface closely with baking parchment to stop a skin forming and leave to cool.

Heat the reserved beurre noisette in a sauté pan until foaming, then add the diced artichokes and fry until they start to caramelise. Drain the artichokes in a colander, then transfer to a bowl, cover and refrigerate until ready to serve.

Poached globe artichokes

4 globe artichokes
Finely grated zest and juice of
  1 lemon, plus the juice of another
  lemon for acidulating
100ml double cream
1 tsp citric acid
1 sprig of rosemary
½ tsp salt

To prepare the artichokes, have ready a bowl of cold water acidulated with the juice of 1 lemon. Trim each artichoke, removing the base and inedible leaves. Scoop out the hairy choke with a teaspoon and immerse the artichoke heart in the acidulated water to prevent discoloration.

Drain the prepared artichoke hearts and place them in a vacuum-pack bag with the cream, lemon zest and juice, citric acid, rosemary sprig and salt. Vacuum-seal the bag under maximum pressure and cook in a water-bath at 80°C for 40 minutes.

Lift out the bag and immerse in iced water to cool quickly. Once cooled, open the bag, drain the cooked artichokes and wipe off the cream, then slice them into thin wedges.

Smoked oil mayonnaise

1 medium free-range egg yolk
1 tbsp Dijon mustard
1 tsp white vinegar
200ml smoked rapeseed oil
Juice of ½ lemon
Sea salt and freshly ground pepper

Whisk the egg yolk, mustard and wine vinegar together in a bowl. Slowly whisk in the smoked oil, until you have a thick mayonnaise. Add the lemon juice and season with salt and pepper to taste. Pour into a container, cover and keep in the fridge until needed.

Burnt rosemary butter

185g unsalted butter
15g rosemary sprigs

Gently melt the butter in a small pan, just to clarify it.

Lay the rosemary on a baking tray and wave a cook's blowtorch all over the surface until the whole sprigs are smouldering and charred. Add the charred rosemary to the clarified butter and set aside to infuse in a warm place for 30 minutes.

Pour the butter through a fine chinois into a bowl to strain off the rosemary. Keep warm, but allow the butter to settle and separate.

Skim off the clarified butter and keep warm to one side, ready to brush on the cracker before serving.

Rye cracker

300g dark rye flour, plus extra
*   for dusting*
100g strong white bread flour
4g sea salt
8g demerara sugar
360ml tepid water
12g fresh yeast

Put the flours, salt and sugar into a
mixer fitted with a dough hook. Pour
the warm water into a jug, crumble
in the yeast and stir until the yeast is
dissolved. Turn the mixer on, then
add the yeast liquid. Mix to combine
and continue to work the dough for
6 minutes until smooth and elastic.

Remove the dough hook, cover the
bowl with cling film and leave to
prove for about 40 minutes until
increased in volume by one-third.

Preheat the oven to 200°C/Fan
180°C/Gas 6. Tip the dough onto
a baking sheet lined with a silicone
mat. Lightly flour the surface and roll
the dough out to a 5mm thickness.

Dust the thin sheet of dough with
a little more rye flour, then press the
handle end of a pastry brush into it
at close intervals to leave small round
indentations all over the surface.
Score the dough into large triangles,
using a pizza cutter.

Bake for 20 minutes, then lower the
oven setting to 180°C/Fan 160°C/Gas
4 and bake for a further 10 minutes
to dry and crisp the cracker. Remove
from the oven and leave to cool.

Once cooled, break the cracker into
the cut triangles and store in an
airtight container until ready to serve.

For the artichoke mix

150g Jerusalem artichoke purée
*   (see opposite)*
30g banana shallots, peeled
*   and finely diced*
400g cooked diced Jerusalem
*   artichokes (see opposite)*
200g cooked diced globe artichokes
*   (see opposite)*
½ red chilli, deseeded and
*   finely diced*
2 tbsp chopped flat-leaf parsley
75ml smoked oil mayonnaise
*   (see opposite)*
Sea salt and cayenne pepper

In a saucepan, warm the artichoke
purée, then add the shallots and
both the cooked diced Jerusalem
artichokes and the artichoke heart
wedges. Warm through gently, to
take the chill off the veg, then add
the red chilli, parsley and smoked
mayonnaise. Season with salt and
cayenne to taste.

To assemble & serve

100ml butter emulsion (see page 403)
100g trompettes, cleaned
24 sprigs of wild chervil
8 thin slices of Alsace bacon
8 thin slices of lardo
*   (8cm square, 4mm thin)*
4 tbsp pork sauce (see page 401)
1 small Périgord truffle
Sea salt and freshly ground pepper

Heat the butter emulsion in a small
pan and season with salt and pepper.
Add the trompettes and poach for
1 minute.

Meanwhile, divide the artichoke mix
between warmed heatproof serving
bowls. Drain the mushrooms on a
tray lined with a J-cloth, then scatter
them over the artichoke in the bowls.
Scatter over the chervil sprigs.

Lay the bacon slices over the top,
then cover with the lardo slices. Place
the bowls under the salamander or
grill, just to melt the fat.

Drizzle a little pork sauce over each
portion to enrich the dish. Grate over
the black truffle and sprinkle with
salt and pepper to finish. Brush the
rye crackers with rosemary butter
and serve alongside.

Torchon of quail

with crispy quail leg, verjus & Matson sauce

———————— SERVES 4 ————————

We've always served traditional terrines, but the continuing challenge is to move them on and make them even more special. As you know, I'm partial to gala pie (see page 87), and coming up with a fancy version is a natural way to go for The Hand & Flowers.

At the heart of this dish is a ballotine – a quail's egg (cooked very, very gently to keep its middle lovely and soft), surrounded by foie gras mousse and spinach, which is then wrapped in quail and a layer of pancetta. So that's all very classic. But then it's lifted, made modern, by serving it with a tempura of quail leg; so, you have elements that are hot and cold in the dish. And there's a splash of spice from our Matson sauce.

I'm proud of this beautiful dish. Not just because it's delicious (which it is) but because it came from Dave Scott, one of our former sous chefs at The Hand & Flowers. It shows that he understood the exact style of food, texture, balance and flavour profile of our cooking. I'd be happy if I had created it myself!

Verjus jelly

3 sheets of bronze leaf gelatine
180ml verjus (we use Minus 8)
25g caster sugar

Soak the leaf gelatine in a shallow dish of cold water to soften for 5–10 minutes.

Heat the verjus and sugar in a pan to dissolve the sugar and bring to the boil. Take off the heat. Immediately squeeze out the excess water from the gelatine leaves, then add them to the verjus liquor and stir until fully melted.

Pass through a fine chinois into a jug. Cover and chill until needed (to glaze the quail).

Foie gras mousse

125g skinless boneless chicken breast
125g foie gras
10g sea salt
A pinch of cayenne pepper
12ml truffle oil
1 medium free-range egg

Chill a jug blender goblet.

Trim the chicken breast of any sinew and de-vein the foie gras. Cut both into 1cm pieces and place in the freezer for 20 minutes.

Put the chilled chicken breast and foie gras into the blender, add the salt, cayenne and truffle oil and blend to a paste. Remove the lid and scrape down the sides. Now, with the motor running, add the egg and blend to form a smooth paste.

Scrape the mousse into a Pacojet beaker and freeze. Churn when you are ready to assemble the ballotines.

Foie gras ballotine

2 quail's eggs
100g foie gras mousse (see left)
About 8 spinach leaves (depending on size)

Add the quail's eggs to a small pan of boiling water and cook for 2 minutes and 10 seconds to soft-boil. Lift out and immerse in a bowl of iced water to cool quickly. When cold, peel the shells – be careful not to break the eggs.

Divide the foie gras mousse into 2 portions and place each in the middle of a sheet of cling film. Flatten to the thickness of a £1 coin, place a quail's egg in the middle and mould the foie gras mousse around the egg filling (as you would a Scotch egg) to make 2 ballotines, each 3cm in diameter and 4cm long. Wrap each tightly in the cling film.

Place in the steamer at 62°C and steam for 45 minutes then remove and cool quickly over ice.

Lay the spinach leaves on a steamer tray and steam for 1 minute, then cool quickly in the blast chiller (or over a bowl of iced water). Pat dry with kitchen paper.

Lay 4 spinach leaves overlapping on a sheet of cling film. Unwrap a ballotine and place in the middle of the spinach sheet. Bring the spinach up around the ball to enclose it, trimming away any excess spinach leaf. Pull the cling film up around the spinach to form a tight seal, leaving no gaps. Repeat to wrap the other ballotine in spinach. Refrigerate until needed.

To prepare the quail

2 quail
400ml brine (10% solution)
15g curry powder
40g butter, melted
4 slices of pancetta
2 foie gras ballotines (see opposite)
Verjus jelly (see opposite)

Remove the legs and wings from the quail, then de-bone the quail: split the skin down the backbone and butterfly the breasts. Remove the thigh bone from the legs.

Immerse the butterflied breasts and quail legs in the brine for 2 hours. Remove the quail, drain and pat dry.

Put the quail legs into a vacuum-pack bag with 5g of the curry powder and the melted butter. Immerse in a water-bath at 88°C for 1 hour. Lift out and chill, then take the legs from the bag and French-trim the bone.

Place 2 sheets of cling film on a clean surface and lay 2 pancetta slices side by side on each, so there are no gaps between them. Dust the flesh side of the quail breasts with curry powder then wrap each foie gras ballotine in a butterflied quail's breast, ensuring the meat is evenly distributed. Place on the pancetta and wrap around the quail parcel to enclose fully, then roll tightly in the cling film to seal.

Immerse in a water-bath at 64°C for 1 hour, then remove and place in an ice-bath to cool quickly and chill.

To serve, bring the quail parcels to room temperature. Slice in half through the middle to bisect the yolk. Glaze with some verjus jelly.

Tempura batter

250ml cold water
1g xanthan gum
45g rice flour
80g cornflour
5g salt

Put the water and xanthan gum into a blender and blend until thickened. Add all of the other ingredients and blend until combined. Pass through a fine chinois into a bowl, cover and chill thoroughly.

Pour the chilled batter into the ISI cream whipper, charge with two charges and shake well. Set aside until you are ready to coat and fry the quail legs.

Deep-fried quail legs

Vegetable oil for deep-frying
4 poached quail legs (see left)
20g rice flour, for dusting
Tempura batter (see above)
Sea salt and freshly ground pepper

Just before serving, heat the oil in a deep-fryer to 180°C. Dip the poached quail legs into the rice flour and turn to coat all over; shake off any excess.

Now dip the quail legs into the batter, carefully add to the hot oil and deep-fry for 3–4 minutes until crisp and golden. Remove and drain on kitchen paper then season lightly; keep hot.

To serve

Matson sauce (see page 89)
1 white chicory bulb
1 red chicory bulb
8 red seedless grapes, halved
8 semi-dried white grapes (partially dried in the dehydrator for 6 hours)
8 sour grapes (unripe white grapes)
30g spiced peanuts, halved

Pipe a little cold Matson sauce into the centre of each plate and sit a quail parcel on top. Arrange red and white chicory leaves, halved red grapes, sour grapes, semi-dried grapes and spiced peanuts around the torchon of quail and add a little verjus jelly.

Serve the hot Matson sauce and a deep-fried quail leg in a warmed ramekin alongside, garnished with chicory, grapes and nuts.

Swede & haggis tart

with chantilly de chèvre, crispy lamb & mushroom

Swede isn't the most commonly used vegetable, but it has a wonderful earthy sweetness and takes massive flavours and fat really well. I love it. We used to have a delicious, crushed swede side dish with loads of rich butter and cracked black pepper on the menu. It was fantastic and I wanted to find a way of transforming it into a starter. But I couldn't quite get my head around elevating this particular side dish until I went to Gleneagles and was blown away by a lunch of neeps, tatties and haggis.

Fortunately, about the same time, I rediscovered an old but incredible Cheddar pastry recipe, which I learnt in the early 1990s while I was working for Stephen Bull in London. Basically, it's a cheese sablé recipe adapted to make a tart base using a tangy, powerful Cheddar – you know, one of those Cheddars that almost stings!

When you bake the tart cases, you have to cook the pastry all the way through so that it caramelises properly. You're aiming for the kind of flavour you get when you put cheese on toast under the grill but leave it just a little bit too long. You get a crispness that really drives the salty, sharp cheese content into the pastry. All you've got to do then is to fill the tart with ultra-sweet and savoury salt-baked swede and great, earthy haggis and make it look pretty!

The final layer of loveliness is a little rocher of smooth, creamed goat's cheese and crème fraîche on top. It's got a touch of vanilla that binds everything together and the gently melting rocher trickles a hint of pepperiness into the tart.

Cheddar pastry cases

*170g 'T45' plain flour, plus extra
    for dusting*
1 tsp salt
A pinch of cayenne pepper
*170g unsalted butter, in pieces,
    softened*
170g mature Cheddar, finely grated

Put the flour, salt and cayenne into
a bowl and rub in the butter until
the mixture resembles breadcrumbs.
Add the cheese and mix to combine
and bring the dough together. Form
the dough into a ball, wrap in cling
film and leave to rest in the fridge
for 1 hour.

Line a baking sheet with parchment
and sit 8 individual tart rings, 8cm in
diameter, on it. Roll out the pastry on
a lightly floured surface and cut out
8 discs, using a 10cm pastry cutter.
Use to line the tart rings, pressing the
pastry carefully into the edges. Line
each pastry case with 3 sheets of
cling film and add a layer of baking
beans. Place in the freezer to rest and
chill for 1 hour.

Preheat the oven to 190°C/Fan
170°C/Gas 5 and bake the pastry
cases for 15–20 minutes until golden.
Remove the beans and cling film and
leave the pastry cases to cool.

Once cool, store the pastry cases in
a single layer in an airtight container
until ready to assemble.

Salt-baked swede

*250g plain flour, plus extra
    for dusting*
75g salt
1 medium free-range egg white
105ml water
1 large swede, about 700g
*Clarified butter (see page 403)
    for brushing*

Put the flour and salt into a mixer
fitted with the paddle attachment.
Add the egg white and water and mix
together to form a smooth dough.
Wrap the dough in cling film and
leave to rest in the fridge for 1 hour.

Preheat the oven to 180°C/Fan
160°C/Gas 4. Take the dough out of
the fridge and roll it out on a lightly
floured surface to the thickness of
a £1 coin. Place the swede in the
middle of the dough and wrap the
dough around it to enclose and seal.
Place on a baking tray and bake in
the oven for 2 hours.

Take the swede from the oven and
allow to cool, then remove the pastry
crust and cut away the skin from the
swede. Halve the swede and cut two
barrels from each half, using a 5cm
round cutter. Save the trimmings for
the purée (see right). Cut the barrels
into fine slices, using a mandoline.

Place 8 individual tart rings, 8cm in
diameter, on a baking tray. Fan the
swede slices out in the tart rings so
each ring has a rosette of swede
petals. Brush with clarified butter
and chill in the fridge.

Swede purée

*200g salt-baked swede trimmings
    (see left)*
60ml double cream
50g unsalted butter

Chop the swede trimmings into
roughly even sized pieces. Heat the
cream and butter in a small pan, add
the swede trimmings and simmer for
10 minutes.

Transfer the mixture to a blender and
blitz to a purée. Pass through a fine
chinois into a piping bag and place in
the fridge until ready to serve.

Haggis

75g shoulder of lamb, minced
25g lamb's liver, minced
25g lamb heart, minced
25g lamb lung, minced
20g lamb suet, minced
25g cooked diced onions
1g ground allspice
3g cracked black pepper
3g salt
15g oatmeal
20g jumbo oats
3ml Worcestershire sauce
A little vegetable oil for frying

Put all of the haggis ingredients into a bowl and mix together thoroughly until well combined and the mixture comes together.

Place the haggis mixture on a board covered with a sheet of cling film. Roll up the haggis in the cling film to form a thick sausage, about 5cm in diameter, and twist the ends of the cling film to seal. Cook the haggis in a steamer for 30 minutes or until cooked through. Remove from the steamer and allow to cool.

Just before serving, slice the haggis into 1cm thick discs and fry in a little oil until crisp.

Crispy lamb breast

200g minced lamb breast
Sea salt and freshly ground pepper

Place a frying pan over a high heat. When it is hot, add the lamb mince and fry, stirring, until browned and crisp. Remove from the pan and season with salt and pepper.

Spread the browned mince out on a dehydration tray and place in the dehydrator overnight to dry fully.

Chantilly de chèvre

200g rindless goat's cheese
100g thick crème fraîche
1 vanilla pod, split and seeds
  scraped
25ml whole milk
Sea salt and freshly ground pepper

Beat the goat's cheese, crème fraîche and vanilla seeds together in a bowl until smooth, then fold in the milk. Season with salt and pepper to taste and transfer to a small container. Cover and chill until needed.

To assemble & serve

120ml lamb sauce (see page 401)
8 button mushrooms
A small handful of lemon
  thyme leaves

Preheat the oven to 180°C/Fan 160°C/Gas 4. Put a disc of fried haggis into each pastry case, then pipe the swede purée around it. Top with the fanned rosette of swede and bake in the oven for 6 minutes.

Place a swede and haggis tart on each warmed serving plate and sauce the tart with a little lamb sauce. Add a generous spoonful of crispy lamb breast, then top with a rocher of chantilly de chèvre. Grate over the button mushrooms and finish with a sprinkling of thyme leaves.

Baked potato 'risotto'

with ceps & wild garlic pesto

— SERVES 4 —

Everyone loves baked potatoes, and the combination of potato, garlic and mushrooms is simple but lush. That said, at The Hand & Flowers, everything is geared to flavour-plus – ingredients tasting of what they're supposed to, but more so. A beautiful baked potato stock, with Maris Piper potatoes, girolles and wild garlic makes this an absolutely gorgeous dish, particularly when it's finished with melting mozzarella and Parmesan. It's like a hugely indulgent and amazing risotto, but without the rice.

The recipe is inspired by my amazing friend Claude Bosi of Bibendum in London, who serves an incredible 'risotto' of his own using celeriac (which he dices to look like rice) and stock-infused, roasted celeriac skins, so that you end up with that wonderful, risotto-like texture and an intense flavour kick of celeriac.

At The Hand, we dice the potatoes to the same size as rice grains and cook them at 72°C for 32 minutes. At that point, the starch sets, which means that you can't overcook the potatoes until they disintegrate; it's almost failsafe. We then bake the potato skins separately to make the stock.

It's a great concept and creates such a beautiful, light and flavoursome dish. Not surprisingly, it has spawned many other equally delicious forms of 'risotto' across the entire Kerridge restaurant business.

Baked potato stock

150g baked potato skins
(from jacket potatoes)
500ml chicken stock (see page 400)

Preheat the oven to 200°C/Fan 180°C/Gas 6. Lay the potato skins on a baking tray, spreading them out evenly. Bake in the oven for 35 minutes until crisp and a dark, even colour.

Bring the stock to the boil in a saucepan, add the potato skins and leave to infuse for 30 minutes.

Pass the infused stock through a chinois, then through a sieve lined with 3 layers of muslin into a jug. Refrigerate until needed.

Risotto potato dice

3 large Maris Piper potatoes

Wash and peel the potatoes, then slice into large, thin discs, using a mandoline. Square off the edges of the slices, then cut into 4mm dice (to imitate the size of rice grains). Tip the potato dice into a chinois and rinse thoroughly under cold running water to wash off the potato starch.

Drain the potatoes and tip them into a medium vacuum-pack bag. Spread the potato dice evenly in the bag and vacuum-seal on full pressure to compress the potato. Immerse in a water-bath at 72°C and cook for 32 minutes.

Lift out the vacuum bag and plunge it into a bowl of iced water to cool the potato dice quickly.

Once cold, if serving straight away, open the bags and transfer the potato dice to a small container; otherwise leave the potatoes in the sealed bag.

Potato skin crisps

1 large Maris Piper potato
Sea salt

Wash the potato and pat dry, then peel, removing the skin in long strips. Put the potato skin strips into a bowl and season evenly with a little salt.

Preheat the oven to 205°C/Fan 185°C/Gas 6–7 and line a baking tray with baking parchment. Lay the potato skin strips on the tray, placing them skin side down and spreading them out so they are not touching each other. Bake in the oven for 8–10 minutes until dark golden.

Remove from the oven and leave to cool and crisp up. Once cooled, keep in an airtight container.

Poached garlic

1 large garlic bulb (or 2 cloves per person)
Olive oil for poaching

Break the garlic bulb into individual cloves and place them in a small saucepan. Pour on enough water to cover and bring to the boil. Drain the garlic and immerse in a bowl of iced water to refresh. Repeat this process twice more, using fresh water.

After the final blanch and refresh, drain the garlic cloves and allow them to cool.

Carefully peel the garlic and place in a clean small saucepan. Pour on enough olive oil to just cover and warm gently over a low heat until the garlic is soft. Remove from the heat and set aside to cool.

Wild garlic pesto

100g wild garlic leaves, stem removed
200g picked parsley leaves
5g garlic, grated
20g pine nuts, toasted
30g Parmesan, grated
6g sea salt
200ml olive oil

Immerse the wild garlic and parsley leaves in a pan of boiling salted water and blanch for 1 minute until soft. Drain and plunge into a bowl of iced water to refresh. Drain the leaves and squeeze out excess water, then place on a board and lightly run your knife through them.

Tip the roughly chopped herbs into a high-powered jug blender (Vitamix) and add all the remaining ingredients. Blitz to a purée then spoon into a Pacojet beaker. (You will have more pesto than you need for this dish; refrigerate the rest in a jar, covered with a layer of oil.)

Chive oil

200ml non-scented oil (sunflower or rapeseed)
75g chives, roughly chopped
Sea salt and freshly ground black pepper

Gently heat the oil in a small saucepan to 150°C. (Use a digital probe to check the temperature.)

Put the chives into a high-powered jug blender (Vitamix). Pour on the warm oil and blend to a purée. Pass through a sieve lined with 2 layers of muslin into a jug and season with salt and pepper to taste.

Chill the chive oil in the blast chiller (or stand the jug in a bowl of iced water) to cool quickly and retain its vibrant green colour, then pour it into a squeezable plastic bottle, ready for serving. (You will have more chive oil than you need; refrigerate any you're not using straight away.)

Potato risotto

20g unsalted butter
80g shallot, finely diced
400ml baked potato stock
  (see page 107)
200g cooked risotto potato dice
  (see page 107)
50g Parmesan, freshly grated
30g buffalo mozzarella (we use
  Laverstoke Park Farm), diced

Melt the butter in a medium saucepan over a medium-low heat until foaming, then add the diced shallot and sweat until soft.

Pour in the infused potato stock and simmer to reduce until it starts to thicken. Add the cooked potato dice and continue to simmer until you have a risotto-like consistency.

Season with the Parmesan and set aside (ready to add the mozzarella just before serving); keep warm.

To assemble & serve

2 firm, medium ceps
Vegetable oil for cooking
25g unsalted butter
70ml chicken sauce (see page 400)
8 garlic cloves
4 oyster leaves
Sea salt and freshly ground
  black pepper

Halve the ceps and lightly score the surface in a criss-cross pattern. Heat a splash of oil with the butter in a frying pan and add the ceps. Fry for 2–3 minutes until tender and lightly caramelised, then add the chicken sauce and turn the ceps to glaze.

Lay the garlic cloves on a baking tray and season with salt and pepper. Warm gently under a low salamander or grill.

Meanwhile, start to assemble the dish. Churn the wild garlic pesto. A minute before the garnish will be ready, gently warm the risotto through over a low heat and stir through the diced mozzarella.

Drain the ceps and place them on a cloth-lined tray to dry, along with the grilled garlic cloves. Sprinkle with a little flaky salt.

Divide the risotto base between 4 warmed serving bowls and arrange the ceps and grilled garlic cloves on top. Using a hot teaspoon, add a generous rocher of the wild garlic pesto to each portion.

Drizzle chive oil around the plates and place an oyster leaf and a potato skin crisp on each portion to serve.

Truffle en croûte

with foie gras & port

Essentially, this is a posh gala pie with a truffle instead of an egg in the middle. It's a very, very simple idea but, I have to admit, the French got there first! They call this style of dish 'en croûte' (baked in pastry) and places like the Roux's Le Gavroche restaurant in London do amazing ones with chicken mousse or foie gras encasing the truffle.

Our British version came about because of a supplier – a little Italian guy who would turn up at the kitchen door with whatever he had in season. One day, he dropped by with an impressive load of really small English truffles. I bought the lot: all 20kg!

The trouble is, summer truffles don't always have the biggest flavour, so we needed to figure out how to make them taste amazing. We vacuum-packed them, then came up with this recipe, which I basically think of as a pork pie with a mushroom in it!

You have to think about creating a dish that works for service in a restaurant like The Hand & Flowers and this one is a perfect example. It minimises the room for error in our super-busy kitchen, because it calls for a lot of pre-service preparation. That way, we can bake it to order at the last minute.

So, truffles are pre-poached; a foie gras and boudin mix is made and left to cool well ahead; the truffles are wrapped in the foie gras mix and chilled in advance; pastry is added and egg washed; oven timings worked out to the nanosecond for perfection. That's it! You've got the pies made, all you're doing is waiting for the order and sticking one in the oven. As a guest you just see a beautiful tiny pie with amazing pastry and a fantastic centre, which melts magically in your mouth.

Poached truffles

100ml red wine
100ml Madeira
100ml brandy
1 tsp truffle oil
8 small truffles, cleaned

Put the red wine, Madeira, brandy and truffle oil into a small saucepan and bring to a simmer. Remove from the heat and allow to cool.

Put the cooled liquor and truffles into a small vacuum-pack bag and seal tightly. Immerse in a water-bath at 88.2°C and poach for 10 minutes. Lift the bag out of the water-bath and immediately plunge into a bowl of iced water or place in the blast chiller to cool quickly.

Once cooled, remove the truffles from the bag and drain, reserving the liquor. Set aside to dry.

Pass the liquor through a muslin-lined sieve and reserve 30ml for the filling.

Foie gras mousse

125g skinless boneless chicken breast
125g foie gras
10g sea salt
A pinch of cayenne pepper
12ml truffle oil
1 medium free-range egg

Chill a jug blender goblet. Trim the chicken breast of any sinew and de-vein the foie gras. Cut both into 1cm pieces and place in the freezer for 20 minutes.

Put the chilled chicken breast and foie gras into the blender, add the salt, cayenne and truffle oil and blend to a paste. Remove the lid and scrape down the sides. Now, with the motor running on a low speed, add the egg, blending to emulsify.

Pass the smooth mixture through a drum sieve into a bowl, cover and refrigerate until needed.

To build the truffle

8 poached truffles (see left)
Foie gras mousse (see left)

One at a time, weigh each truffle and add enough foie mousse (about 40g) to the scales to make up to 60g. Carefully wrap the truffle in the mousse to form a perfect ball.

Place the wrapped truffles on a tray lined with baking parchment and chill for 2 hours to firm up before wrapping them in the pastry.

Egg glaze

3 medium free-range egg yolks
5g dextrose
2 tsp whole milk

Whisk the egg yolks and dextrose together to combine, then stir in the milk. Leave the egg glaze to rest for an hour before use.

Port glaze

400ml port

Pour the port into a wide saucepan, bring to the boil and let bubble to reduce right down to about 40ml, to form a rich glaze.

Pastry

250g strong white bread flour, plus extra for dusting
50g polenta
½ tsp bicarbonate of soda
½ tsp sea salt
75g lard
90ml water

Put the flour, polenta, bicarbonate of soda and salt in a mixer fitted with the paddle attachment.

Melt the lard with the water in a saucepan over a medium heat and bring to the boil. Immediately pour onto the dry ingredients and mix on a low speed to form a smooth dough.

Remove from the bowl and knead lightly with your hands, just to bring the dough together to form a ball. Divide and shape the pastry into 30g balls; wrap in cling film. Use while still warm.

To assemble

One at a time, unwrap each pastry ball and roll out on a lightly floured surface to a 4mm thick disc.

Place a coated truffle in the centre of each disc and wrap the pastry around it to enclose, trimming off the excess and sealing the edges well.

Roll each ball gently to ensure it is perfectly round. Place the truffle en croûtes in the fridge to rest for an hour before cooking and serving.

To bake & serve

200ml pork sauce (see page 401)
Sea salt

Preheat the oven to 200°C/Fan 180°C/Gas 6.

Brush each truffle en croûte lightly all over with the egg glaze and make a hole in the top of the pastry with a butcher's needle or fine skewer.

Sprinkle with sea salt and place on a baking sheet lined with baking parchment. Bake in the oven for 12 minutes, turning halfway through. Remove from the oven and leave to rest for 5 minutes.

While the pie is resting, heat up the pork sauce and add the 40ml port glaze to finish.

Place each truffle en croûte in the middle of a warmed serving plate and serve the sauce in a jug on the side.

Beef fat brioche

with English mustard butter, Gem lettuce & corned beef

—— S E R V E S 1 2 ——

This dish is in heartfelt praise of that very British wartime favourite, bread and dripping. It reminds me of my mum and of my nan, her mum, who'd lived through the Second World War and taught mum never to waste beef roast dripping. As a kid, I would go ferreting in the fridge and see this little pot of solid, white fat. There was no way I ever wanted to eat it back then! One day, decades later, after I'd saved some beef fat from a Sunday lunch at The Hand & Flowers, I just thought, 'let's live a little,' so I spread it on a piece of toast, took a bite and thought, 'Wow! It's roast beef on toast without roast beef!'

Then began the challenge to elevate dripping to Hand & Flowers standard. We based our dish on a beef dripping brioche, but stuck with the idea of wartime and post-war rationing to give it a big, robust flavour. Corned beef, salad cream and lettuce – and a delicious hit of ox tongue.

I'm lucky to have had the chance to talk to grandparents who lived through the war. But my little man – like most of the chefs in my kitchen – will have no real connection with that time. It's a privilege to create and eat a beautiful dish like this and understand the history that inspired it, and it's up to me to pass that knowledge on.

BEEF FAT BRIOCHE

Crispy beef fat

500g beef cod fat, minced
Sea salt and freshly ground pepper

Put the beef cod fat into a large saucepan over a low heat. As it begins to render, give it a whisk to separate the grains. Keep frying over a low heat so the fat crisps up.

Once you have brown crispy beef fat crumb, pass it through a sieve and lay on a small tray lined with a J-cloth. Season with salt and pepper and leave to cool.

Beef fat brioche

475g 'T45' plain flour, plus extra
for dusting
10g salt
100ml tepid whole milk
15g fresh yeast
30g caster sugar
200g beaten eggs
(about 4 medium free-range)
375g unsalted butter, diced
and slightly softened
10g salted anchovies, diced
20g capers in brine, drained
15g Marmite
Finely grated zest of 1 lemon
1–2 tsp rendered beef fat
100g crispy beef fat (see left),
for the glaze

Put the flour and salt into a mixer fitted with the dough hook and mix briefly.

Pour the warm milk into a jug, crumble in the yeast, add the sugar and stir until the yeast is dissolved. Add the yeast liquid to the mixer with the beaten eggs and mix on a low speed for 4 minutes; the dough will be very firm, glossy and pale yellow in colour.

Keeping the mixer on a low speed, add the softened butter pieces, one by one, at 3–4 second intervals, so each piece is incorporated into the dough before the next is added – this may take a while. Add the anchovies, capers, Marmite and lemon zest and continue to mix until these flavourings are evenly distributed.

Scrape the dough into a floured bowl and cover with cling film. Place in the fridge to rise slowly overnight.

The next day, remove from the fridge, tip the dough onto a lightly floured surface and knock back. Roll into a smooth ball, then into a cylinder the same length as a 900g loaf tin.

Grease the loaf tin with rendered beef fat, then lay the rolled dough in the tin and cover with cling film. Leave to prove in a warm place for about 1 hour.

Preheat the oven to 240°C/Fan 220°C/Gas 9. Brush the top of the brioche with rendered beef fat and sprinkle with the crispy beef fat. Bake in the oven for 10 minutes, then lower the oven setting to 200°C/Fan 180°C/Gas 6. Bake for a further 20 minutes or until a fine skewer, inserted into the middle of the brioche, comes out clean.

Leave in the tin for 5 minutes then tip out onto a wire rack. Leave to cool completely.

Once cooled, cut the brioche into 1.5cm thick slices and lay on a board. Press a 4cm cutter into the middle of each brioche slice to remove a disc. (This will be replaced with the corned beef slices.)

Corned beef

*375g beef brisket, brined for 5 days
    in a 10% brine
600g rendered beef fat
½ tsp salt
½ tsp cracked black pepper*

Lift the brined brisket out of the liquid and rinse under cold running water for 20 minutes.

Put the brisket and beef fat into a vacuum-pack bag and vacuum-seal on full pressure. Immerse in a water-bath at 88.2°C and cook for 8 hours.

Once cooked, take the beef from the bag and drain off the fat, reserving 100g of it. Chill the reserved fat, then grate it.

Flake the beef into a bowl and add the salt, pepper and grated beef fat. Let cool slightly and then bring the mixture together with your hands.

Shape the corned beef into a cylinder, 4cm in diameter, and wrap in cling film. Tie the ends with butcher's twine and chill in iced water to set the shape. Remove from the water and place in the fridge to firm up overnight.

Slice the corned beef into 1.5cm discs and remove the cling film. Press a disc of corned beef into the hole in the middle of each slice of brioche (see opposite).

Mustard butter

*500g unsalted butter, softened
100g English mustard
20g salt*

In a bowl, beat the butter, mustard and salt together until smoothly combined. Scrape the butter into a Pacojet beaker, level the surface and freeze.

Before serving, churn the butter in the Pacojet beaker and leave at room temperature until ready to serve. (You will have more mustard butter than you need. Refrigerate or freeze any you're not using straight away.)

Salad cream

*15g 'T45' plain flour
75g caster sugar
2 large free-range eggs
15g English mustard powder
125ml white wine vinegar
125ml double cream
A generous squeeze of lemon juice,
    to taste
Salt and cayenne pepper*

Put the flour, sugar, eggs, mustard and wine vinegar into a large heatproof bowl. Whisk over a pan of simmering water until thick and increased in volume to form a thick sabayon, and to cook out the flour. Remove the bowl from the heat and leave to cool.

In a separate bowl, whisk the cream to soft peaks. Once the sabayon is cooled, fold in the cream and season with salt, cayenne pepper and lemon juice to taste.

Spoon into a piping bag and keep in the fridge until ready to serve.

Parsley oil

300ml vegetable oil
250g parsley leaves

Heat the oil in a Thermomix to 70°C and add the parsley leaves. Blend for 1 minute at 70°C, then pass the oil through a fine chinois into a bowl and leave to cool. (You will have more parsley oil than you need; refrigerate any you're not using straight away.)

Date purée

250g pitted dates
*4 Granny Smith apples (you need
  200g prepared weight)*
¼ tsp ground ginger
¼ tsp ground nutmeg
¼ tsp ground allspice
*150ml Cabernet Sauvignon red
  wine vinegar*
150ml standard red wine vinegar
200g soft dark brown sugar
Sea salt and freshly ground pepper

With a sharp knife, chop the dates quite small and put into a bowl. Peel and coarsely grate the apples. Weigh out 200g apple and add to the dates. Mix in the ground spices.

Put the wine vinegars into a pan with the sugar and heat to dissolve. Bring to the boil and pour onto the date and apple mix. Cover with cling film and leave to cool; the dates will absorb some liquid and become soft.

Tip the mixture into a heavy-based pan and cook over a very low heat for 1½ hours until soft and pulpy. Remove from the heat and blitz in a jug blender until smooth. Season with salt and pepper to taste.

Pass through a fine chinois into a bowl or jar, cover and keep in the fridge until needed. Bring to room temperature before serving.

Poached Gem lettuce

6 Little Gem lettuces
75ml parsley oil (see left)
*300ml butter emulsion
  (see page 403)*
Sea salt and freshly ground pepper

Halve the lettuces vertically and remove any damaged outer leaves. Using a paring knife, turn the root end of each lettuce half to round it.

Place the lettuce halves in a vacuum-pack bag and pour in the parsley oil. Vacuum-seal on full pressure and place in the fridge for 2 hours.

When ready to serve, remove the lettuce halves from the bag. Heat the butter emulsion in a pan and season with salt and pepper. Add the lettuce halves and poach for 2 minutes. Drain on a tray lined with kitchen paper.

Place the lettuce halves, cut side up, on a metal tray and wave a cook's blowtorch over the surface to char the lettuce.

Braised ox tongue

1 ox tongue, about 1kg, brined
for 5 days in a 10% brine
300g caster sugar
50ml water
50ml soy sauce
20g Marmite

Lift the brined ox tongue out of the brine and rinse under cold running water for 30 minutes.

Put the caster sugar into a heavy-based saucepan and melt over a medium heat, then increase the heat and cook to a golden caramel. Take off the heat and immediately add the water and soy to stop the caramel cooking, followed by the Marmite. Whisk until smooth.

Tip the caramel into a large vacuum-pack bag and leave to cool. When cool, add the ox tongue and vacuum-seal under full pressure to remove all air. Immerse in a water-bath at 88.2°C and poach gently for 8 hours.

Remove the poached tongue from the water-bath and leave until cool enough to handle. Pass the cooking liquor through a fine chinois and set aside.

Once cooled enough, remove the tongue from the vacuum bag, reserving the liquor, and carefully peel away the membrane. Place in a clean vacuum-pack bag and pour the cooking liquor back over it. Re-vacuum and chill until needed.

When ready to serve, drain the ox tongue, reserving the liquor, and cut into 5mm thick slices.

To serve

Rendered beef fat for frying
Vegetable oil for cooking
12 quail's eggs
3 tsp chopped chives
Sea salt and freshly ground pepper

Preheat the oven to 205°C/Fan 185°C/Gas 6–7. Heat a little rendered beef fat in a frying pan and gently fry the brioche slices until golden brown on both sides. Place on a tray in the oven for 3 minutes to keep warm.

Meanwhile, fry the ox tongue slices in the fat remaining in the frying pan until lightly caramelised on both sides. Add the reserved cooking liquor to the glaze.

At the same time, heat a little oil in a frying pan, carefully add the quail's eggs and fry over a very low heat for about 3 minutes until the whites are set and the yolks are still soft. Season with salt and pepper to taste. Use a cutter to trim and neaten the eggs.

Remove the toast from the oven and lay on a draining tray. Lay a glazed ox tongue slice on one corner of each brioche slice and top with a fried quail's egg. In the opposite corner, place a little scoop of date purée.

Position a blowtorched lettuce half on a third corner and a piece of crispy beef fat on the opposite corner. Place a rocher teaspoonful of mustard butter on the beef fat. Spoon some salad cream on top of the lettuce and sprinkle with chives.

Carefully transfer the built brioche toasts to warmed plates and serve.

Crispy pig's head

with black pudding, rhubarb & pork crackling

—— SERVES 8 ——

The meat from a pig's head is super, super tasty. That alone is enough to get a chef excited. But coming from the West Country also means I'm very proud of our pig-farming heritage – just think of the Gloucester Old Spot, anything bearing our regional name makes me a happy boy!

The thought of buying and cooking a pig's head can be intimidating if you're not a chef. People get a bit queasy. But if you eat sausages, that's not so different. Once you braise the head and start taking the meat off the skull itself, mixing it all together, it's just fantastic. Press it, cut it, pané it and deep-fry it. I promise you, it really is delicious.

This recipe was inspired by our great friend, Nottingham-based chef Sat Bains. He used to do a phenomenal Japanese-influenced pig's head croquette with kombu seaweed, which our former head chef, Aaron Mulliss, tasted when he was on a stage at Sat's. We do something a little bit different – more British in style with a bit of Channel hopping to France. We start by braising the pig's head with a classic mirepoix and a dash of English mustard, which give a fabulous porky taste to the meat. The piggy-ness doesn't stop there, though, because there's a lovely little cube of fried black pudding served alongside the deep-fried pig's head meat, which explodes in your mouth when you bite into it: soft and gooey in the middle and deliciously crispy on the outside.

All that rich porky-ness is offset by a sprinkle of nutty, oaty crumble, a pork crackling stick (very simple to do) and the acidic hit of rhubarb. I use rhubarb a lot; it's great for cutting through the flavour of rich food. We've got it two ways here: pickled and puréed into a kind of ketchup.

I'm particularly pleased with the clean crisp taste of chickweed that finishes the dish. Chickweed tastes of the grass that it grows with, which makes me think of pigs in a field… all very connected!

To braise the pig's head

½ pig's head
2 tbsp coriander seeds
2 tbsp black peppercorns
½ bunch of thyme
½ bunch of rosemary
1 onion, peeled and roughly chopped
1 carrot, peeled and roughly chopped
1 celery stick, roughly chopped
2 tbsp salt
100ml white wine vinegar
100g Dijon mustard
Sea salt and freshly ground pepper

Place the half pig's head in a suitably sized ovenproof pan and cover with water. Bring to the boil, then pour off the water and cover the pig's head with fresh cold water. Repeat this process twice more.

Meanwhile, tie the coriander seeds and black peppercorns in a muslin bag. Preheat the oven to 150°C/Fan 130°C/Gas 2.

As you cover the pig's head with fresh water for the third time, add the muslin spice bag, herbs, diced vegetables, salt and wine vinegar. Bring to the boil and cover the pan with foil. Place the pan in the oven for 6–8 hours until the pig's head is cooked through.

Lift the pig's head out of the liquor onto a board. When cool enough to handle, flake all the meat and skin, including the tongue. Mash it all together with your hands then place in a bowl. Add the mustard and season with salt and pepper to taste. Mix thoroughly.

Press the seasoned meat in a tray lined with cling film, cover and place in the fridge for 12 hours. Remove from the tray before portioning.

Rhubarb purée

375g rhubarb, sliced
125g caster sugar
Juice of ½ lemon
50g unsalted butter, diced and chilled

Put the rhubarb into a saucepan with the sugar, lemon juice and a splash of water. Place over a very low heat and cook for about 15 minutes until soft.

Transfer to a blender and blitz until smooth, then pass through a fine chinois into a clean pan; the purée should be quite thick.

Return to a low heat and add the butter, a few pieces at a time, stirring vigorously to emulsify. Set aside.

Black pudding

1 small pig's heart
95g double cream
1 medium free-range egg
20g fresh white breadcrumbs
75g lardo, cut into 5mm dice
*100g smoked streaky bacon, cut
   into 5mm dice*
150g onion, peeled and finely diced
20g fine ground oatmeal
500g pig's blood (clot free)
½ tsp ground mixed spice
8g salt
1 tsp brown sugar
40ml dark rum

Put the pig's heart into a small pan, cover with cold water and bring to the boil, then drain off the water. Repeat this process twice more, then return the pig's heart to the pan, cover with fresh cold water and bring to the boil again. Lower the heat and simmer for 4–5 hours until tender.

Leave the pig's heart to cool in the liquid, then drain and chop into 5mm dice.

In a bowl, lightly whisk the cream and egg together to combine, then add the breadcrumbs and give it a stir. Leave the breadcrumbs to soak for 30 minutes.

In a large saucepan over a low heat, render the fat from the lardo. Lift the lardo from the pan with a slotted spoon and set aside.

Add the bacon to the rendered fat in the pan and fry until evenly coloured. Remove with a slotted spoon and add to the lardo.

Add the onion to the fat remaining in the pan and fry until soft without colouring. Remove the pan from the heat and let cool slightly.

Add the breadcrumb mix, oatmeal, pig's blood, braised heart, spice, salt, sugar and rum to the onion. Return the pan to a low heat and stir to mix thoroughly. Heat to 40°C (check the temperature with a digital probe).

Pour the warm black pudding mixture into a small tray lined with 3 layers of cling film. Cover the tray with foil and place in a steam oven at 100°C for about 2 hours until it reaches a core temperature of 75°C (check with a digital probe), indicating it is cooked.

Remove from the steam oven and press the black pudding using another (slightly smaller) tray. Place in the blast chiller, or in the fridge overnight, to set and cool quickly. Remove from the tray before cutting.

Oat crumble

50g plain flour
50g caster sugar
50g jumbo oats
5g honey
35g unsalted butter, diced

Preheat the oven to 180°C/Fan 160°C/Gas 4. Put all of the crumble ingredients into a mixer and mix until well combined.

Gather the mixture together and roll it out directly on a baking sheet to form an even 5mm thick sheet.

Bake in the oven for 20 minutes until golden and crisp. Allow to cool, then break or chop the crumble into small pieces. Keep in an airtight container until needed.

Pickled rhubarb

140ml white wine vinegar
35ml water
175g demerara sugar
2 bay leaves
½ cinnamon stick
¼ tsp freshly grated nutmeg
½ tsp ground mace
1½ tsp white peppercorns
1½ tsp salt
4 sticks of rhubarb, peeled

For the pickling mix, put the wine vinegar, water, sugar, bay leaves, spices and salt into a small saucepan and bring to the boil. Remove from the heat, cover and leave to infuse in a warm spot for 1 hour. Pass the pickling liquor through a fine chinois and set aside to cool.

Cut the rhubarb into 5cm lengths and place in a vacuum-pack bag. Cover with the cold pickling liquor and vacuum-seal under high pressure. Cook in a water-bath at 80°C for 10 minutes, then immerse the bag in a bowl of iced water to stop the cooking.

Drain the pickled rhubarb batons and cut 3 fine slices off each one. Set these aside, with the rhubarb batons, ready for serving.

Pork crackling sticks

1 pig skin, from the belly
(we use skin destined to be
cured for bacon)
Sea salt

Place the pork skin in a vacuum-pack bag and vacuum-seal under full pressure. Immerse in a water-bath at 70°C and cook for 24 hours. Lift out the bag and chill thoroughly.

Preheat the oven to 205°C/Fan 185°C/Gas 6–7.

Remove the cooked pork skin from the bag and cut it into long, thin strips. Season all over with salt (this helps it to crackle). Place on an upturned baking sheet and lay a second baking sheet on top. Bake in the oven for 15 minutes.

Remove from the oven and leave to cool. The pork crackling sticks will release from the trays as they cool. Set aside.

To finish & serve

50g plain flour, for dusting
3 medium free-range eggs, beaten,
for eggwash
100g panko breadcrumbs
Vegetable oil for deep-frying
8 slices of fine-quality pancetta
40ml beurre noisette (see page 403)
8 tbsp pork sauce (see page 401)
24 sprigs of picked chickweed
Sea salt

Cut the pressed braised pig's head into 8 x 3 x 3cm pieces. Coat with flour, then dip into the eggwash and finally into the breadcrumbs, turning to coat all over.

Heat the oil in a deep-fryer to 180°C. Carefully lower in the pig's head pieces and deep-fry for 3–4 minutes. Remove and drain on kitchen paper, then season with salt; keep hot.

While the pig's head is frying, heat a little oil in a frying pan. Cut the black pudding into 2cm squares and coat in flour, then add to the pan and fry until coloured and crisp on all sides. Drain and keep hot.

Lay one strip of sliced pancetta just off-centre in each warmed serving bowl. Add a quenelle of the rhubarb purée and a pickled rhubarb baton.

Warm the black pudding under the grill, then add a cube to each bowl along with 1 tsp beurre noisette and 1 tbsp pork sauce. Lay the crispy pig's head against the pickled rhubarb baton and add a piece of oat crumble. Finish with 3 fine slices of pickled rhubarb, 3 sprigs of chickweed and a pork crackling stick. Serve at once.

Braised hare & pearl barley

with foie gras & pickled quince

SERVES 6

Hare has such a strong, gamey flavour, it's one of those ingredients that people love or hate. It works brilliantly with pearl barley, which is a favourite at The Hand & Flowers. It gives this particular dish a great texture, the kind you get in a risotto. And actually, pearl barley is a very British ingredient, so that sits beautifully with what we do at the restaurants. This is an ideal dish for autumn and winter when customers are dreaming of log fires and wholesome food to fill them up.

Quince is another thing that's cropped up for centuries in British cooking. Flavour-wise, it's not dissimilar to that lovely, perfumed taste of pear, but texturally it's more robust. It has such a short season, I feel it's really important to use it when it's around. We poach the quince in pickling liquor and then add it, once drained, to the pearl barley, along with flaked, braised hare – they liven it up a treat!

On top of the base of pearl barley, we serve beautifully sliced hare loin and a piece of pan-seared foie gras. Okay, so foie gras isn't really British, but hare has zero fat in it and you need a counterbalance of lush richness to provide real comfort. Our customers always appreciate eating a strong, robust dish cooked with delicacy.

Braised hare & pearl barley

Vegetable oil for cooking
2 hare legs
About 1 litre chicken stock
(see page 400)
Pared zest of ½ orange
3 sprigs of lemon thyme
3 sprigs of rosemary
300g pearl barley, soaked in cold
water for 24 hours
50g honey
25ml soy sauce
Sea salt and freshly ground pepper

Heat a little oil in a large frying pan. Season the hare legs with salt and add them to the pan. Colour on both sides, until golden brown. Preheat the oven to 160°C/Fan 140°C/Gas 3.

Transfer the hare legs to a flameproof casserole and pour on enough stock to just cover. Add the orange zest, lemon thyme and rosemary, bring to a simmer over a medium-low heat then put the lid on the casserole and transfer to the oven. Braise for 2–2½ hours until the meat is tender and falling away from the bone.

In the meantime, wash the soaked pearl barley under cold running water until the water runs clear. Put the pearl barley into a saucepan and cover with fresh water. Bring to the boil over a medium heat, lower the heat and simmer for 25–30 minutes until tender but still with a little bite.

Tip the cooked pearl barley into a sieve to drain and refresh under cold running water. Transfer to a bowl, cover and refrigerate until needed. (You will need 4 tbsp of this for the puffed pearl barley garnish.)

Once the hare is cooked, lift the legs out of the casserole, reserving the liquor, and flake the meat off the bone. Place in a bowl, cover and refrigerate until ready to serve.

Heat the honey in a saucepan over a medium heat to caramelise to a rich dark brown, then add the soy. Carefully add the reserved cooking liquor and reduce by one-third. Pass through a sieve into a bowl and keep in the fridge until needed.

Pickled quince

250g white wine vinegar
125g caster sugar
3 star anise
5 white peppercorns
10 coriander seeds
1 cinnamon stick
1 quince

For the pickling liquor, put the wine vinegar, sugar and spices into a small saucepan and bring to the boil. Set aside to cool and infuse, then pass through a sieve into a clean pan.

Peel the quince, cut into quarters and remove the core. Add to the pickling liquor and bring to a simmer. Lower the heat and simmer for 30–35 minutes until tender.

Remove from the heat and chill the quince, in the liquor. Before serving, drain the pickled quince and cut into 2cm dice.

Puffed pearl barley

*4 tbsp cooked pearl barley
  (see opposite)
Vegetable oil for deep-frying
Sea salt and freshly ground black
  pepper*

Pat the cooked pearl barley dry with kitchen paper. Heat the oil in a deep-fryer to 180°C. Add the pearl barley and deep-fry for 1 minute or so until crisp. Drain on kitchen paper and season with salt and pepper. Reserve for the garnish.

To assemble & serve

*75g unsalted butter
Vegetable oil for cooking
2 hare loins, trimmed
6 slices of frozen rouge foie gras
1 tsp lemon thyme leaves
Finely grated zest of 1 orange
6 tsp chopped chives
Sea salt and freshly ground pepper*

Preheat the oven to 205°C/Fan 185°C/Gas 6–7.

Put the braised pearl barley into a saucepan with 300ml of the reserved cooking liquor and the butter. Place over a medium heat and cook until the liquor thickens and emulsifies.

Heat a splash of oil in an ovenproof frying pan and sear the hare loins over a high heat for about 1 minute on each side until dark golden. Transfer the pan to the oven and cook for a further 3 minutes until medium-rare. Set aside in a warm place to rest for 5 minutes.

Meanwhile, place another ovenproof frying pan over a high heat. When hot, add the foie gras slices and sear for 40 seconds on each side or until golden brown. Transfer the frying pan to the oven for 2–3 minutes to finish the cooking.

Add the flaked braised hare and drained quince to the warmed barley, along with the lemon thyme leaves and most of the grated orange zest (save a little for the garnish). Warm through and season with salt and pepper to taste.

Carve each hare loin into 9 slices and season with salt. Spoon the pearl barley mixture into warmed serving dishes and arrange the hare loin slices and foie gras on top. Sprinkle the chopped chives and reserved orange zest on top of the foie gras and finish with the puffed pearl barley. Serve at once.

Pork & mushroom terrine

with dill pickles

———— SERVES 12 ————

It's a nice way to spend an afternoon, making terrines; you finish lunch service, then, having got all your ingredients prepped and ready in the morning, you put together an incredible terrine. It's the nearest you get to calm and civilised during a working day in the kitchen!

When I created this terrine for The Hand & Flowers, I wanted something rustic; a farmhouse-style terrine. I went through loads of recipes. Classic French ones. Larousse. Escoffier. The lot. This recipe is a mash-up of them all. It's based around pork (now there's a surprise!), but I wanted the kind of joy you get when you see a terrine in a little pot in Selfridges Foodhall; you know, the kind that has a little jelly on top.

So I went for a dry duxelles mix finished with port, which adds incredible richness when it's spread on top of the terrine. Then, for a bit of finesse, I added a poultry jelly to sit on top; a beautifully brown, rich, clear gel. When it's sliced, you get a stunning-looking terrine.

You just need to serve it simply. A little sharpness with cucumber pickle, a crunch of yeasty sourdough bread, some indulgent truffle butter. Every element has to be perfect. It's a typical Hand & Flowers dish: simple food that everyone understands, but the absolute best it could possibly be.

Pork terrine

Vegetable oil for cooking
200g onions, peeled and diced
500g pork belly, diced
500g pork shoulder, diced
250g bacon, diced
350g pig's liver, diced
¾ tsp thyme leaves
1 bay leaf
6 juniper berries
1 tbsp cracked black pepper
2 cloves
10g saltpetre
15g table salt
30ml brandy
30ml red wine

Chill the mincer attachment for your mixer in the fridge for a minimum of 4 hours.

Heat a little oil in a pan over a medium heat, add the onions and cook until soft without colouring. Remove from the heat and set aside to cool.

When the mincer is thoroughly chilled, fit a coarse plate. Mix all the pork, bacon and offal together and press through the mincer into a large bowl. Add the softened onions and mix well.

Blitz the herbs, spices and salts together in a spice grinder to a fine powder then add to the minced meat and onion along with the brandy and red wine. Mix thoroughly.

Preheat the oven to 90°C/Fan 70°C/ lowest Gas. Line a 1.3 litre terrine mould with 3–4 layers of cling film, leaving at least 5cm overhanging the sides and ends.

Spoon the pork mixture into the lined terrine, packing it in tightly. Fold over the overhanging cling film to seal.

Cook in the oven until the core temperature reaches 70°C indicating it is cooked (check with a digital probe); this takes 8–12 hours.

Once cooked, place a tray (or similar item) that just fits inside the tin on top of the terrine and press firmly with an appropriate weight (about 500g). Chill overnight.

Mushroom layer

1kg button mushrooms
250ml ruby port

Preheat the oven to 95°C/Fan 85°C/ lowest Gas (with zero humidity). Put the mushrooms into a food processor and pulse until finely chopped.

Spread the chopped mushrooms out on a baking tray lined with baking parchment. Place in the oven until fully dehydrated; this can take up to 12 hours.

Put the dehydrated mushrooms into a saucepan and pour on the port. Place over a low-medium heat for about 5 minutes to reconstitute the mushrooms until soft.

Poultry jelly

*1 turkey drumstick, meat removed
   from the bone and cut into
   2cm dice, bone chopped (ask
   your butcher to do this)*
50g runny honey
100ml soy sauce
2 litres chicken stock (see page 400)
4 shallots, peeled and chopped
4 celery sticks, chopped
½ red pepper, deseeded and chopped
3 sheets of leaf gelatine

Preheat the oven to 205°C/Fan 185°C/Gas 6–7. Place the turkey meat and bone in a roasting tray. Roast in the oven for 25–30 minutes until golden brown. Transfer the turkey bone and diced meat to a suitable saucepan.

Place the roasting tray on the hob over a medium heat, add the honey and stir until caramelised to a rich dark brown. Add the soy sauce and a splash of the chicken stock to deglaze the tray, scraping up all the roasting juices and sediment. Add to the saucepan containing the turkey.

Pour on the rest of the chicken stock to cover and bring to the boil over a high heat. Add the shallots, celery and red pepper, lower the heat to a simmer and reduce the stock down by one-third.

Pass the stock through a fine chinois into another pan and reduce by one-third again to 600ml.

Meanwhile, soak the gelatine in a shallow dish of cold water to soften for 5–10 minutes.

Pass the reduced stock through a muslin-lined sieve into a bowl. Squeeze the excess water from the gelatine then add it to the hot stock, whisking until fully melted. Use warm, to assemble the terrine.

To build the terrine

Carefully remove the cooked terrine from the mould, scraping away any impurities or fats from the surface, and place on a wire rack. Smooth a thin layer of the mushroom and port mix on the top of the terrine, then transfer to a tray. Carefully ladle some of the warm jellied stock over the mushrooms and place in the fridge to set.

Once the poultry jelly layer is set, repeat the process. Continue in this way until you have a layer of jelly roughly 1cm thick. Chill thoroughly for 2 hours then, with a hot knife, trim the sides to neaten.

Wrap the terrine in cling film and refrigerate until ready to serve.

Truffle butter

150g unsalted butter, softened
10g black truffle, finely chopped
5g truffle oil
Sea salt

In a bowl, mix the butter together with the chopped truffle and truffle oil until evenly combined and season with salt to taste.

Using a warm teaspoon, rocher the truffle butter into portions, cover and store on a tray in the fridge until needed. Bring back to room temperature before serving.

Pickle garnishes

500ml wine white vinegar
250g caster sugar
10 white peppercorns
½ cinnamon stick
4 star anise
2 tsp coriander seeds
2 tsp fennel seeds
10–12 baby onions, peeled
40g dill sprigs
½ cucumber, halved lengthways
　and deseeded
12 button mushrooms

For the pickling liquor, put the wine vinegar, sugar and spices into a small saucepan and bring to the boil. Set aside to infuse until cool, then pass through a sieve into a jug.

Place the baby onions in a vacuum-pack bag and cover with one-third of the pickling liquor. Vacuum-seal under full pressure and cook in a water-bath at 70°C for 30 minutes until tender. Lift the bag out of the water-bath and chill.

Put half of the remaining pickling liquor into a jug blender with the dill and blend until smooth. Cut the cucumber into 2cm wide batons and place in a vacuum-pack bag. Pour in the green liquor and vacuum-seal on full pressure. Leave in the fridge.

Warm the remaining pickling liquor. Put the mushrooms into a bowl, pour on the warm liquor and leave to cool, then keep, covered, in the fridge.

Just before serving, drain the onions, cucumber batons and mushrooms. Cut the mushrooms into quarters.

To assemble & serve

3 button mushrooms, finely sliced
2 small truffles, finely sliced
36 small sprigs of dill
12 thick slices of sourdough,
　freshly toasted

Slice the terrine and stand a slice on each plate. Arrange the pickled onions, cucumber and quartered mushrooms next to the terrine and add the raw mushroom slices, truffle slices and dill sprigs.

Serve with the toasted sourdough and rocher of truffle butter.

MAINS

When we opened The Hand & Flowers, I knew we needed to include steak and chips on the menu (because that's what pubs do) and I also wanted to put a fish dish, a white meat dish and a game dish on there.

In this chapter, you'll find the techniques that became really important to me right from the beginning of my career. For example, when I started out many top-end restaurants would serve prime cuts of meat pink – it was always a rack of lamb or a fillet of beef or a grouse breast – and that was considered to be good cooking. But for me, the best flavour comes from braising; from long, slow cooking. It's the caramelisation of the shin of beef recipe on page 261 that drives the flavour forward. I also like to braise the different elements within certain dishes – perhaps a pie or ragout.

It was clear that we needed a great 'sauce' section in the kitchen to make the menu work – sauce chefs do the hot food and they are a different breed! They work in the hottest, most challenging and frantic section of the kitchen. If you're on the sauce section, you're under pressure to deliver as soon as the check is in: the moment the order comes through, you cook that piece of meat immediately, so that it has enough time to rest before it is sent out.

I love the zone you get into when you're doing the basic things, like cooking with butter; gaining an understanding of temperature and how to work with your stove; organising your section, your space. Because part of the kick is setting yourself up properly. You have to get your pans sorted so that you know where they are without even looking. If you don't do that, the section will collapse, and it's the jeopardy of failing badly that keeps you constantly on top of your game.

When you're on sauce, you see your job a bit like a professional sportsman – you're going out there to win! But that doesn't mean you ditch finesse. You need to understand the art of what you're doing so you can finish a dish with a beautiful touch. And you need to literally touch an ingredient during the cooking process if you want to get, for instance, perfectly crispy fish every single time.

That is where sauce chefs separate themselves from the pack with their ability to run with the pressure and to hold on to their craft. They're the ones who know how to party late into the night and get up earlier than everyone else the next morning! And they're the ones who are, just slightly, on the next level as chefs, because if you have the ability to cook 75 or 80 perfect fish or meat covers a night, then you are a very, very good cook.

Lemon sole grenobloise

Old and new – that's what this dish is about. Grenobloise is a traditional, brown-butter-rich French sauce, with the sharp cut of capers, but how we hold the stuffed lemon sole in this dish together during cooking is bang up-to-date. We use glue!

Let me explain. The glue we are talking about is transglutaminase, aka 'meat glue', a protein that comes from tuna. Its use in this country was pioneered by my friend Heston Blumenthal at his famous restaurant, The Fat Duck, in Bray. Many years ago, I came across a dish served there of two fillets of mackerel, which had been stuck together with meat glue. A simple dusting of the transglutaminase enabled the two fillets to be sealed together along their edges to create a pouch for stuffing. It blew my mind.

Essentially, cooking with the 'glue' opens up a whole new world for us chefs: one in which you're able to give guests a big, chunky fillet of flat fish that would normally be bisected by a large backbone, without any pesky bones. That's priceless, because bone-dodging really stops a lot of people from eating and enjoying fish like sole.

I've gone for two fillets of lemon sole here, sandwiching a line of spinach and shallots between them; the final product is beautiful and the grenobloise sauce is a perfect accompaniment. The end result is a dish based on incredible classic flavours, which just happens to be cooked with a dash of modern know-how.

Stuffed lemon sole

4 lemon sole, about 600–800g each, filleted, dark skin removed
500ml brine (10% solution)
Rapeseed oil for cooking
50g onion, peeled and finely diced
100g cavolo nero, roughly shredded
10g salted anchovy fillets (we use Ortiz), chopped
Finely grated zest of ½ lemon
A pinch of freshly grated nutmeg
2 tbsp meat glue transglutaminase
Sea salt and freshly ground pepper

Submerge the sole fillets in the brine for 20 minutes, then remove and pat dry with kitchen paper. Briefly rinse off the brine under cold running water. Set the fish aside.

For the filling, heat a little rapeseed oil in a medium saucepan, add the onion and sweat over a medium-low heat for about 10 minutes until soft, with no colour.

Add the cavolo nero and wilt with the onion, then add the chopped anchovies, lemon zest and nutmeg. Season with salt and pepper to taste and transfer to a bowl. Cool quickly, in a blast chiller (or over ice).

Lay the 4 unskinned sole fillets on a board, white skin side down. Spoon the cavolo filling along the middle to fill the backbone cavity.

Put the meat glue into a small sieve and dust the edges of the fillets with the glue. Lay the other sole fillets on top, skinned side uppermost, then wrap tightly in cling film.

Place in the fridge for at least 2 hours to activate the sealant.

Brown butter hollandaise

250g unsalted butter
2 medium free-range egg yolks
2 tbsp double cream
1 tbsp shallot purée (see page 404)
A splash of Cabernet Sauvignon red wine vinegar, to taste
Juice of ½ lemon, or to taste
Sea salt and cayenne pepper

Melt the butter in a heavy-based saucepan over a medium-low heat and cook until the butter turns nut brown and releases a toasty nutty aroma. Pour into a measuring jug and leave to cool slightly.

Meanwhile, put the egg yolks, cream and shallot purée into a heatproof bowl and set over a bain-marie. Whisk until pale and thickened to create a thick sabayon. Add a splash of hot water.

Remove from the heat and slowly ladle the warm nutty butter into the sabayon, whisking constantly as you do so.

Once the hollandaise sauce is fully emulsified, season with salt, cayenne, wine vinegar and lemon juice to taste. Pass through a chinois into a container and keep warm until ready to serve.

Brown bread croûtons

200g wholemeal cereal loaf (we use NPAV2 Delice de France), crusts removed, frozen
50g beurre noisette (see page 403)
Sea salt

Preheat the oven to 205°C/Fan 185°C/Gas 6–7. Take the bread from the freezer and cut into 5mm cubes.

Toss the bread cubes in the nut brown butter with a little salt. Bake in the oven for 8–10 minutes until golden and crisp. Set aside to cool until ready to serve.

Confit lemon zest

3 unwaxed lemons
100ml non-scented oil (sunflower or grapeseed)

Using a small, sharp knife, cut the rind off the lemon in rectangular pieces. Square off any uneven edges, as this will help to get perfect dice. Remove most of the white pith, leaving just a thin layer. Cut into 5mm perfect dice.

Bring a small pan of water to the boil. Add the lemon zest dice and boil for 1 minute. Drain and refresh in iced water. Repeat the process twice more, using fresh boiled water.

Once cooled, transfer the blanched lemon zest to a bowl and pour on the oil. Cover and place in the fridge until needed.

Remove from the fridge about 20 minutes before serving, to bring up to room temperature.

Crispy deep-fried capers

4 tbsp small capers in brine, drained
Vegetable oil for deep-frying

Put the capers into a small sieve or chinois. Heat the oil in a deep-fryer to 180°C.

Carefully lower the capers into the hot oil and fry for up to 1 minute until they stop bubbling. Remove and drain on kitchen paper. Leave to cool and crisp up.

Anchovy fritters

100g self-raising flour
30g Trisol (wheat starch)
85ml sparkling water
Vegetable oil for deep-frying
2 salted anchovy fillets (we use Ortiz), split lengthways
25g plain flour, for dusting

For the batter, mix the flour and Trisol together in a bowl and whisk in the water to make a smooth coating batter. Cover and refrigerate until ready to use.

Heat the oil in a deep-fryer to 180°C. Dust each anchovy fillet in flour to coat and shake off any excess.

Dip the anchovy fillets into the batter to coat and then immerse in the hot oil. Fry for 2–3 minutes until golden and crisp. Remove and drain on kitchen paper.

To cook & serve the fish

Vegetable oil for cooking
50g plain flour, for dusting
80g unsalted butter, diced
A squeeze of lemon juice
A little chopped flat-leaf parsley
4 deep-fried parsley sprigs
4 tbsp chicken sauce (see page 400)
Sea salt and freshly ground pepper

Mix equal parts of the brown bread croûtons, confit lemon zest and deep-fried capers together in a bowl and set aside.

Heat a plancha or non-stick heavy-based frying pan over a medium heat and oil lightly. Unwrap the fish then dip the fillets into a tray of seasoned flour to coat the skin side; pat to remove any excess.

Lay the fish skin side down on the plancha or frying pan and cook slowly for 5–6 minutes until the fillet is cooked about two-thirds of the way through. Carefully turn the fish and finish cooking for a minute or two.

Add the butter to the plancha or pan and allow it to melt and colour to become buerre noisette. Brush the butter over the fish, add a squeeze of lemon and baste this over the fish too.

Transfer the sole fillets from the plancha or pan to a board. With a serrated knife, trim the edges off the fish, then top with an even layer of the croûton, lemon and caper mix. Finish with chopped parsley.

Place a sole fillet in the centre of each warmed plate and add a dropped quenelle of brown butter hollandaise to one side.

Top each sole fillet with an anchovy fritter and a deep-fried parsley sprig. Drizzle the chicken sauce around the plate and serve at once.

Spiced monkfish

with roasted cauliflower & peanut crumble

SERVES 4

This dish is a Hand & Flowers milestone; it was the first dish to feature a 'swipe' of purée! One Saturday lunchtime, maybe eight years ago, we were all standing around the pass and Jamie May (who's now our head chef) swiped roasted cauliflower purée across the plate. Until that point, we'd just done little rochers (scoops) of purée, but swipes were starting to become fashionable in kitchens. It may seem hard to believe, but we then built this entire dish around that one swipe.

Monkfish (which we cure with salt and spices, poach, then pan-roast in foaming butter and flash under the grill) was an obvious choice of fish because it's got an amazingly dense texture and isn't overpowered by spice. Cauliflower is the veg equivalent. I've always loved using cauliflower, even before it became trendy. It's got great texture, caramelises nicely and works brilliantly with robust spices. To counterbalance the spices, we add sweet raisins and a shallot dressing.

Interestingly, when we construct a dish like this in the kitchen, we often find ourselves marrying nuts, fish, spices and raisins. It's a natural gravitation for us, as these ingredients work so well together. The trick is to use them to add complexity and surprise, with flavour and texture layering. A peanut crumble, with a hint of satay about it, does that.

This dish has also become the basis for one of our vegetarian options. We've transformed it into a caramelised cauliflower risotto with exactly the same flavours, exactly the same spices. It also epitomises how we work at The Hand & Flowers: collaboratively.

SPICED MONKFISH

Cured monkfish

1.2kg monkfish tail (middle-cut),
* skin removed and cleaned*
100g sea salt
100g cumin seeds
100g coriander seeds

Trim off any excess skin, fat and
bloodline from the monkfish tail.
Sprinkle evenly all over with the salt
and leave to cure in the fridge for
2 hours.

Meanwhile, toast the spice seeds
in a dry frying pan until fragrant. Tip
them onto a plate and allow to cool
slightly then grind to a powder using
a spice grinder.

Rinse the monkfish thoroughly under
cold running water to remove the
salt and pat dry. Using a sharp knife,
cut the monkfish into 4 portions
through the bone to make darnes.

Sprinkle the monkfish darnes with
the ground spice mix and place them
individually in small vacuum-pack
bags. Set aside until ready to cook.

Roasted cauliflower purée

1 medium cauliflower
250g unsalted butter
100ml double cream
Sea salt and freshly ground pepper

Chop the cauliflower into small
pieces. Heat half the butter in a large
frying pan over a medium heat
until melted and foaming. Add the
cauliflower pieces and fry until fully
caramelised (you may need to do this
in batches). Add the rest of the butter
to the pan, in pieces, as needed.

Drain the roasted cauliflower in
a colander, then transfer to a
Thermomix and pour in the cream.
Set the Thermomix to 90°C and
purée the cauliflower for 20 minutes.

Pass through a fine chinois into a
bowl and season the purée with salt
and pepper to taste. Cover and keep
in the fridge until needed.

Roasted cauliflower

1 small cauliflower
4 tbsp vegetable oil
Sea salt

Break the cauliflower into large
florets and halve these vertically.
Heat a plancha or heavy-based frying
pan over a medium-high heat and
drizzle with the oil.

Lay the cauliflower florets cut side
down on the hot plancha or pan and
season with salt. Fry quickly to char
and roast the cauliflower but don't
overcook it. Remove from the heat
and allow to cool.

Peanut crumble

1 tsp table salt
½ tsp ground cumin
¼ tsp cayenne pepper
¼ tsp ground turmeric
1 tbsp water
250g skinned unsalted peanuts
75g unsalted butter

Preheat the oven to 200°C/Fan 180°C/Gas 6. In a bowl, mix the salt together with all of the spices, then add the water and mix to a paste.

Add the peanuts and turn them to make sure they get a good coating. Spread the spice-coated nuts out on a baking tray and bake in the oven for 5 minutes.

Stir the nuts and then return them to the oven for another 5 minutes. Repeat the process once or twice more until the spice paste has dried onto the nuts and they are fully toasted. Allow to cool a little, then chop the nuts finely.

Heat the butter in a pan over a medium heat until melted and foaming. Cook until it turns nut brown then take off the heat. Add the nuts and stir until fully coated.

Roll the mixture between 2 sheets of baking parchment to a thin even layer. Place in the freezer until ready to serve.

To cook & serve

A splash of vegetable oil
A large knob of unsalted butter
4 tbsp Chablis shallots
   (see page 404)
2 tsp chopped chives
2 tbsp verjus (we use Minus 8)
4 tbsp extra-virgin olive oil
   (we use Leblanc)
20 semi-dried white grapes
   (partially dried in the dehydrator
   for 6 hours)

Immerse the vacuum-pack bags of monkfish in a water-bath at 60°C and cook for 8 minutes.

Remove the monkfish darnes from the bags. Heat the oil and butter in a large frying pan until melted and foaming. Add the monkfish darnes and cook for about 2 minutes on each side until lightly golden. Remove and drain.

Top half of each monkfish portion with peanut crumble. Flash the monkfish under the grill to melt the crumble onto the fish.

For the dressing, in a small bowl, whisk together the shallots, chives, verjus and extra-virgin olive oil.

Place a large spoonful of roasted cauliflower purée in the middle of each warmed plate and swipe across. Arrange the semi-dried grapes around the purée. Place a monkfish darne and a roasted cauliflower floret on the cauliflower purée and finish with the dressing. Serve at once.

Sea bass with roasted peppers,

tomato fondue, sweet & sour aubergine & black olive caramel

SERVES 8

Showcasing wonderful Mediterranean ingredients like aubergines, olives and tomatoes, this is one of my favourite fish recipes at The Hand & Flowers; it sings summertime to me.

Of course, nothing showcases those Med-style flavours better than Provençal cuisine, and this dish was created very much with French cookery in mind – a little bit Pierre Gagnaire, if you like. It's the product of our current head chef Jamie May, our former head chef Aaron Mulliss, and me combining forces, tossing some ideas around and coming up with this winning recipe. It instantly stole my heart!

The aubergine element – sweet and sour aubergine wedges – was dreamt up by Jamie and references his time working at the Australian restaurant Circa, The Prince in the St Kilda suburb of Melbourne, where he made a lamb dish featuring a similar garnish. Jamie's approach to food is comparable to my own passion for taking great ingredients and letting them shine.

The black olive caramel on the plate is made from glossy Kalamata olives, and this element comes from Aaron, inspired by something he saw on his travels. It gives the dish an authentic Provençal flavour, as do the roasted peppers, which help to make the dish look so beautiful.

Together with the aubergine, tomatoes and olives, the peppers say, 'this is summer.' They contrast beautifully with the delicious, white wild sea bass that takes the lead role.

Sweet & sour aubergine

*2 large Dutch aubergines,
    quartered lengthways*
10g table salt
1 tsp cumin seeds
1 tsp mustard seeds
1 tsp coriander seeds
4 tbsp vegetable oil
1 medium chilli, diced
*1 garlic clove, peeled and grated
    (use a Microplane)*
*10g peeled root ginger, grated
    (use a Microplane)*
30g dark muscovado sugar
75ml white wine vinegar
150ml chicken stock (see page 400)

Lay the aubergine wedges on a perforated steamer tray (with a tray beneath to catch the liquid extracted on salting). Sprinkle the aubergine with the salt and then toss to make sure it is evenly distributed. Cover and place in the fridge for 24 hours.

The next day, tip the aubergine wedges into a colander and wash off the salt under cold running water for 5 minutes. Drain thoroughly and pat dry with kitchen paper, making sure the aubergine wedges are fully dried.

Preheat the oven to 200°C/Fan 180°C/Gas 6. Toast the spice seeds in a dry frying pan for a minute or so until they release their aroma. Tip onto a plate to cool then grind to a powder in a spice grinder.

Heat 3 tbsp oil in a large heavy-based frying pan over a medium-high heat. Add the aubergine wedges and turn to colour and caramelise on all sides. Transfer the aubergines to a roasting tray in which they fit in one layer.

Wipe the frying pan out with some kitchen paper, then add 1 tbsp oil and place over a medium heat. When hot, add the ground spices, chilli, garlic and ginger and fry for 30 seconds or so.

Add the sugar and take to a light caramel (145°C), then add the wine vinegar to deglaze, stirring and scraping the base of the pan. Let it reduce down to a syrup, then add the chicken stock and bring to the boil.

Pour the reduced liquor over the roasted aubergine wedges. Braise in the oven for 10–15 minutes until the aubergines are cooked but not falling apart. Leave to cool in the liquor.

Tomato fondue

10 ripe plum tomatoes, halved
Olive oil for cooking
*2 Spanish onions, peeled, halved
    and sliced*
6 garlic cloves, peeled and sliced
*50ml Cabernet Sauvignon red
    wine vinegar*
200ml red wine
Sea salt and freshly ground pepper

Preheat the oven to 205°C/Fan 185°C/Gas 6–7. Lay the tomatoes cut side up on an oven tray and roast in the oven for 20–25 minutes until slightly charred and dehydrated.

Meanwhile, heat a splash of olive oil in a large saucepan over a medium-low heat, add the onions and garlic and cook until soft and translucent; this will take around 10–15 minutes.

Add the wine vinegar and reduce down to a glaze then pour in the wine and reduce by half. Add the roasted tomatoes to the pan and simmer for 45 minutes–1 hour.

Tip the tomatoes and sauce into a high-powered jug blender (Vitamix) and purée until smooth, adding a little olive oil if needed to make the purée smooth and glossy. Season with salt and pepper to taste.

Pass the tomato fondue through a chinois into a saucepan or container and cover the surface with a sheet of baking parchment. Either keep warm or refrigerate if serving later, ready to reheat for serving.

Black olive caramel

100g caster sugar
100g Kalamata olives in brine,
  drained and chopped
A little olive oil (if needed)

Put the sugar into a heavy-based saucepan and melt over a medium heat, then increase the heat and cook to a dark caramel. Take the pan off the heat and immediately add the chopped olives.

Pour the mixture into a high-powered jug blender (Vitamix) and purée until smooth, adding a little olive oil if needed. You should have a glossy black olive caramel.

Pass the caramel through a fine chinois and spoon into a piping bag or squeezable plastic bottle, ready for serving.

Roasted peppers

4 large green peppers
4 large red peppers
4 large yellow peppers
2 tbsp olive oil

Preheat the oven to 220°C/Fan 200°C/Gas 7. Place the peppers on a baking tray, drizzle with the olive oil and roast for 8–10 minutes until the skins have blistered, making them easier to peel. Transfer the peppers to a bowl, cover with cling film and leave to cool.

Once cooled, remove the cling film and peel away the skin from the peppers, then open them up with a sharp knife and remove the seeds.

Lay the opened peppers on a board and cut rounds, using a 3cm cutter; you will need 24 of each colour.

To cook & serve the fish

8 portions of wild sea bass,
  150g each, skin scored
A large knob of unsalted butter
A generous squeeze of lemon juice
8 tbsp extra-virgin olive oil
  (we use Leblanc)
2 tsp thyme leaves, to garnish

Heat up a plancha or non-stick heavy-based frying pan to a medium heat.

Place the sweet and sour aubergine wedges on an oven tray and spoon over a little of their cooking liquor. Heat through in the oven at 205°C/Fan 185°C/Gas 6–7 for 5 minutes or so, basting them with the liquor as they heat to give them a lovely sheen.

Add the fish to the plancha or pan, skin side down, and cook nice and slowly for about 8–10 minutes so that the skin crisps up perfectly.

Meanwhile, warm the roasted pepper discs, drizzled with a little olive oil, under the salamander or grill.

Spoon 1 tbsp warm tomato fondue onto the centre of each plate and spread across with a stepped palette knife. Lay an aubergine wedge across the fondue and arrange the pepper discs on the plates. Finish with a few lines of warm black olive caramel.

Finally turn the fish and add the butter to the plancha or pan. Once the butter is melted and foaming, baste the fish with it, then baste it with the lemon juice. Place a sea bass fillet in the centre of each plate, resting slightly on the aubergine, and sprinkle with thyme leaves. Finish with a drizzle of olive oil and serve.

Cod with chicory gratin,

grape sauce & ham hock butter

Quite a few Hand & Flowers dishes combine nuts and grapes with fish. There's a reason for that! The balance of roasted, nutty, savoury flavours from hazelnuts or walnuts is perfect with a sweet burst of grapes, and together they lift a piece of fish to something special.

In warmer climates, like the Mediterranean, fish is often cooked very simply and served lightly, with a bit of lemon, but at The Hand, I like to treat it differently. I tend to think of fish almost like poultry or pork and use similar flavour combinations when I cook it.

This approach works particularly well with North Sea fish, like cod, which is more robust than Mediterranean fish. It's had to swim in our colder seas, so it's like the SAS of fish. It can take most things you fling at it, including the bitterness of chicory, or endive (which does the job lemon would normally do by bringing sharpness to this dish).

A black grape sauce gives a sweet balance to the dish and there's richness from the ham hock butter and beurre blanc. Chicory and toasted hazelnuts provide a contrasting crunchy texture. Like the other fish dishes at The Hand & Flowers, this isn't necessarily your usual light option. You will leave feeling satisfyingly full!

Cured cod

1kg cod loin fillet, skinned and pin-boned
1 litre brine (10% salt solution)

Trim the cod fillet to a perfect shape, about 20cm long and about 800g in total. Submerge the cod fillet in the brine and place in the fridge to cure for 2 hours.

Rinse the fish under cold running water to remove the brine, then wrap the fish in a clean cloth to dry it thoroughly. Remove the cloth and wrap the fish tightly in cling film to set the shape.

Gruyère & hazelnut crust

200g brioche crumbs
75g unsalted butter, softened
75g Gruyère, grated
20g chives
1 tsp truffle oil
A pinch of sea salt
100g hazelnuts, toasted and chopped

Put all of the ingredients into a blender and blitz to a coarse paste. Roll out between two sheets of baking parchment to a thin sheet. Place in the freezer until needed.

Grape sauce

60g unsalted butter
1 red onion, sliced
1 tbsp redcurrant jelly
2 tbsp blackberries (fresh or frozen and thawed)
500g black grapes, halved and deseeded
175ml ruby port
75ml red wine
A pinch of sea salt

Melt the butter in a saucepan, add the sliced red onion and sweat over a medium heat for 10–15 minutes until soft.

Add the redcurrant jelly, blackberries, black grapes, port, red wine and salt. Bring to the boil, then turn the heat down to a simmer and cook for 25–30 minutes until the sauce has reduced by half.

Tip the sauce into a jug blender and blend until smooth, then pass through a fine chinois into a bowl. Cover and keep in the fridge until ready to serve.

Pickled red chicory

2 medium red chicory bulbs
100ml pickling liquor (see page 404)

Put the chicory into a vacuum-pack bag, pour in the pickling liquor and vacuum-seal, then cook in a water-bath at 88°C for 15 minutes.

Lift out the bag and plunge into a bowl of iced water to cool quickly. Once cooled, remove the chicory and halve lengthways.

Chicory gratin

Remove the top sheet of parchment from the Gruyère crust. Place the pickled chicory halves, cut side down, on the crust and cut around the chicory so that the crust is the same shape and size.

Transfer the chicory halves to a baking tray, ready to warm up. Remove the other sheet of parchment from the Gruyère crust then position the crust on top of the chicory. Keep in the fridge until needed.

Ham hock butter

125g unsalted butter, at room
temperature
1 banana shallot, peeled and
finely chopped
150g crispy ham hock
2 tbsp English mustard
1 tbsp toasted yellow mustard seeds
½ tsp curry powder
½ tbsp chopped chervil
1 tbsp chopped parsley
1 medium free-range egg yolk

Mix all of the ingredients together in a bowl until evenly blended. Scrape the butter onto a piece of cling film and roll into a small cylinder, 1.5cm in diameter. Twist and tie the ends to seal and place in a bowl of iced water to set the shape.

Cut the ham hock butter roll into 1cm thick slices and remove the cling film. Lay the slices on a small tray, cover with cling film and keep in the fridge until needed.

To cook & serve the fish

Vegetable oil for cooking
A knob of unsalted butter
12 red chicory leaves
Olive oil to drizzle
A squeeze of lemon juice
16 hazelnuts, toasted and halved
24 semi-dried black grapes
(partially dried in the dehydrator
for 6 hours)
4 tbsp beurre blanc (see page 403)

Preheat the oven to 205°C/Fan 185°C/Gas 6–7. Unwrap the cod and slice into 4 even portions.

Place a large ovenproof frying pan over a medium heat and line with 4 squares of baking parchment. Drizzle with a little oil and lay a cod portion on each square. Cook for about 4 minutes until the fish starts to colour. Add a little butter to the pan and then transfer it to the oven for 4 minutes.

While the fish is cooking, place the chicory gratins in the oven to warm through. Once warm, pop them under the grill to toast and colour. Warm the grape sauce through. Drizzle the fresh chicory leaves with a little oil.

Remove the fish from the oven, squeeze in a little lemon juice and baste the fish. Lift the cod portions out of the pan and drain on a tray lined with kitchen paper.

Spoon some grape sauce onto the centre of each warmed serving plate and place a portion of cod and a chicory gratin on top. Lay a slice of ham butter on each cod portion.

Scatter the grapes, hazelnuts and fresh chicory leaves around the plates and finish with the beurre blanc. Serve straight away.

Fish & chips

with pea purée & tartare sauce

—————— SERVES 4 ——————

Fish and chips is an archetypal British dish. At its heart, The Hand & Flowers is a classic British pub. Need I say more?

However, if you put fish and chips on a menu you have to overcome the preconception that, because it is so easy to get on the high street, it's cheap. We have to elevate it into something special as a dish – though, to my mind, there's actually more to fish and chips than its cost. It evokes memories…days at the seaside, chippy teas at the weekend. And people don't typically cook it at home, do they? So, there's a little bit of the treat about it.

Truthfully, a classic fish and chips is an amazingly balanced dish from a chef's point of view. Everything you look for, fish and chips already has: protein, texture, crunch, carb, acidity, sweetness and a rich sauce. All we did for our version was to come up with what we think is the best fish and chips.

Everyone loves chips, whether you're a gourmand or a geezer who's never been to a Michelin-starred restaurant in his life. Triple-cooking them means you get the best chip ever; we've got my friend Heston Blumenthal to thank for refining that technique.

Our Hand & Flowers fish and chips is very special in a personal way, too, for Beth and myself. Shortly after opening the pub, we were lucky enough to be shortlisted in the 'best fish and chips' category at an industry awards ceremony. We closed the restaurant for the evening and hired a great, big Hummer stretch-limo to take some of the team to the presentation – it was such a lovely, fun thing to share with them. Especially as we won.

Triple-cooked chips

10 large chipping potatoes, peeled
Vegetable oil for deep-frying
Sea salt
A little very finely chopped parsley

Cut a slice from the top and bottom of each potato, then press an apple corer through from top to bottom to make round cylinder chips. Put the cut chips under cold running water to wash of some of the starches.

Now lay the chips out on a steamer tray and season with salt. Steam for 30 minutes until cooked, then place in the blast chiller to cool quickly and draw out the excess moisture (or place somewhere cool and dry).

Once the chips are cool, heat the oil in a deep-fryer to 140°C. Lower the chips into the hot oil in a wire basket and deep-fry for 10 minutes. Remove the chips from the fryer, drain and leave to cool until needed.

When ready to serve, heat the oil to 180°C and deep-fry the chips for about 6–7 minutes until golden and very crispy. Remove the chips from the fryer and drain on kitchen paper. Season with salt and sprinkle with chopped parsley.

Coating batter

300g self-raising flour
100g Trisol (wheat starch)
260ml sparkling water

Mix the flour and Trisol together in a bowl and whisk in the water to make a smooth batter. Cover and refrigerate until ready to use.

Pea purée

15g unsalted butter
1 small banana shallot, peeled
  and sliced
½ tsp sea salt
250g frozen petits pois, defrosted
10g caster sugar
60ml boiling water
A handful of mint leaves

Melt the butter in a medium saucepan, add the shallot and salt and sweat over a medium heat for about 10 minutes until softened.

Add the petits pois and sugar, pour on the boiling water and bring back to the boil, then take off the heat and add the mint leaves.

Tip the pea mixture into a blender and blitz to a purée, then pass through a fine chinois into a bowl containing freezer blocks or set over ice.

Scrape the pea purée into a Pacojet beaker and freeze. Churn to use as required.

Tartare sauce

2 medium free-range egg yolks
1½ tsp Dijon mustard
1½ tbsp white wine vinegar
250ml vegetable oil
1 small shallot, peeled and
  finely diced
1 tbsp baby capers in brine, drained
1 tbsp cornichons
1½ tbsp chopped curly parsley
1 medium free-range egg,
  hard-boiled, shelled and
  finely chopped

Put the egg yolks, mustard and wine vinegar into a blender and blend briefly to combine. With the motor running, slowly pour in the oil and blend until emulsified to a thick, glossy mayonnaise.

Transfer the mayonnaise to a bowl and stir in the shallot, capers, cornichons, parsley and chopped boiled egg. Cover and refrigerate until ready to serve.

To cook & serve the fish

Vegetable oil for deep-frying
4 whiting fillets, 150g each
50g plain flour, for dusting
Sea salt
2 lemons, halved and tied in muslin,
  to serve

Heat the oil in a deep-fryer to 180°C. Dip the fish fillets into the flour and turn to coat all over; shake off any excess. Now dip the fish into the batter, carefully add to the hot oil and deep-fry for 4 minutes until cooked.

While you are frying the fish (and the chips for the final time), warm the pea purée through.

Remove the fish from the oil, drain on a tray lined with kitchen paper and season with salt.

Pot up the chips, tartare sauce and pea purée. Lay the fish fillets on the plate and serve with the lemon halves for squeezing.

'Fish du jour'

with Banyuls butter sauce, rosemary potato, artichoke & caper purée

SERVES 8

Fish cookery should never be overcomplicated. The methodology needs to be simple to allow the flavour of the fish to shine. You only need to answer the following questions: what's the starch and sauce? Is there a purée? Where's the crunch and texture coming from?

This dish – featuring glorious turbot, garnished with hasselback Red Duke potatoes and a caper and artichoke purée – illustrates that philosophy perfectly. And nowhere more so than in the beautiful sauce, which sits under the fish. It's a rich, butter (almost beurre-blanc-style) sauce, with the addition of red Banyuls dessert wine taking it to a new level. A spoonful of Beluga caviar adds texture and a touch of luxury to the sauce. It's substantial and rich… delicious.

Red Duke is a heritage potato and flavoursome in spades. We sous-vide the potato first and then skewer and slice it to get the beautiful hasselback (ridged) effect. It's a detail that helps to make the dish special, and for me, details make dishes.

Further flavour layering comes in the form of the artichoke and caper purée, instead of lemon for acidity to cut through the sauce, and little Grelot onions and sea purslane, briefly poached in butter emulsion, offer crunch. Of course, you have to adapt details to the seasons. When Grelot onions are not in season, baby leeks or spring onions work just as well. Simple methodology, lateral thinking; that equals a lush fish dish.

Bonne femme base

2 tbsp olive oil
125g Spanish onions,
    peeled and sliced
100g leeks, cleaned and sliced
125g celery, sliced
125g fennel, sliced
125g button mushrooms, sliced
1½ star anise
5g coriander seeds
5g fennel seeds
1 bay leaf
150ml white wine
1 litre fish stock (see page 400)
250ml double cream

Heat the olive oil in a saucepan over a medium heat and add the onions, leeks, celery and fennel. Sweat for a few minutes until the vegetables are softened, then add the mushrooms, spices and bay leaf and cook, stirring from time to time, for 5 minutes.

Deglaze the pan with the wine and reduce the liquor to a glaze. Add the fish stock and reduce by half, then pour in the cream and reduce to a sauce consistency.

Pass through a fine chinois into a bowl, squeezing out as much flavour as possible from the vegetables. Cover and chill until needed.

Banyuls shallots

4 banana shallots, peeled
    and finely diced
200ml Banyuls wine

Put the shallots and wine into a saucepan, bring to the boil and reduce the wine down until it is the same volume as the shallots. Remove from the heat.

Banyuls & caviar sauce

250ml bonne femme base (see left)
50ml Banyuls wine
200g unsalted butter, diced,
    at room temperature
Juice of 1 lemon, or to taste
4 tbsp Banyuls shallots (see above)
4 tbsp Beluga caviar
Sea salt and freshly ground pepper

Reduce the bonne femme down until the cream starts to thicken and the bubbles slow.

Add the wine, then whisk in the butter, a piece at a time, to emulsify and give the sauce a shine. Add lemon juice and season with salt and pepper to taste.

Pass the sauce through a chinois into a bowl. Keep warm until needed. When ready to serve, stir in the Banyuls shallots and caviar.

Artichoke & caper purée

600g Jerusalem artichokes, peeled
    (400g prepared weight)
150g raisins, soaked in warm water
    for 30 minutes and drained,
    liquid retained
100g small capers in brine, drained
Sea salt and freshly ground pepper

Slice the Jerusalem artichokes roughly and place in a vacuum-pack bag with a pinch of salt. Vacuum-seal on full pressure and immerse in a water-bath at 88.2°C. Leave to cook overnight until softened.

Preheat the oven to 205°C/Fan 185°C/Gas 6–7. Once cooked, open the bag, drain off any liquid from the artichokes, then tip them into a roasting tin. Roast in the oven for 15 minutes to slightly dry and caramelise them.

Tip the roasted artichokes into a high-powered jug blender (Vitamix) and add the drained raisins and capers. Blend to a smooth, thick purée, adding a little of the raisin soaking liquid to make it easier to purée if necessary.

Pass through a fine chinois into a bowl, season with salt and pepper and keep in the fridge until needed.

Burnt rosemary butter

3 sprigs of rosemary
150g unsalted butter

Lay the rosemary on a baking tray and wave a cook's blowtorch all over the surface until the whole sprigs are smouldering and charred.

Melt the butter in a saucepan, add the charred rosemary and remove from the heat. Leave to infuse for 30 minutes. Strain the butter through a fine chinois into a bowl, cover and set aside until needed.

Crispy deep-fried capers

4 tbsp small capers in brine, drained
Vegetable oil for deep-frying

Put the capers into a small sieve or chinois. Heat the oil in a deep-fryer to 180°C.

Carefully lower the capers into the hot oil and fry for up to 1 minute until they stop bubbling. Remove and drain on kitchen paper. Leave to cool and crisp up.

Rosemary potatoes

8 medium Red Duke potatoes,
  washed
100g rosemary butter (see left)
Vegetable oil for cooking
Sea salt and freshly ground pepper

Put the whole potatoes into a large vacuum-pack bag, along with a pinch of salt and the infused rosemary butter. Vacuum-seal on full pressure then immerse in a water-bath at 88°C for 20 minutes to part-cook.

Transfer the bag to a bowl of iced water to cool the potatoes quickly. Once cooled, remove the potatoes from the bag. One at a time, skewer each potato along the bottom then slice thinly down to the skewer, to hold the potato intact at the base. Set aside for serving.

When ready to serve, preheat the oven to 205°C/Fan 185°C/Gas 6–7. Put the potatoes into a roasting tin with a generous splash of oil and season with salt and pepper. Toss to coat well and place in the oven. Roast for 30–40 minutes, turning every 5 minutes until the potatoes are crispy and fully cooked. Serve hot.

To cook & serve the fish

50g unsalted butter
8 skinned boneless portions of turbot,
  120g each
8 Grelot onions
200g butter emulsion (see page 403)
32 picked sea purslane leaves
24 hazelnut halves, toasted
8 deep-fried tarragon sprigs

Heat the butter in a large frying pan until melted and foaming. Add the turbot and cook for about 6 minutes, turning the portions halfway through cooking and making sure the presentation side is a good colour.

Meanwhile, in a small pan, poach the Grelot onions in the butter emulsion for 3 minutes, then drop in the sea purslane. Remove the onions and purslane from the pan.

Warm the artichoke purée through. Place a quenelle on each warmed plate and top with the toasted hazelnut halves and crispy fried capers. Place a potato alongside and drape a Grelot onion over it. Garnish with the sea purslane leaves.

Sauce the plate with the Banyuls and caviar sauce and place a roasted turbot portion on top. Finish with the deep-fried tarragon sprigs and serve at once.

Hake wrapped in vine leaves

with sweet & sour grapes

SERVES 4

This dish was born when we were sent a bottle of verjus by Minus 8 Vinegar, a family-owned vineyard in Niagara, Canada. The taste was absolutely stunning and got me thinking about classic sole Veronique: grilled lemon sole, butter sauce and the lovely sweetness of peeled grapes. But, unless you've got a load of commis chefs to help prep the grapes – which we didn't back in the early days – Veronique isn't a goer. It's just too time-consuming. So, I had to ask myself, 'how do we get everything that's delicious out of that dish without it being too much like hard work?' The answer was to dehydrate a load of grapes – the intensified sweetness you derive from the dried fruit is amazing.

Keen to use the brilliant verjus, too, we made a butter sauce. A fellow chef, Ed Wilson, used to serve a butter sauce with diced shallots running through it at a pub called the Green Man and French Horn in London. For our version, we could do a beautiful butter sauce with the lovely addition of verjus, perhaps actual grapes, too… Outside The Hand & Flowers, we happened to have some vines and I started picking the little grapes from them: they were sour, which added a level of acidity that balanced out the dish.

The final layer comes from wrapping the fish – we use hake – in vine leaves, which helps to steam and flavour it. Part of the cod family, hake's a fantastic fish. It's robust but not too powerful taste-wise and it takes on flavours brilliantly, which means the grapes, the vine leaves and the sauce can really shine.

Cured hake

1 side of hake 900g, skinned
4 large fresh vine leaves (if available)
  or from a jar (packed in brine)
Sea salt

Check the hake for pin-bones. Place a large sheet of cling film on your work surface and sprinkle with a fine layer of flaky sea salt. Place the side of hake on top and sprinkle the surface with a fine layer of salt.

Wrap the fish tightly in cling film and place on a tray in the fridge to cure for 1½ hours. This process draws moisture from the fish, and seasons and firms the flesh.

When the curing time is up, wash off the salt and pat the fish dry. Cut the fish into 4 equal portions.

Drain the vine leaves (if packed in brine) and cut out any thick pieces of stalk. Wrap each hake portion in a vine leaf, making sure that it is completely enclosed.

Now wrap each parcel tightly in cling film, to help set the vine leaves in place, and place in the fridge to firm up for at least 2 hours.

Potted crab pie

1 cooked large cock crab, cooled
1 tbsp Chablis shallots (see page 404)
1 Granny Smith apple, peeled and
  diced
120g pomme purée (see page 182)
2 tsp chopped chives

Brown crab mayonnaise:
100g brown crab meat (from above)
1 egg yolk
1 tsp Dijon mustard
1 tsp Pernod
1 tsp orange juice
200ml vegetable oil
1 drop of white truffle oil
Sea salt and cayenne pepper

Pick the white and dark meat from the crab; you need 100g of each. Flake the white meat and set aside.

For the mayonnaise, put the brown crab meat, egg yolk, mustard, Pernod and orange juice into a blender and blend to a paste. With the motor running, slowly pour in the oil and blend to emulsify. Add the truffle oil and salt and cayenne pepper to taste. Pass through a fine chinois into a bowl, pressing firmly with the back of a ladle. Place in the fridge.

When ready to serve, gently warm through the Chablis shallots with the white crab meat, then stir in 75g of the brown crab mayonnaise and remove from the heat. Stir through the diced apple.

Divide most of the crab mix between 4 individual serving pots and pipe on the warm pomme purée. Add the rest of the crab mix and top with the chives. Serve warm.

To cook & serve the fish

30g Chablis shallots, plus liquor
  (see page 404)
100ml warm beurre blanc
  (see page 403)
1 tbsp verjus (we use Minus 8)
Extra-virgin olive oil (we use
  Leblanc), for brushing
20 white seedless grapes, peeled
20 semi-dried white grapes
  (partially dried in the dehydrator
  for 6 hours)
12 sour grapes (unripe white grapes)
Sea salt and freshly ground pepper

Bring a fairly deep, wide pan of water to the boil. Put the cling-film-wrapped fish portions into a vacuum-pack bag, vacuum-seal and immerse in the boiling water. Simmer for 7 minutes.

For the verjus sauce, warm the Chablis shallots through in a pan, then add to the warm beurre blanc. Finish the sauce with the verjus and season with salt and pepper to taste.

Remove the cling film from the fish and brush the vine-leaf wrapping with olive oil.

Spoon some verjus sauce onto the centre of each warmed plate and dress the plate with the peeled fresh grapes, dried grapes and sour grapes. Place a vine-leaf-wrapped fish portion in the middle. Serve at once, with the potted crab pie on the side.

Cod with artichoke purée,

smoked cod's roe, hazelnuts & golden raisins

SERVES 4

Confession time. Late-night munchies (and a local producer) are responsible for this dish! I've been a huge fan of taramasalata for ages – it's often in my fridge for after service – and when some sheep's sorrel was brought into the kitchen by a local producer who regularly supplied us with bits and bobs, I got to thinking.

Sorrel leaves, which dress this dish, have an amazing but incredibly sour and bitter flavour. They're a super-popular ingredient now; you just have to be careful not to overuse them. I liked the idea of incorporating sorrel as a garnish to counterbalance Jerusalem artichokes, which have a lovely earthy flavour and texture and form the purée for this dish. The artichokes aren't heavy, either; there's a lightness to them, but flavour-wise they're robust. They bring a lot to the dish.

The artichoke purée is topped with a piece of oven-roasted cured cod, sitting alongside a roasted brandade cube. We decorate the plate with little mounds of smoked cod's roe, delicately positioned toasted hazelnuts and homemade raisins. A delicious chicken sauce is then drizzled on top, along with some rapeseed oil. And, finally, the dish is finished with wafer-thin raw artichoke slices.

It's a dish that was very much part of our two-star journey – I can clearly remember creating it in between the award of one and two stars – I love how utterly timeless and elegant it is, and it will always bring a smile to my face knowing that it was inspired by a night-time snack!

Cured cod

*1 side of a large Cornish cod,
about 1.5kg*
100g sea salt

Remove and discard the skin from
the cod, clean and fillet it, trimming
off the belly and both ends to give a
thick piece sufficient for 4 portions;
reserve the cod trimmings for the
brandade mix (see opposite).

Lay the prepared cod fillet on a sheet
of cling film and sprinkle lightly and
evenly on both sides with sea salt.
Wrap in the cling film and leave to
cure in the fridge for 2 hours.

Tip the cod into a colander and rinse
off the salt under cold running water
for about 5 minutes. Drain well and
pat dry with kitchen paper.

Wrap in cling film to form a cylinder
shape and place in the fridge until
ready to cook.

Jerusalem artichoke purée

300g Jerusalem artichokes
Juice of 2 lemons
A good knob of unsalted butter
½ white onion, peeled and sliced
150ml white wine
150ml double cream
Sea salt and freshly ground pepper

Peel and slice the artichokes,
immersing them in a bowl of cold
water with the lemon juice added as
you do so, to prevent discoloration.

Melt the butter in a saucepan over a
medium-low heat, add the onion and
sweat for about 10 minutes until soft.

Drain the artichokes and add them
to the onion. Pour on the wine and
reduce by three-quarters, then pour
on the cream and cook until the
artichokes are very soft.

Drain the artichokes, reserving the
liquid, and tip them into a high-
powered jug blender (Vitamix).
Blend to a smooth purée, adding
enough of the reserved liquor to give
the desired consistency.

Pass the artichoke purée through a
chinois into a bowl and season with
salt and pepper to taste. Cover and
refrigerate until ready to serve.

Smoked cod's roe

1 slice of white bread, crusts removed
200g smoked cod's roe
*1 garlic clove, peeled and
roughly chopped*
250ml pomace olive oil
Juice of ½ lemon, or to taste

Place the bread in a dish, cover with
cold water, then immediately drain
and squeeze out the excess water.

Put the bread into a blender with the
smoked cod's roe and garlic and
blend until smooth, slowly adding
the olive oil as if making mayonnaise.
Add lemon juice to taste.

Spoon into a piping bag and set aside
in the fridge, ready for serving.

Brandade

100g cod trimmings (see opposite)
40g sea salt
40g caster sugar
100ml white wine
250ml extra-virgin olive oil
75g dry mashed cooked potato,
*   put through a potato ricer*
A pinch of saffron strands
50g plain flour, for dusting
2 medium eggs, beaten
100g panko breadcrumbs

Cut the cod trimmings into fairly evenly sized pieces. Mix the salt, sugar and wine together in a bowl, add the cod trimmings and leave to cure in the fridge for 50 minutes.

Preheat the oven to 200°C/Fan 180°C/Gas 6. Tip the cod trimmings into a sieve and rinse off the cure under cold running water. Drain well and transfer to a small baking dish. Pour on the extra-virgin olive oil to cover, then seal the dish with foil and cook in the oven for 15–20 minutes.

Drain the cod, discarding the oil, and mix with the dry mash and saffron.

Line a small tray with cling film. Transfer the cod mixture to the tray and spread it evenly, pressing the mixture to compact it. Leave in the fridge until set.

Once set, cut 4 nice-sized brandade cubes. Roll each cube in flour to dust all over, then dip into the beaten eggs and finally into the breadcrumbs to coat. Set aside, until ready to serve.

Golden raisins

200g white seedless grapes

Take the grapes off their stems and lay them on a baking sheet. Dry the grapes in the oven at 90°C/Fan 80°C for 12 hours or in a food dehydrator at 65°C for 24 hours.

To cook & serve the fish

Vegetable oil for deep-frying
Olive oil for cooking
4 knobs of unsalted butter
5 tbsp chicken sauce (see page 400)
8–12 hazelnuts, halved and toasted
Cold-pressed extra-virgin rapeseed
*   oil, to dress*
16 sheep sorrel leaves
1–2 Jerusalem artichokes, peeled and
*   finely sliced on a mandoline*

Preheat the oven to 205°C/Fan 185°C/Gas 6–7. Heat the oil for deep-frying in a deep-fryer to 180°C.

Portion the cod into 4 equal pieces. Remove the cling film and place the cod portions on a baking tray lined with baking parchment. Drizzle with a little olive oil and place a knob of butter on each portion. Bake in the oven for 6–8 minutes, basting halfway through cooking.

Meanwhile, warm the artichoke purée and chicken sauce. Add the brandade cubes to the hot oil and deep-fry for 1½ minutes, then drain on kitchen paper.

Spread a large spoonful of artichoke purée in the centre of each plate. Pipe 3 small mounds of smoked cod's roe around the purée and arrange a few toasted hazelnuts and raisins in between. Place a cod portion on the purée, along with a brandade cube.

Drizzle the chicken sauce and rapeseed oil around the garnish and finish with a few sheep sorrel leaves and wafer-thin raw artichoke slices.

Halibut poached in red wine

with bourguignon garnish

SERVES 4

My right-hand man in the Kerridge empire, Chris Mackett, is responsible for this dish. He and I go way back to when I was head chef at Adlard's in Norwich and I recruited him as my sous chef. He's this big beast of a bloke and when he walked through the door I thought, instantly, 'I love this guy.' He's a machine, has incredible drive and enthusiasm and he loves food. He's a great, bullish character, and a genuinely lovely guy.

When it came to opening The Hand & Flowers two years later, Chris and Luke Butcher (our 16-year-old apprentice at Adlard's at the time, who is now Glynn Purnell's head chef in Birmingham) decided that they both wanted to come on the journey with me and Beth. But with just three of us in the kitchen, we needed to work out how to do 50 covers of quality food in a way that would make service as easy as possible.

Our bourguignon garnish is perfect for quick service. If you've got everything cooked just before starting, you can finish the sauce pretty much *à la minute*. Then you only need to poach the fish, wilt a bit of spinach, add some lovely buttery mash and you're done.

We chose halibut because of its gorgeous, lush 'meaty' texture. We went for red wine as the poaching liquor – reducing it down by two-thirds to get the deep, rich red colour in the fish we were aiming for. But it became the most expensive dish in the world: it took about 10 bottles of reduced wine to get the equivalent of three! Plus, at the end of service, the natural waters from the fish had diluted the reduction, so we had to throw that away. If we did it now, of course, we would vacuum-seal the fish in a bag with the reduction and save on a lot of red wine!

That said, I loved the dish so much, it was on the menu for ages. Now that we've revisited it for this book, I think we'll get it back on the menu: but in version 2.0.

HALIBUT POACHED IN RED WINE

Braised bacon

*200g piece of streaky bacon,
    skin removed*

Put the bacon into a vacuum-pack
bag and vacuum-seal on full pressure.
Immerse in a water-bath at 72°C and
cook for 12 hours.

Once the bacon is cooked, lift the bag
out of the water-bath and place it on
a tray. Place a second tray on top
and weight down with some heavy
weights, so that the bacon is pressed
flat. Leave to cool.

Once cooled, remove the bacon from
the bag and clean away any jellied
ham stock. Cut the bacon into lardons
and set aside until required.

When ready to serve, simply add the
lardons to a hot non-stick frying pan
and fry until caramelised and crisp.

Red wine poaching liquor

*75cl bottle red wine
1 bay leaf
1 garlic clove, peeled and sliced
2 black peppercorns
100ml chicken stock (see page 400)*

Pour the wine into a saucepan, bring
to the boil over a medium heat and
reduce by half. Add the bay leaf,
garlic, peppercorns and stock. Bring
to the boil and lower the heat to a
gentle simmer. Leave to infuse over
the heat for 5 minutes.

Pass the liquor through a fine chinois
into a wide deep-sided pan and keep
at 70°C for poaching.

Pomme purée

*750g Desirée potatoes
150ml double cream
200ml milk, warmed
85g unsalted butter, diced, chilled
Sea salt and freshly ground pepper*

Preheat the oven to 200°C/Fan
180°C/Gas 6. Bake the potatoes in
the oven for about 1 hour until soft.

Meanwhile, pour the cream into a
saucepan and simmer to reduce by
half; keep warm.

When the potatoes are cool enough
to handle, halve them and scoop out
the flesh from the skins.

Pass the potato flesh through a drum
sieve into a pan and beat in the warm
cream and milk. Beat in the diced
butter and season with salt and
pepper to taste.

Heat the pomme purée through
when you are ready to serve.

Baby onions

24 baby onions, peeled but left whole
30g unsalted butter
2 sprigs of thyme
Sea salt

Put the baby onions into a vacuum-pack bag and add the butter, thyme sprigs and a pinch of salt. Seal, then pop it into a steamer at 100°C for 8 minutes.

Once cooked, remove the bag from the steamer and immerse in a bowl of iced water to quickly cool and refresh the onions.

Open the bag and tip the baby onions into a container. Set aside until ready to serve.

To cook & serve the fish

4 skinned, boneless portions of
  Scottish prime-cut halibut,
  about 130g each
A knob of unsalted butter
  for cooking
300g mixed wild mushrooms
  (girolles, trompettes, baby ceps)
80g spinach, wilted and seasoned
100ml red wine sauce (see page 402),
  warmed
Sea salt and freshly ground pepper

Add the halibut portions to the red wine poaching liquor and poach very gently for 8–10 minutes, depending on the thickness of the fish portions (make sure the temperature of the liquor doesn't drop below 60°C).

Meanwhile, heat the butter in a frying pan until melted and foaming. Add the steamed baby onions and wild mushrooms and cook for about 10 minutes until the onions are golden and the mushrooms are tender. Remove from the pan and keep warm.

Warm the spinach through, then drain and squeeze out any moisture. Spoon the spinach into the middle of the warmed serving plates. Carefully lift the halibut portions out of the pan, reserving the liquor. Drain the fish and season with salt, then place on top of the spinach.

Place the baby onions, lardons and wild mushrooms around the fish, then ladle the poaching liquor over them. Glaze the fish with the hot red wine sauce and serve, with pomme purée on the side.

Stuffed red mullet

with braised oxtail, bay & beef fat dressing

SERVES 4

Oxtail is such a special cut of beef. I love it. I think it's a childhood thing: from when I used to have oxtail soup. It takes a fair amount of work to get the meat off the bone but the taste is outstanding. And red mullet packs a big, flavoursome punch, so the two work really nicely together in a super-rich combination.

You need to put a lot of graft in to prepping the fish. The way we fillet and then stuff it (with the oxtail) is a skilful process. It's a cheffy technique, involving removing the fish's ribcage and backbone and careful pin-boning. It needs practice to get it right. You end up with a filleted fish looking like it's got a skeleton; but that skeleton is the oxtail stuffing.

There are a few other tricks of the trade involved in getting things perfect. A bit of transglutaminase (meat glue) to seal the stomach cavity together; vacuum sealing (with beef dripping) and cooking in a water bath; a blast of the blowtorch to crisp the fish skin before serving. That sort of thing!

Another little touch that makes this dish so amazing is a French-style dressing made with Cabernet Sauvignon vinegar and beef fat instead of olive oil. Very satisfying.

Braised oxtail stuffing

1 oxtail, cut into 4 pieces
75cl bottle red wine
4 tbsp vegetable oil
500ml chicken stock (see page 400)
40g fresh horseradish, peeled
  and grated
Sea salt and freshly ground pepper

Marinate the oxtail pieces in the red wine for 24 hours.

Preheat the oven to 160°C/Fan 140°C/Gas 3.

Drain the oxtail, reserving the wine. Heat a flameproof casserole over a medium-high heat and add the oil. When it is hot, add the oxtail pieces and sear, turning, until brown on all sides.

Bring the red wine to the boil in a separate saucepan and skim off any impurities from the surface. Pour the wine and stock over the oxtail and bring to the boil over a high heat. Cover with the lid and transfer to the oven. Braise for 3 hours.

Leave the oxtail to cool in the liquor, then drain, reserving the liquor. Pass the cooking liquor through a chinois, then through a sieve lined with 6 layers of muslin into a clean pan. Reduce to a sauce consistency.

When cool enough to handle, flake all the meat off the bone and place in a bowl with the horseradish. Mix well and use just enough of the oxtail sauce to bind the flaked meat. Season with salt and pepper to taste. Cover and place in the fridge until needed.

Refrigerate the rest of the oxtail sauce, ready to reheat for serving.

Stuffed red mullet

4 red mullet, 300g each, descaled,
  gutted and boned (ribcage
  removed, head and tail intact)
4 large slices of pastrami, 5mm thick
Meat glue (transglutaminase)
  for sealing

Line the cavity of each red mullet with the pastrami slices and then stuff with the oxtail mixture. Dust the edges of the opening with meat glue and bring them together to seal in the stuffing. Wrap in cling film and place in the fridge overnight to set the glue.

Bay & beef fat dressing

125g beef fat
10g bay leaves
25ml Cabernet Sauvignon red
  wine vinegar
Sea salt

Put the beef fat into a saucepan over a low heat to render. Once melted, add the bay leaves and leave to infuse over a very low heat for 1 hour.

Pass the fat through a fine chinois into a bowl.

Set aside one-third of the fat for cooking the fish (see right).

For the dressing, stir the wine vinegar into the rest of the fat and season with salt to taste.

To cook & serve the fish

4 bay leaves, finely diced

Remove the cling film from the red mullet and place them individually in vacuum-pack bags with the reserved beef fat. Cook in a water-bath at 70°C for 30 minutes.

Warm the bay and beef fat dressing and stir in the diced bay leaves.

Remove the fish from the vacuum-pack bags and blowtorch the skin until golden.

Place a fish in the middle of each warmed plate. Drizzle the dressing and the oxtail sauce over and around the fish, then serve.

John Dory & cuttlefish dolma

with artichoke gratin & burnt lemon purée

I'm a big fan of Greek food and this dish is inspired by the fabulous stuffed vine leaves and wonderful squid you get in Greece. I know, I've substituted the squid with cuttlefish, but there's a reason. It packs a great taste punch. It's like squid on steroids in terms of flavour and texture; plus it takes to long, slow cooking so much better than squid (a cooking technique you need to use to make the dolma). If you braise cuttlefish for ages, it softens beautifully and gives you a big, robust flavour and texture.

Vine leaves are quite robust and slightly sour, and they're a perfect match with the cuttlefish. It's something they have in common with Jerusalem artichokes, so the two work very well together, as well as with the same complementary ingredients. The roasted artichoke in this dish features a lovely gratin crust with a hint of hazelnuts.

Add to that the kick of the burnt lemon purée and you've got a fish dish with a super-individual character. We owe the lemon purée to a great chef, Ben Howarth, who worked with us for a number of years and learnt the technique while working in Copenhagen. He used beer and burnt lemons to create this beautiful ketchup, which ties in so well with the dolma. The result: an incredible plate of fish that's both autumnal and Greek.

Cuttlefish fish braise

200ml rapeseed oil
1 bay leaf
2g fennel seeds
2g coriander seeds
Finely pared zest of ¼ lemon
2 cleaned cuttlefish, about 350g each,
*   with tentacles*

Pour the oil into a pan, add the bay leaf, spices and lemon zest and warm gently to 60°C (use a digital probe to check the temperature). Remove from the heat and leave the oil to cool and infuse.

Pass the infused oil through a fine chinois into a measuring jug. Pour 50ml of the infused liquid into a large vacuum-pack bag and add one cleaned cuttlefish, along with the tentacles. Vacuum-seal on full pressure to remove all the air. Repeat with the other cuttlefish.

Immerse the vacuum-pack bags in a water-bath at 82°C and cook for 4 hours until tender. Once cooked, remove from the water-bath and refrigerate the cuttlefish in the bags.

Dolmas

20ml olive oil
40g onion, peeled and finely diced
50g long-grain rice
50ml cuttlefish braising liquor
*   (see left)*
100ml water
30g spring onion, sliced
10g chopped parsley
10g chopped dill
3g chopped mint
1 tbsp vegetable oil
350g braised cuttlefish, diced
*   (see left)*
30g unsalted butter
25ml lemon juice
10g dried herbes de Provence
4 fresh vine leaves (if available)
*   or from a jar (packed in brine)*
Extra-virgin olive oil (we use
*   Leblanc), to dress*
Sea salt and freshly ground pepper

Heat the olive oil in a medium pan over a medium heat, add the onion and cook for 5 minutes or so. Add the rice and cook for a further minute. Add the cuttlefish braising liquor and water and bring to the boil. Put the lid on and simmer until the liquor is absorbed and the rice is cooked. Stir in the spring onion and chopped fresh herbs, remove from the heat and leave to cool.

Heat the vegetable oil in a heavy-based saucepan, add the diced braised cuttlefish and sear until it starts to brown, then add the butter. Cook until the butter is melted, foaming and nut brown, then deglaze with the lemon juice and stir in the dried herbs. Remove from the heat and allow to cool, then chill in the fridge for 20 minutes.

To assemble the dolmas, mix 140g of the diced cuttlefish with 60g of the cooked rice and season with salt and pepper to taste.

Lay each of the 4 vine leaves out on a sheet of cling film. Place 50g of the dolma filling along the middle of each leaf, then roll tightly into a cylinder, 2.5cm in diameter. Tie the ends to secure and place in the fridge until needed.

When ready to serve, steam the dolmas for 6 minutes then remove the cling film. Trim off the ends to neaten and brush the dolmas with extra-virgin olive oil.

Burnt lemon purée

8 lemons
130g caster sugar
100g muscovado sugar
130ml water
290ml Sleeping Lemons beer
  (from the Wild Beer Company)
30ml lemon juice
7g salt
5g charcoal powder

Heat up a plancha or non-stick heavy-based frying pan. Add the whole lemons and colour, turning as necessary, until soft and evenly charred all over; this will take about 15 minutes.

Meanwhile, put the sugars, water, beer, lemon juice and salt into a heavy-based saucepan, heat to dissolve the sugars and bring to a simmer. Take off the heat.

Once the lemons are soft, transfer them to a high-powered jug blender (Vitamix). Blend until smooth, gradually pouring in enough of the hot lemon syrup to give a thick purée consistency. Add the charcoal powder and blitz to combine.

Pass the burnt lemon purée through a fine chinois into a bowl. Cover the surface with cling film to prevent a skin from forming and pop into the fridge to chill.

Gruyère & hazelnut crust

200g brioche crumbs
75g unsalted butter, softened
75g Gruyère, grated
20g chives
1 tsp truffle oil
A pinch of sea salt
100g hazelnuts, toasted and chopped

Put all of the ingredients into a blender and blitz to a coarse paste. Roll the mixture out between two sheets of baking parchment to form a thin sheet. Place in the freezer until needed.

When ready to assemble, remove the crust from the bag and place on a board. Using a cutter the same diameter as the Jerusalem artichoke tops (see right), press out 4 rounds.

Jerusalem artichoke gratin

4 medium Jerusalem artichokes,
  scrubbed clean
A pinch of sea salt
4 Gruyère and hazelnut crust discs
  (see left)

Place the whole artichokes in a vacuum-pack bag with the pinch of salt and vacuum-seal on full pressure. Cook in a water-bath at 88°C for 2 hours until tender, then drain and refresh in cold water. Top and tail the artichokes.

When ready to serve, preheat the oven to 205°C/Fan 185°C/Gas 6–7. Top each baked artichoke with a Gruyère and hazelnut crust disc and bake in the oven for 8 minutes, then colour under a hot grill if necessary.

Wheat beer dressing

6 banana shallots, peeled and
  finely diced
300ml wheat beer
80ml buerre blanc (see page 403)

Put the shallots into a saucepan, pour
on the wheat beer and bring to the
boil. Lower the heat to a simmer and
reduce until the liquor has almost
totally evaporated, then remove from
the heat.

When ready to serve, drain the
shallots and add to the warm buerre
blanc; keep warm.

To cook & serve the fish

4 fillets of John Dory, about 120g
  each
Olive oil for brushing
12 hazelnuts, halved and toasted

Preheat the grill in the oven to
medium. Place the John Dory fillets,
skin side up, on the grill rack and
brush liberally with olive oil. Cook
under the grill for 4–5 minutes,
basting frequently with the oil.

Meanwhile, place a dolma and
a gratin-topped artichoke on each
warmed plate and pipe on a little
mound of burnt lemon purée. Add
a portion of fish and finish with the
wheat beer dressing and toasted
hazelnuts. Serve at once.

Spiced tuna

with poppy seed crusted turnip, roasted ceps
& lime beurre noisette

SERVES 4

As a chef, my work mostly celebrates British food and ingredients and I'm known for creating meat-based dishes. Okay, so tuna's not a British fish and it's not meat, but its texture is super-dense; you treat it like a steak (hot-seared and very pink in the middle). And, trust me, it takes being served with ingredients that withstand meaty flavours, like cep and turnip.

While the recipe is unusual, it has all the hallmarks of a great Hand & Flowers dish. A bit of spice, a crunch of toasty poppy seeds, a taste of the sea and a hit of the earth. Visually, it's us all over: three things on a plate, packed with flavour.

The tuna is dusted with ground, toasted cumin and coriander seeds and seared in a really hot pan, before being joined on the plate by poached turnips rolled in poppy seeds, and beautiful, juicy ceps – cooked in butter and a reduced chicken sauce. The dish is then finished with a zesty lime beurre noisette, a little herb sauce, and a single oyster leaf.

Strikingly simple, it emits the most incredible flavour. I'm happy to push my comfort zones and I love the idea of other amazing cuisines – South American, Scandinavian, Chinese – but this dish really says 'me' because it highlights the style I have driven towards over the years.

Spiced tuna

*600g prime tuna loin, with
 no bloodline*
100g coriander seeds
100g cumin seeds

Trim the tuna loin and roll tightly
in cling film to set the shape. Place in
the fridge until ready to cook.

Toast the spices in a hot pan until
they release their aromas, then grind
to a fine powder, using a spice
grinder or pestle and mortar. Pass
through a fine chinois and set aside
until ready to cook.

Poppy seed crusted turnips

4 medium round turnips
100g unsalted butter
200ml butter emulsion (see page 403)
30g black poppy seeds, toasted
Sea salt and freshly ground pepper

Peel the turnips and rub with a
scourer to remove all peel lines, so
that the turnip looks perfectly round.
Put them into a vacuum-pack bag
along with the butter and some salt
and pepper. Vacuum-seal on full
pressure and immerse in a water-
bath at 82°C. Cook the turnips for
45 minutes.

Remove the bag from the water-bath
and drop into a bowl of iced water to
refresh the turnips.

When ready to serve, take the turnips
out of the bag and reheat in the
butter emulsion for about 5 minutes.
Remove from the pan and toss in the
poppy seeds to coat all over.

Roasted ceps

6 firm medium ceps, cleaned
1 tbsp vegetable oil
50g unsalted butter, in pieces
50ml chicken sauce (see page 400)

Halve the ceps. Heat a large frying
pan over a medium heat and add the
oil. When it is hot, add the ceps, cut
side down, and fry until caramelised
to a rich golden colour. Turn the ceps
over and add the butter and chicken
sauce to the pan. Baste the ceps with
the buttery sauce to glaze. Remove
from the pan and keep warm until
ready to serve.

Lime beurre noisette

To cook & serve the tuna

100g unsalted butter, diced
Juice of 2 limes

Heat the butter in a small saucepan over a medium heat until melted and starting to foam. Continue to cook until the butter is nut brown in colour and starts to smell biscuity.

Remove from the heat and add the lime juice, scraping up all of the toasted butter solids from the bottom of the pan. Season with salt to taste; keep warm.

Vegetable oil for cooking
4 tbsp herb sauce (see page 402)
4 oyster leaves

Slice the tuna into 4 equal portions, remove the cling film and lay on a tray. Using a small sieve, lightly dust the tops of the tuna steaks with the toasted spice mix.

Heat a generous splash of oil in a non-stick frying pan over a medium-high heat. When the pan is hot, add the tuna steaks and sear for 1–2 minutes on each side, depending on size.

Transfer the tuna to a grill rack and place under a low grill or salamander for 2–3 minutes, just to warm the middle of the tuna; don't overcook it.

Place a tuna steak on each warmed plate with a poppy-crusted turnip and a few cep halves. Dress with the lime beurre noisette and a little herb sauce and finish with an oyster leaf.

Drinks

Our wine list has developed over time and we like to offer interesting bottles that people may not have heard of – English wine, for instance, as well as wine from small producers and suppliers all over the world.

A lovely wine with great food is wonderful, but we've always encouraged customers to drink real ales with their Michelin-starred meals, too. I love the fact that people feel comfortable and adventurous enough in The Hand to go off-piste with food-and-drink matching.

When you meet brewers it's hard not to be blown away by how passionate they are about what they do. They absolutely understand their own process, the way a beer's flavours can change at different times of the year because of the nuances in hops, or barley, or malt. And serving is affected by so many things – from cellar temperature to how long a beer has been tapped for before serving (are you drinking it straight away, or leaving it for three days to settle?). All of these elements affect the beer and its flavour profile.

For me, creating the perfect cellar environment and looking after our beers is very important. They deserve the same love as my ingredients get! At the same time, The Hand & Flowers is still a pub at heart, which means people can come in whenever they want to have a pint of their local Hand & Flowers ale, or Rebellion – a very good beer from a local Marlow brewery.

Or they might order a gin and tonic, because over the last decade gin has become massively popular. A lot of that popularity is down to the fact that gin has a long association with Britain. Its resurgence took off around the same time as people started growing their own vegetables and getting into baking – traits that stood strong in a post-war Britain. It can also be seen as something of a healthier option; gin and slimline tonic, for example, is relatively low in calories and so some see it as a health-conscious choice.

We created our own gin with the Portobello Road Gin company in London – it's a celery-based gin and it's delicious! The way we shine a light on the small, artisan producers who supply the kitchen with fantastic ingredients is no different to the way we treat the suppliers whose products we showcase in the bar: with admiration and gratitude.

Chicken in beer & malt

with salt-baked celeriac & confit garlic

This recipe is rooted in my first ever experience of going out for a meal, back in the 1980s. It's based on a meal in a Berni Inn restaurant that my mum took me to in the centre of Gloucester. I clearly remember having half a chicken, roasted, with chips and peas.

You never forget those first treats, do you? So, this dish is my reflection on my early dining years and childhood memories; and my tribute to just how lovely something like chicken and chips can be, done in a pub, if it's lifted out of the ordinary by using the best ingredients you can get hold of.

Our chicken includes Abbot Ale beer and links up with our local brewery. We get malt and hops – and all the other bits – from there and then use them to make a brine liquor, which eventually gets reduced and used as a glaze when the chicken is ready to serve.

We've added one or two other flavour layers to take the dish forward: a swirl of vanilla mayonnaise, a mushroom tuile and a generous jug of oak sauce – made from chicken stock infused with oak chips – on the side. For me, it's a lovely dish that brings back delightful childhood memories.

CHICKEN IN BEER & MALT

To brine the chicken

2 free-range chickens, 1kg each
1 litre brine (10% solution)

Remove the knuckles and wings from the chickens, then halve them lengthways through the breastbone. Using a pair of sharp poultry scissors, cut away the backbone, then tie the leg bone to the French-trimmed wing bone.

Submerge the portioned chickens in the brine solution for 6 hours. After this time, rinse off the brine under cold running water.

Oak sauce

25g oak chips
200g chicken sauce (see page 400)

Preheat the oven to 200°C/Fan 180°C/Gas 6 and line a baking sheet with baking parchment. Scatter the oak chips on the prepared baking sheet and bake for 5–10 minutes until lightly toasted.

Bring the chicken sauce to the boil in a saucepan, add the toasted oak chips and remove from the heat. Cover the pan with cling film and set aside to infuse for 5 minutes.

Pass the sauce through a muslin-lined sieve into a jug and keep warm.

Confit garlic

1 garlic bulb
100ml olive oil
Sea salt and freshly ground pepper

Separate the garlic into cloves, then trim off the hard root end with a paring knife. Place the garlic cloves in a saucepan and cover with cold water, bring to the boil and then drain and refresh in iced water. Repeat this process 5 times.

After the final blanch, drain the garlic thoroughly and place in a container. Pour on the olive oil to cover and set aside.

When ready to serve, preheat the oven to 200°C/Fan 180°C/Gas 6 and line a small baking tray with baking parchment. Drain the oil from the garlic and lay the cloves on the baking tray. Season them with salt and pepper. Bake in the oven for 10 minutes until the garlic starts to caramelise. Keep warm.

Malt glaze

125ml Abbot Ale
20g malt extract

Mix the beer and malt extract together in a saucepan and bring to the boil. Simmer to reduce to a sticky glaze, then pour into a container and leave to cool to room temperature.

Mushroom tuiles

10g dried mushrooms
100g Isomalt

Blitz the dried mushrooms to a powder in a blender.

Melt the Isomalt in a saucepan over a medium-low heat and heat to 130°C (check the temperature with a digital probe). Stir in the dried mushroom powder until evenly combined.

Pour the mixture onto a silicone mat and spread thinly and evenly with a palette knife.

Leave the tuile sheet to cool and firm up, then break into 4 large pieces (to lay on top of the chicken). Set aside, ready for serving.

Tuile garnish

30g sourdough crumbs
Vegetable oil for dressing and
deep-frying
30g Sosa Airbag Granet dehydrated
pork skin, broken into small pieces
2 tsp thyme leaves
10g malt glaze (see opposite)
Sea salt and freshly ground pepper

Preheat the oven to 205°C/Fan 185°C/Gas 6–7 and line a baking sheet with baking parchment.

Dress the sourdough crumbs with a little oil and season with salt and pepper. Scatter on the prepared baking sheet. Bake for 15 minutes, stirring every 5 minutes.

Heat the oil in a deep-fryer to 190°C. Add the pork skin pieces and fry for about 40 seconds. Remove from the oil with a slotted spoon, drain on kitchen paper and season with salt.

Combine the fried pork skin pieces, baked sourdough crumb and thyme leaves in a bowl.

Just before serving, brush the mushroom tuiles with a little malt glaze and sprinkle over the pork crumb mix.

Vanilla mayonnaise

2 egg yolks
2 tsp Dijon mustard
2 tsp white wine vinegar
2 vanilla pods, split and
seeds scraped
250ml vegetable oil
Sea salt and cayenne pepper

Put the egg yolks, mustard, wine vinegar and vanilla seeds into a blender and blend briefly to combine.

With the motor running, slowly pour in the oil and blend until emulsified to a thick, glossy mayonnaise. Season with salt and cayenne pepper to taste.

Spoon the mayonnaise into a piping bag, ready for serving.

Celery jam

250ml water
150g caster sugar
4 celery sticks, peeled and sliced
Juice of ½ lemon, to taste

Put the water and sugar into a small heavy-based saucepan and heat to dissolve the sugar, then bring to the boil. Add the sliced celery, lower the heat and simmer slowly for about 30 minutes until reduced and thickened to a jam-like consistency.

Add the lemon juice to taste. Allow to cool and set aside.

Celeriac royale

1kg peeled celeriac, diced
400ml milk
150g butter
20g salt
20ml truffle oil
2 medium free-range eggs
7 medium free-range egg yolks
200ml double cream
4 tsp celery jam (see left)
20 celery leaves
2 crispy chicken skins (see page 206),
broken into shards

Put the celeriac, milk, butter, salt and truffle oil into a large vacuum-pack bag. Place on a steamer tray and cook in a steamer at 100°C for 40 minutes.

Open the bag and tip the contents into a blender. Blitz until smooth, then pass through a fine chinois into a bowl. Cover and refrigerate.

Measure 300g of the celeriac purée and place in a bowl with the eggs and extra yolks. Whisk to combine and then stir in the cream.

Pour the mixture into a Thermomix, heat to 80°C and hold at that temperature for 5 minutes.

Divide the celeriac royale between 4 individual staub dishes, cover with cling film and keep warm.

When ready to serve, finish with the celery jam, celery leaves and crispy chicken skins.

Salt-baked celeriac

*1 batch of salt crust dough
   (see page 405)
1 celeriac (unpeeled)
50g unsalted butter
50g fresh yeast, crumbled
A little vegetable oil for frying*

Preheat the oven to 190°C/Fan 170°C/Gas 5. Roll out the salt crust dough to a round, about 5mm thick. Wrap the celeriac in the salt crust dough and press the edges together to seal. Bake in the oven for 2 hours.

Remove from the oven and leave the celeriac to cool in the crust. Once cooled, break away the crust. Remove the skin from the celeriac and cut into wedges. Keep to one side.

When ready to serve, warm the butter and yeast together in a small pan until the butter is melted and the yeast is dissolved; take off the heat.

In a large frying pan over a medium-high heat, heat a little oil then add the celeriac wedges and caramelise, turning them as necessary to colour all over. Baste with the yeast butter to glaze.

To cook the chickens

*250ml Abbot Ale
40g malt extract
4 brined chicken halves
   (see page 204)
4g hops, divided between 4 muslin
   bags (as for a bouquet garni)*

Mix the beer and malt extract together. Place each brined chicken half in a medium vacuum-pack bag and add 60ml of the beer liquor and 1 hop bag to each. Vacuum-seal at full pressure.

Immerse in a water-bath at 70°C and cook for 2 hours until the chicken is cooked through. (In the meantime, prepare the crispy chicken skins and fried thyme garnish.)

Remove the cooked chicken from the bags, reserving the liquor. Set the chicken aside to rest in a warm place. Pour the liquor into a saucepan and reduce to a rich glaze.

Just before serving, blowtorch the chicken to give the skin a deep golden brown colour then brush the chicken all over with the beer glaze.

Crispy chicken skins

*Skins from 6 chicken legs
Sea salt*

Preheat the oven to 190°C/Fan 170°C/Gas 5 and line a baking sheet with baking parchment. Lay the chicken skins out on a board and scrape away any excess fat to leave translucent skins.

Lay the chicken skins out on the prepared baking sheet and season them lightly with salt. Bake in the oven for 15–20 minutes until crisp and golden.

Use two of the crispy chicken skins to finish the celeriac royale; use the rest to garnish the assembled plates.

Deep-fried thyme sprigs

Vegetable oil for deep-frying
4 large sprigs of soft-leaved thyme

Heat the oil in a deep-fryer or deep, heavy pan to 180°C. Add the thyme sprigs and deep-fry for 30 seconds or until they stop bubbling.

Remove the thyme sprigs with a slotted spoon, drain on kitchen paper and season with salt.

To serve

Place the glazed chicken on warmed plates and add a wedge of salt-baked celeriac to each. Pipe a mound of vanilla mayonnaise alongside and add a confit garlic clove.

Lay a crispy chicken skin on the celeriac and a fried thyme sprig across the vanilla mayonnaise. Top the chicken with the garnished mushroom tuile. Serve the celeriac royale and oak sauce on the side.

Slow-cooked duck

with duck fat chips & gravy

——— SERVES 4 ———

Some dishes end up defining you, chef and restaurant. This is one of them. I cooked it at the Great British Menu banquet for Prince Charles and the Duchess of Cornwall in 2010. That raised our profile into the stratosphere: everybody suddenly wanted to book a table at The Hand & Flowers and order duck and chips!

We already had a great little business, but Great British Menu became one of the most pivotal moments in the pub's history. The programme is very special: it shines the spotlight on quality British produce and showcases food and restaurants around the UK, which is brilliant because that underlines that our world isn't just about London and the Southeast.

To get to the final, you compete in 'heats', and in 2010, my cook-off location was Waddesdon Manor, which is near Aylesbury. So, to me, the obvious thing to cook was something with Aylesbury duck. These ducks taste amazing and they're from a small-scale producer – everything Great British Menu is about. Since an important part of our Hand & Flowers menu includes chips on the side (we're a pub, after all), I decided to make the ultimate chips, cooked in duck fat.

I needed peas, too. So, I went down the route of *petits pois à la française*, except, instead of using bacon, which you'd normally do, I used crisp-fried duck leg confit. And then I finished the dish with a gravy that uses honey from the Waddesdon estate.

It all added up to a winner. I remember one Saturday night after the banquet was televised, we did 84 covers and served 78 portions of duck in one sitting. The success of this dish has been extraordinary.

To prepare the duck

2 large Aylesbury ducks, about
    2kg each
3 tsp ground mace

Remove the legs and wings from
the ducks and take out the wishbone
(reserve for the faggots, gravy etc.,
see right and overleaf). Remove the
excess fat and skin, placing it all in
a frying pan. Now carefully cut away
the backbone; you should be left with
the crown.

Place the pan of fat and skin over
a low heat to render the fat out. Set
aside for later use.

Score the skin on the duck crowns
and rub in the mace. Heat a heavy-
based frying pan over a medium-
high heat. Add the duck crowns and
sear on all sides for 5–10 minutes
to render the fat and give the skin
a good golden colour. Remove the
duck crowns from the pan and allow
to cool.

Put each duck crown into a large
vacuum-pack bag and vacuum-seal
on full pressure. Immerse in a
water-bath at 62°C and cook for
1½ hours.

Lift out the vacuum-pack bags and
remove the ducks. Carefully cut the
breasts from the crowns. Cover and
refrigerate until ready to cook.

Duck gravy

500g duck bones and wings, chopped
A little vegetable oil for cooking
4 carrots, peeled and chopped into
    3cm pieces
4 celery sticks, cut into 3cm pieces
1 onion, peeled and diced into
    3cm pieces
1 garlic bulb, cut across in half,
    through the equator
150g runny honey
4 cloves
2 litres chicken stock (see page 400)
50ml soy sauce
About 500g unsalted butter
Lemon juice, to taste (optional)
Sea salt and freshly ground pepper

Preheat the oven to 205°C/Fan
185°C/Gas 6–7. Put the chopped
duck bones and wings into a roasting
tray and roast in the oven for about
25–30 minutes until golden brown
and caramelised.

Heat a little oil in a large heavy-based
saucepan over a medium-high heat.
Add the chopped carrots and colour
until darkly caramelised. Add the
celery, onion and garlic and similarly
colour until well browned.

Remove the duck bones and wings
from the roasting tray and add them
to the saucepan. Drain off the excess
fat from the roasting tray, then add
the honey and cloves to the tray.
Place over a medium heat and take
the honey to a dark golden caramel.

Add a splash of the chicken stock
and the soy sauce to deglaze the tray,
stirring to scrape up the sediment.
Add the liquor to the duck bones and
vegetables. Pour in the rest of the
chicken stock and reduce down by
half, to 1 litre.

Pass the liquor through a muslin-
lined sieve into a clean pan and skim
off any excess fat from the surface.
Add 250g butter to every 500ml duck
liquor and reduce down until it has
emulsified into the sauce.

Season with salt and pepper and add
a little lemon juice if required. Set
aside for serving.

Duck faggots

250g minced duck leg (skin on)
50g minced chicken liver
50g breadcrumbs
1 medium free-range egg
5g salt
2g cracked black pepper
100g caul fat, soaked in cold
   water for 30 minutes

Put all the faggot ingredients into a bowl and mix well until evenly combined. Divide and shape the mixture into 50g balls. Wrap each one in caul fat to enclose.

Steam the duck faggots at 100°C for 20 minutes. Remove from the steamer and allow to cool, then chill until needed.

When ready to serve, preheat the oven to 205°C/Fan 185°C/Gas 6–7. Place the faggots on a baking tray and bake for 8 minutes.

Hold the faggots in the duck gravy until ready to plate up.

Duck legs & peas

2 duck legs
1 star anise
½ cinnamon stick
10 black peppercorns
1 tsp coriander seeds
1 tsp fennel seeds
1 tbsp rock salt
2 bay leaves
About 300ml duck fat
500g freshly podded peas
4 tbsp runny honey
A little vegetable oil for cooking
2 large banana shallots, peeled
   and finely diced
100ml chicken stock (see page 400)
2 Gem lettuces, finely sliced
20 small mint leaves

Preheat the oven to 150°C/Fan 130°C/Gas 2. Put the duck legs into a large ovenproof pan or flameproof casserole. Tie the spices together in a muslin bag and add them to the pan with the rock salt and bay leaves. Pour on enough duck fat to cover and bring to the boil over a medium heat.

Transfer the pan to the oven and cook for 3½ hours or until the duck legs are soft. Leave them to cool in the duck fat. Once cooled, remove from the fat and place in the fridge.

Meanwhile, add the peas to a pan of boiling salted water, bring back to the boil and blanch for no longer than 1 minute. Immediately drain and refresh in iced water. Drain and set aside.

Preheat the oven to 205°C/Fan 185°C/Gas 6–7. Place an ovenproof heavy-based frying pan over a medium-high heat. Add the duck legs, skin side down, and place in the oven for 10–12 minutes to crisp up. Remove the duck legs to a plate and add the honey to the pan. Allow to caramelise, then pour over the duck legs and allow to cool.

When ready to serve, heat a little oil in a saucepan over a medium heat. Add the diced shallots and sweat for 10–15 minutes until softened but not coloured. Add the peas and stock and bring to a simmer.

Meanwhile, flake the duck leg. Stir the duck meat into the peas with the lettuce and mint. Divide between 4 small serving pots.

Duck fat chips

15 large potatoes for chipping
2.5 litres duck fat for deep-frying

Cut a slice from the top and bottom of each potato, then press an apple corer through from top to bottom to make round cylinder chips. Put the cut chips into a colander under cold running water to wash off some of the starches.

Now add the chips to a pan of boiling salted water, bring back to a simmer and poach for about 10 minutes until just soft, but still holding their shape. Drain on a perforated tray and leave to cool.

Heat the duck fat in a deep-fryer to 140°C. Lower the chips into the hot fat in a wire basket and deep-fry for 8–10 minutes until the oil stops bubbling. Remove the chips from the fryer, drain and leave to cool. Set aside until needed.

When ready to serve, heat the duck fat to 180°C and deep-fry the chips for about 6–7 minutes until golden and crispy. Remove, drain on kitchen paper and season with salt.

To serve

Vegetable oil for cooking
2 tbsp runny honey
50g unsalted butter
Pea shoots, to garnish

Just before serving, preheat the oven to 200°C/Fan 180°C/Gas 6. Heat a little oil in a heavy-based ovenproof frying pan over a medium-high heat. Add the duck breasts, skin side down, and fry for 3–4 minutes to crisp up the skin, then place in the oven for 4–5 minutes to heat through.

Pour off any excess fat from the pan, then add the honey and butter and turn the duck around in the pan to coat in the honey glaze.

Remove the duck breasts to a warmed plate and rest in a warm place. Increase the heat under the pan to caramelise the honey glaze then pour it over the duck breasts.

Serve the duck breasts with the duck legs and peas, duck faggots, gravy and chips. Finish with a garnish of pea shoots.

Spiced duck breast

with dukka & duck confit tart & apricot gel

This is a Middle-Eastern-influenced dish flavoured with a Baharat spice mix featuring classic ingredients: we're talking coriander, cinnamon, cardamom, cloves, cumin, paprika. The duck breast is immersed in a spiced brine for 4 hours, then after cooking we glaze it with caramelised honey and butter and give it a final dusting of Baharat spice.

The recipe is one that's constantly evolving. There's always a tart case – comprising layers of feuille de brick pastry brushed with duck fat and salt – that we fill with a rich, dark duck ragout, confit duck and whatever veg is in season. Here the veg is pickled radicchio, but in the summer that might be peas or broad beans. We have even used rhubarb and topped it with a savoury oat crumble. The dukka topping on this tart is another Middle Eastern touch.

The recipe, like many Hand & Flowers dishes, is a team creation and Jamie May, our head chef, is responsible for the pickled radicchio. He was looking at incorporating a bitter leaf into the dish and asked Fabrizio, an Italian chef in the brigade, how his mum would cook radicchio at home. It turns out she would chiffonade it (cut it into long, fine strips or ribbons) and cook it in sugar and vinegar. So, Jamie evolved that, wilting the leaves in our pickling liquor before placing them in the tart.

A fresh, tart, apricot gel is the finishing touch for this dish – it cuts through the richness of the duck perfectly.

Brined duck breasts

1 litre cold water
100g table salt
50g Baharat spice mix
4 duck breasts

In a bowl, whisk the water, salt and spice together to dissolve the salt and make a brine. Pour into a shallow container. Add the duck breasts and place in the fridge for 4 hours.

Remove the duck breasts from the brine and pat dry. Place individually in vacuum-pack bags and vacuum-seal. Immerse in a water-bath at 62°C for 45 minutes.

Once the duck breasts are cooked, lift the bags out and plunge them into a bowl of iced water to cool the duck breasts quickly. Drain and refrigerate until serving.

Confit duck legs

6 duck legs
10g cumin seeds
3g fennel seeds
7g coriander seeds
½ cinnamon stick
3 cardamom pods, cracked open
4 cloves
9g mild curry powder
105g mixed table and sea salt
  (equal quantities)
100g dried apricots, diced
200ml melted duck fat
Sea salt and freshly ground pepper

Have the duck legs ready at room temperature. Toast the whole spices, 4g of the curry powder and the salt mix together in a dry frying pan over a medium heat for a minute or so until fragrant. Tip onto a plate and allow to cool, then blitz in a blender to a fine seasoning.

Coat the duck legs in the toasted spice mix and place on a tray in the fridge to cure for 10 hours.

Wash off the spice mix and pat the duck legs dry with kitchen paper. Place in vacuum-pack bags, vacuum-seal and immerse in a water-bath at 88.2°C for 8 hours until tender.

Once cooked, drain off the cooking juices and reserve. Remove the duck meat from the bone, flake and place in a bowl with the remaining 5g curry powder, diced apricots and duck fat. Mix well, adding the reserved cooking juices, and season with salt and pepper to taste.

Weigh 160g of the confit duck and set aside for the ragout (overleaf).

Place the rest of the mixture in a vacuum-pack bag and seal, leaving 1cm margin at the end. Roll the mixture in the bag to form a cylinder, then freeze.

When ready to serve, remove the confit duck cylinder from the bag and cut into 4cm discs. Warm through under a salamander or grill.

Duck ragout

Vegetable oil for cooking
260g minced duck leg meat
5 star anise, tied in a muslin bag
20g shallot, cut into 3mm dice
20g carrot, cut into 3mm dice
50ml red wine
50ml Madeira
200ml pork sauce (see page 401)
160g confit duck leg (see page 217), warmed
5g ground mixed peppercorns (black, pink, pimento, white and green)
Sea salt

Heat a large heavy-based frying pan over a medium-high heat and add a splash of oil. When it is hot, add the duck leg mince, along with the bag of star anise. Cook, stirring frequently, until the mince is well browned. Add the shallot and carrot dice, lower the heat and sweat until softened.

Add the wine and Madeira and allow to bubble until reduced right down, then add the pork sauce and flaked duck confit. Season with the mixed pepper and salt to taste. Cover and place in the fridge until needed. Reheat to serve.

Dukka mix

25g salted pistachio nuts
25g blanched skinned hazelnuts
10g black sesame seeds
5g coriander seeds
5g fennel seeds
2g caraway seeds
2g cracked black peppercorns

Preheat the oven to 200°C/Fan 180°C/Gas 6. Place all the nuts, seeds and cracked pepper on a baking tray and roast together for 8–10 minutes until golden brown. Leave to cool.

Using a cook's knife, halve or slice the nuts. Keep the dukka mix in a dry container.

Tart cases

4 sheets of feuille de brick pastry
100ml melted duck fat

Brush the brick pastry sheets generously with duck fat and then layer, one on top of another, on a board. Cover with another board to press the pastry and place in the fridge for an hour.

Preheat the oven to 190°C/Fan 170°C/Gas 5. Cut four 8cm rounds from the pressed brick pastry and use to line 4 fluted individual brioche moulds, pressing the pastry into the flutes of the moulds. Stack them on top of each other, placing an empty mould on the top one. Bake for 15 minutes until golden and crisp. Trim the edges to neaten.

Transfer the tart cases to a wire rack and leave to cool. Keep in an airtight container until needed.

Apricot gel

250g apricot purée (Boiron)
125ml apple juice
5g agar agar
60ml cider
60ml cider vinegar

Put the apricot purée, apple juice and agar agar into a Thermomix, heat to 100°C and hold for 3 minutes. Pour onto a tray and leave to set.

Once cooled and set, dice the jelly. Place in a high-powered jug blender (Vitamix) and add the cider and cider vinegar. Blend to a smooth purée and pass through a fine chinois into a bowl. Refrigerate until needed.

To finish the duck breasts & serve

20g Baharat spice mix, for dusting
30ml runny honey
50ml pickling liquor (see page 404)
½ radicchio, chiffonade
100ml duck gravy (see page 211)

Preheat the oven to 205°C/Fan 185°C/Gas 6–7. Unwrap the duck breasts and score the skin. Place a heavy-based ovenproof frying pan over a medium heat, add the duck breasts, skin side down, and render the fat slowly.

Once the fat is rendered and the skin is crisp, transfer the pan (with the duck still skin side down) to the oven for 4–5 minutes just to warm the meat through.

Remove from the oven and give the duck breasts a final dusting of spice, then place, skin side up, on a resting tray in a warm spot and leave to rest.

Return the pan to the heat and add the honey. Bring to the boil and cook to a dark caramel, then pour over the duck breasts to glaze.

While the duck is resting, bring the pickling liquor to the boil. Drop in the chiffonade radicchio briefly to wilt, then remove. Layer the warm duck ragout and confit duck discs in the tart cases with the radicchio. Top with the dukka.

Place a duck breast and a tart on each warmed serving plate. Add a drop quenelle of the apricot gel to each plate and finish with the duck sauce.

Pigeon & foie gras en croûte

with Gem lettuce & pickled girolles

SERVES 4

Pies have become quite fashionable now, and we've been doing them as a main course for more than a decade. They tick all the boxes of what we do at The Hand & Flowers and they have helped to define our style. Pies may be humble on the outside – but once you cut into them, you see care, attention, a beautiful product, and a lot of love.

This recipe in particular is a definitive Hand & Flowers dish. It's special because it represents the moment when the kitchen team and I began to take ownership of our own particular style of food; that is cuisine which is robust in soul, yet refined in manner.

Essentially, yes, this is a pie. But it's a decadent pie with a lot of finesse: duxelles, chicken mousse, crépinette wrapping, pastry, glaze. It takes a lot of practice to perfect all of the elements and achieve consistency. The hard work is all in the mise-en-place – the preparation, in other words. Time and care in the mise takes the risk out of service.

Actually, I have to confess, before we became super-confident with the dish, we sometimes cooked two pies for one portion because we were worried that when we sliced it in half it might not be quite right! When it is right, the pigeon and foie gras are beautiful, almost mosaic-like.

The dish has traditional French roots (you see versions of it on many three-Michelin-starred menus) and in many ways it feels like a summary of all my training in classic French cookery. It's very much our Hand & Flowers take, though. Yes, it has the classic richness of flavour you get from squab pigeon and foie gras. But you also get this amazing Gem lettuce with roasted onions and pickled girolles, which cuts through that wonderful lushness. We've done it our way, to coin a phrase.

To prepare the pigeon

*2 large squab pigeon crowns,
    from 600g pigeons*
4 sprigs of thyme

Remove the legs and wings from the pigeons and take out the wishbone. Carefully cut away the backbone; you should be left with the crown. Keep the bones for the sauce (see right).

Put each pigeon crown into a large vacuum-pack bag with 2 thyme sprigs and vacuum-seal. Cook in a water-bath at 62°C for 45 minutes. Transfer the bags to a bowl of iced water to refresh.

Once the pigeons are cooled, take them out of the bags and remove the skin. Carefully take off the pigeon breasts, lay them on a tray lined with a J-cloth, wrap in cling film and place in the fridge until ready to serve.

To prepare the foie gras

A little vegetable oil for cooking
4 slices of frozen rouge foie gras

Heat a non-stick heavy-based frying pan over a high heat and oil lightly.

Lay the frozen foie gras in the hot pan for about 40 seconds until caramelised on the surface and cooked one-third of the way up. Flip the foie gras slices over and cook for another 30 seconds.

Remove from the pan and chill on a tray in the fridge until ready to build the pigeon en croûte.

Pigeon sauce

*250g pigeon bones, chopped
    (see left)*
1 litre chicken stock (see page 400)

Preheat the oven to 205°C/Fan 185°C/Gas 6–7. Put the chopped pigeon bones and wings into a roasting tray and roast in the oven for about 20 minutes until they are richly caramelised.

Transfer the pigeon bones to a saucepan and pour on the stock. Bring to the boil and simmer for 45 minutes to draw out the flavour from the bones.

Pass the stock through a fine chinois, then through 4 layers of muslin. Return the pigeon stock to the pan, bring to a simmer and reduce to a glossy, rich sauce consistency.

Gem lettuce parcels

A little vegetable oil for cooking
2 onions, peeled and thinly sliced
100g small girolles
*1 small shallot, peeled and finely
    diced*
25ml pickling liquor (see page 404)
2 Gem lettuces
Sea salt and freshly ground pepper

Heat a little oil in a heavy-based saucepan over a medium-high heat. Add the onions and cook for about 10–15 minutes until soft and well caramelised. Remove from the heat and leave to cool. Cover and set these Lyonnaise onions aside until needed.

Heat a little oil in a heavy-based frying pan, add the girolles and sauté for 1–2 minutes. Add the shallot and cook for a few minutes to soften. Deglaze with the pickling liquor then remove from the heat.

Separate the lettuce leaves. Add them to a pan of boiling salted water and blanch for 20–30 seconds until just wilted. Immediately drain and refresh in iced water.

Drain the lettuce leaves and lay them on a tray lined with kitchen paper to dry off any excess liquid, then wrap in cling film and place in the fridge until ready to assemble and serve the parcels.

Chicken mousse

2 skinless boneless chicken breasts,
  diced
½ tbsp flaky sea salt
½ tsp cayenne pepper
½ tbsp dried herbes de Provence
1 medium free-range egg
2 tbsp truffle oil
250ml double cream

Put the diced chicken breast into a
blender with the salt, cayenne and
dried herbs and blitz thoroughly.
Add the egg and pulse to combine,
then add the truffle oil and pulse
again. Finally, with the motor
running, pour in the cream and
bring together.

Pass the chicken mousse through
a drum sieve into a bowl, cover and
chill until needed.

Portobello duxelles

10 large Portobello mushrooms,
  peeled and roughly chopped
1 tsp dried herbes de Provence
50ml red wine
100ml double cream
A good pinch of cayenne pepper,
  to taste
3 drops of black truffle oil
Sea salt

Put the chopped mushrooms into a
blender or food processor and blitz
briefly to a coarse texture (not a
purée or paste).

Heat a pan over a medium heat and
add the blitzed mushrooms with the
dried herbs. Cook for about 20–30
minutes until the mushrooms release
their liquid and it is fully evaporated.
(You want them fully dehydrated
– almost like a mushroom tobacco.)

Pour in the wine and let it reduce
until fully evaporated. Pour in the
cream and reduce until the mixture
becomes very thick and the cream is
no longer visible. Season with salt,
cayenne and black truffle oil.

Spoon the duxelles into a container
and cool quickly in the blast chiller
or fridge.

Pastry

400g 'T45' plain flour
A pinch of sea salt
A pinch of dextrose
A pinch of baking powder
125g unsalted butter, diced
2 medium free-range egg yolks
150ml cold water

Sift the flour, salt, dextrose and
baking powder together into a bowl,
then add the butter and rub in until
the mixture resembles breadcrumbs.

Beat the egg yolks with the water,
then add to the rubbed-in mixture
and mix to combine and bring
together to form a smooth dough.

Wrap the dough in cling film and
leave to rest in the fridge for an hour
before using.

Egg glaze

3 medium free-range egg yolks
5g dextrose
2 tsp whole milk

Whisk the egg yolks and dextrose
together to combine, then stir in the
milk. Leave the glaze to rest for an
hour before use.

To assemble & bake the pigeon en croûte

250g Portobello mushroom duxelles (see page 223)
250g chicken mousse (see page 223)
4 caramelised foie gras slices (see page 222)
4 poached pigeon breasts (see page 222)
100g pig's caul fat, washed
Pastry (see page 223)
Egg glaze (see page 223)
Plain flour, for dusting
Sea salt and freshly ground pepper

In a bowl, mix the mushroom duxelles and chicken mousse together thoroughly to bind together. To test the seasoning, take 1 tbsp of the mixture, wrap it in a sheet of cling film, roll into a little sausage and tie the ends to seal. Poach in simmering water for 5 minutes or until cooked. Remove and taste for seasoning. Adjust the seasoning of the duxelles accordingly, adding more salt and/or pepper if needed.

To build the pigeon filling, lay a sheet of cling film on a board and place a generous 1 tbsp of the duxelles and mousse mixture in the centre. Using a stepped palette knife, spread out the mixture so the foie gras will be able to sit proudly on top with a little excess mix to the sides.

Position a slice of caramelised foie gras centrally and place a pigeon breast, skin side up, on top. Then, using a palette knife, spread a good layer of duxelles mix over the breast to cover it completely. Wrap up tightly in the cling film and pop in the fridge to set. Repeat for the 3 remaining pigeon breasts.

Once set, remove the cling film. Divide the caul fat into 4 even sheets. Lay one on a clean board and then place a pigeon parcel in the middle. Wrap up in the caul fat, ensuring there are no gaps. Repeat with the other 3 parcels.

Place in the fridge for an hour or so to dry the caul fat – any reduction of moisture will help to prevent the pastry from cracking.

Divide the pastry into 4 portions. Roll out one portion on a floured surface and place a wrapped pigeon parcel in the middle.

Cut away the corners of the pastry, so it looks like a big cross (this will allow you to fold the ends of the pastry together without enclosing too much excess).

Brush the furthest edge of the pastry all over with egg glaze. Fold the closest pastry edge over the pigeon, then fold the glazed pastry edge on top and press together to seal. Thin out the excess pastry with a rolling pin at the sides and trim away the excess. Brush with egg glaze and fold up the sides, then lay on a tray.

Repeat to wrap the other 3 parcels in pastry and rest in the fridge for 1 hour so that the pastry can set.

Preheat the oven to 205°C/Fan 185°C/Gas 6–7. Brush the pastry evenly with the glaze and bake for 12 minutes, turning at the halfway stage to promote an even bake.

Remove from the oven and leave to rest for 4 minutes.

To serve

Sea salt and freshly ground pepper
Sautéed girolles, to garnish
Boulangère potatoes, to accompany

To assemble the lettuce parcels, heat the Lyonnaise onions, stir through the pickled girolles and season with salt and pepper to taste. Unwrap the Gem lettuce leaves and flash them under a hot grill to warm through. To build the 4 lettuce parcels, wrap the onion and girolle mix in the lettuce leaves, making sure the filling is fully enclosed.

Once the pigeons en croûte are cooked, trim off the ends and cut the en croûtes in half, through the middle of the pigeon and foie gras.

Arrange pigeons en croûte on warmed plates, with the Gem lettuce parcels to the side. Spoon the pigeon sauce over the lettuce parcels and garnish with the sautéed girolles. Serve with Boulangère potatoes.

Gunnerside grouse

with boudin noir purée, roots ragout pie & cow puff

Grouse has a big, strong flavour and people who eat it for the first time can be surprised – and sometimes put off – by that. But it's nice to have it on the menu for those people who do like it: because they love it. We only serve grouse for a brief time in the year, during the shooting season. We cook it in the traditional way, roasted in the oven; not in a bain-marie.

There's something very special about grouse: it's a true wild animal, the ultimate in game bird meat. You can't breed or rear it, like pheasant or partridge. If the heather moors are looked after, the grouse come, so for me, that means it deserves to be cooked in an organic, hands-on, non-science-based way.

Because grouse has such a distinct, gamey flavour, it matches brilliantly with robust ingredients, like beautiful earthy beetroots. When we first created this dish we got wonderful beetroots from Chris Webb, our friend turned supplier, who grew them on his allotment nearby. Vegetables cooked pretty much straight out of the ground are amazing; roast them and the flavour is unique.

Although our grouse is cooked traditionally, that doesn't mean we haven't got a few surprises in the dish. For instance, a cow puff! That's a veal tendon that has been dried, cooked, dehydrated and then deep-fried so it ends up like a beefy Quaver.

And we've got a delicious boudin noir (black pudding) purée inspired by my friend Daniel Clifford, of Midsummer House in Cambridge, who makes his black pudding with apple juice. For our purée, we blend Bramley apples and boudin noir in a Thermomix to produce a smooth, rich purée. It sits fantastically well with the grouse. It also happens to be the first solid my little man, Acey, tasted when he came into The Hand & Flowers kitchen with Beth to say hello one day. He absolutely hated it!

To prepare the grouse

4 grouse

Remove the legs and wings from the grouse and take out the wishbone. Reserve these for the sauce (see below). Carefully cut away the backbone; you should be left with the crown. Place in a vacuum-pack bag, seal and keep in the fridge. Bring back to room temperature before cooking and remove from the bag.

Grouse sauce

*250g grouse bones, chopped
(see above)
1 litre chicken stock (see page 400)*

Preheat the oven to 205°C/Fan 185°C/Gas 6–7. Put the chopped grouse bones and wings into a roasting tray and roast in the oven for about 20 minutes until they are richly caramelised.

Transfer the grouse bones to a saucepan and pour on the stock. Bring to the boil, lower the heat and simmer for 45 minutes to draw out the flavour from the bones.

Pass the stock through a fine chinois, then through 4 layers of muslin. Return the grouse stock to the pan, bring to a simmer and reduce to a glossy, rich sauce consistency.

Cow puff

*10 cleaned veal tendons
Vegetable oil for deep-frying
Sea salt*

Using a sharp knife, remove any excess meat from the end of the tendons. Place the tendons in a pressure cooker and cover with water. Secure the lid and bring up to temperature. Cook for 1½ hours. Take the pan off the heat and leave to cool, then release the pressure and lid. Drain the tendons in a colander, then pick away and discard any meat.

Line a small square mould (that will hold the tendons) with cling film, leaving plenty overhanging the sides. Put the veal tendons into the mould and fold the cling film over to cover them. Place a flat tray that will just fit inside the mould on top and weight it down to press the tendon terrine. Place in the fridge overnight to set.

The next day, remove the weight and place the tendon terrine in the freezer. Once frozen, remove the cling film and slice finely, ideally with a gravity meat slicer. Lay the tendon sheets on a dehydrator tray. Place in the dehydrator at 70°C for 20 minutes, then turn the sheets over and dry for a further 20 minutes. Store the crackers in a container with silica gel, to keep them dry.

When ready to serve, heat the oil in a deep-fryer to 180°C. Add the tendon crackers and deep-fry for 20 seconds or until they puff up. Remove the 'cow puffs' with a slotted spoon, drain on a draining tray lined with kitchen paper and season with salt.

Mushroom ketchup

*750g Paris brown mushrooms
5g sea salt
100g white wine vinegar
40g caster sugar
25ml dark soy sauce
3g gellan gum powder type F
Sea salt and freshly ground pepper*

Blitz the mushrooms with the salt in a blender to a finely chopped texture. Place in a muslin cloth, tie and hang over a bowl to catch the mushroom juice overnight. You will need 300ml.

Put the wine vinegar, sugar and soy sauce into a saucepan, heat to dissolve the sugar and bring to the boil. Take the pan off the heat and allow this gastrique to cool.

Pour the 300ml mushroom juice into a Thermomix and add the gellan powder. Heat to 95°C and blend on level 4. Once it reaches 95°C, hold at this temperature for 2 minutes then transfer the jug to the fridge and leave to set.

Once, set place the jug back on the base, add the gastrique and blend to combine. Season with salt and pepper to taste and spoon into a small bowl.

Place the bowl in the vacuum-pack machine and close the lid. The vacuum will draw the air bubbles out of the ketchup. Store in a small container until needed.

Boudin noir & apple purée

150g Bramley apple, peeled, cored and sliced
150g boudin noir, skin removed and diced
Sea salt and freshly ground pepper to taste

Put the apple and boudin noir into a Thermomix and blend on level 3 at 100°C for 15 minutes.

Once cooked, transfer the purée base to a high-powered blender (Vitamix) and blitz until smooth. Season with salt and pepper to taste.

Pass the purée through a fine chinois into a bowl and cover the surface closely with cling film to prevent a skin forming. Chill in the blast chiller or fridge. Store in the fridge, ready to reheat for serving.

Salt-baked roots

300g salt crust dough (see page 405)
2 or 4 medium beetroot, carrots or turnips, washed
4 baby beetroot (ideally golden baby beets)
200ml butter emulsion (see page 403), to serve

Preheat the oven to 190°C/Fan 170°C/Gas 5. Divide the salt crust dough into 6 or 8 pieces (depending on the number of roots you're using). Roll each piece of dough out to about a 5mm thickness.

Wrap each root veg individually in the salt crust dough and press the edges together to seal. Bake in the oven for about 30 minutes.

Remove from the oven and leave the roots to cool in the crust. Once cooled, carefully break open the crust and take out the roots. Top, tail and peel them. Leave the baby beets whole; halve the larger roots. Keep to one side until ready to serve.

To serve, heat the butter emulsion in a pan, add the salt-baked roots and warm through. Drain to serve.

Lyonnaise onion purée

60g unsalted butter
500g Spanish onions, peeled and sliced
5g table salt

Melt the butter in a heavy-based saucepan over a medium heat. Add the onions, sprinkle with the salt and cook for about 10–15 minutes until softened and darkly caramelised.

Spoon all of the ingredients into a blender and purée until smooth. Transfer to a bowl and allow to cool. Store the onion purée in a vacuum-pack bag until needed.

Celery étuve

2 celery sticks
100ml butter emulsion (see page 403)

Cut the celery sticks in half on the diagonal. Heat the butter emulsion in a pan, add the celery and poach for 2–3 minutes, just to take off the raw edge. Serve warm.

Demi pie game filling

50g vegetable oil
500g venison mince
90g smoked streaky bacon,
   cut into 7mm cubes
75ml red wine
7g salt
2g ground cloves
2g freshly grated nutmeg
150g Lyonnaise onion purée
   (see page 229)
130ml venison sauce (see page 401)
2g ground cinnamon

Heat a large frying pan over a
medium heat and add the oil.
When hot, add the venison mince
and fry until thoroughly and evenly
browned, and crispy.

Add the bacon and cook for a further
5 minutes to render the fat and cook
the bacon cubes until crispy. Drain
off the fat from the pan and return
to the heat.

Add the wine and bring to the boil.
Add the remaining ingredients
and mix well. Taste the filling for
seasoning and adjust as necessary.
Cover and chill until needed.

Pastry

250g 'T45' plain flour
50g polenta
½ tsp bicarbonate of soda
½ tsp sea salt
75g lard
90ml water

Put the flour, polenta, bicarbonate
of soda and salt into a mixer fitted
with the paddle attachment.

Melt the lard with the water in a
saucepan over a medium heat and
bring to the boil. Immediately pour
onto the dry ingredients and mix on
a low speed to form a smooth dough.

Remove from the bowl and knead
lightly with your hands, just to bring
the dough together to form a ball.

Divide the pastry into 4 equal
portions, shape each into a ball and
flatten slightly. Wrap in cling film
and use while still warm.

To build & bake the pies

Demi game pie filling (see left)
100g caul fat, soaked in cold water
   for 30 minutes
Pastry (see left)
Egg glaze (see left)

Divide and shape the pie filling into
30g balls and then wrap each in a
single thin layer of caul fat.

Roll out one portion of warm pastry
to a thin disc. Place a caul-wrapped
ball of filling in the centre and quickly
wrap in the pastry to make a perfectly
round ball, pressing out any creases.
Repeat to shape the rest of the pies.

Allow the pastry to cool and set.
Keep the pies in the fridge until
ready to bake and serve.

When ready to serve, preheat the
oven to 205°C/Fan 185°C/Gas 6–7.
Bake the pies in the oven for
12 minutes, turning at the halfway
stage to ensure even cooking.

Egg glaze

3 medium free-range egg yolks
5g dextrose
2 tsp whole milk

Whisk the egg yolks and dextrose
together to combine, then stir in
the milk. Leave the glaze to rest
for an hour before use.

To cook the grouse & serve

40g sourdough crumbs
Vegetable oil for cooking
4 slices of boudin noir, 1cm thick,
sliced on an angle
100g unsalted butter
4 garlic cloves, peeled and crushed
4 sprigs of thyme
1 tsp thyme leaves
Sea salt and freshly ground pepper

Preheat the oven to 205°C/Fan 185°C/Gas 6–7.

Dress the sourdough crumbs with a little oil and season with salt and pepper. Scatter on a baking tray and bake for 15 minutes, stirring every 5 minutes.

Heat a little oil in a frying pan and add the boudin noir slices. Fry for about 1½–2 minutes until crispy on both sides.

Set a large ovenproof frying pan over a medium heat and add a splash of oil. Place the grouse crowns in the pan straight away, to start gently warming the meat. Add the butter, garlic and thyme sprigs to the pan and heat until the butter is melted and foaming, and the grouse breast skin is lightly coloured, turning as necessary.

Sit the grouse crowns breast side down with the cavity pointing up and fill the cavity with the foaming butter and garlic. Transfer to the oven to finish cooking for 5 minutes, basting at the halfway stage. Remove from the oven and set aside to rest in a warm place for 8 minutes. (At this stage warm through the salt-baked veg etc.)

Carefully cut the grouse breasts from the bone and remove the skin. Brush the grouse breasts with a little grouse sauce and sprinkle over the baked sourdough crumbs, thyme leaves and some salt and pepper.

Place the celery étuve and salt-baked roots on warmed plates and arrange the grouse breasts on top. Add a demi game pie and a quenelle of boudin noir and apple purée to each plate. Drizzle with the grouse sauce and finish with the cow puff. Serve the mushroom ketchup on the side.

Braised leg of rabbit

with dandelion, bacon & summer savory

SERVES 4

This recipe is inspired by an amazing rabbit and squid dish I once ate at Eric Chavot's restaurant in London. It's also a nod to French Lyonnaise salad, which uses *pissenlit* (dandelion) and bacon.

We serve the squid as part of a beautiful salad with dandelion and bacon; and the braised rabbit has a rich, buttery, herby glaze. There are also a couple of less likely ingredients in the form of coffee dust and lime zest, which are sprinkled on a little filo crisp that sits on the side.

The coffee and lime zest give the dish a great lift: a citrus zing and a hint of bitterness from the coffee that you can just taste as an undertone. The combination works unbelievably well with the dandelion, which also has a bitterness (and harks back to a time when rabbit would have been hung out in a field before cooking). It's no secret that I'm a big fan of bitter tones, particularly in main courses. I like the protein element of a dish to be rich and hearty, but then that always needs something to cut through it.

This isn't a dish that came from my formative years at Monsieur Max on Hampton Hill, on the outskirts of southwest London – famous for its bourgeois cuisine – but it could quite easily have sat on the menu there under head chef Alex Bentley. I learnt so much from Alex; about finishing things, how to make beautiful sauces, classic French flavours. And how, with an added little twist, you can enhance things.

At the end of the day, anyone can make a Lyonnaise salad or braise a rabbit. What you have to ask yourself is this: what are you going to do to make the recipe stand out?

Chicken mousse

1 skinless boneless chicken breast,
*   diced*
½ tsp flaky sea salt
¼ tsp cayenne pepper
½ tsp dried herbes de Provence
1 medium free-range egg, beaten
1 tbsp truffle oil
125ml double cream

Put the chicken into a blender with
the salt, cayenne and dried herbs and
blitz thoroughly. Add the egg and
pulse to incorporate, then add the
truffle oil and pulse again.

Finally, with the motor running,
pour in the cream to emulsify and
bring the mixture together.

Pass the chicken mousse through
a drum sieve into a bowl. Cover and
chill until needed.

Cured rabbit legs

4 farmed rabbit legs
200ml white wine
5g salt
1 sprig of rosemary, bruised
100g chicken mousse (see left)
2 garlic cloves, peeled and grated
2 tbsp chopped parsley
Vegetable oil for brushing

Remove the thigh bone from each
leg, by cutting around the bone down
to the knee joint and removing it
to create a cavity for the stuffing.
French-trim the lower leg bone.

Whisk the wine and salt together,
add the rosemary and pour over the
rabbit legs. Leave to cure for 8 hours.

Remove the rabbit legs from the
brine, drain and pat dry then lay
each one on a sheet of cling film.

In a bowl, mix the chicken mousse,
garlic and parsley together until
evenly combined.

Spoon the mixture into a piping bag
fitted with a 1cm plain nozzle. Pipe
into each rabbit bone cavity to fill it,
then lightly roll each leg in the cling
film and tie the ends to seal.

Place the stuffed rabbit legs in
individual vacuum-pack bags and
vacuum-seal. Immerse in a water-
bath at 72°C and cook for 2 hours.
(Meanwhile, prepare the filo crisps
and salad, see opposite.)

Lift the bags out of the water-bath
and take out the rabbit legs. Remove
the cling film, pat the rabbit legs
dry and wipe away any fat proteins.
Brush the rabbit legs with oil and
caramelise with a cook's blowtorch.
Rest in the oven warming drawer
until ready to serve.

Coffee & lime filo crisps

3 sheets of filo pastry
Plain flour, for dusting
100g clarified butter
1 tsp thyme leaves
2 tbsp coarse-ground coffee beans,
  crushed
Grated zest of 3 limes
Sea salt

Lay the filo sheets on a lightly floured surface. Brush with clarified butter and then sprinkle over the thyme leaves, most of the crushed coffee and lime zest, and a little salt.

Layer the filo sheets one on top of another to sandwich the coffee and lime and cut into 4 equal squares. Place in the fridge to set for about 20 minutes.

Preheat the oven to 190°C/Fan 170°C/Gas 5. Line a baking sheet with a silicone mat. Transfer the filo squares to the silicone mat and bake for 10 minutes until golden and crisp. Remove from the oven and leave to cool.

Sprinkle the filo crisps with the remaining crushed coffee and lime zest before serving.

Dandelion & bacon salad

A little vegetable oil for cooking
100g dry-cured bacon lardons
2 medium squid pouches, cleaned
  and sliced into thin rings
3 tbsp Lyonnaise onions
  (see page 404)
2 bunches of dandelion leaves,
  picked and washed in iced water
1 tsp summer savory leaves
Sea salt and freshly ground pepper

Heat a sauté pan over a medium heat and add a splash of oil. Toss in the lardons and fry until evenly coloured and just crisp. Remove with a slotted spoon and place the lardons on a tray lined with kitchen paper to drain.

Add the squid rings to the fat remaining in the pan and sauté very quickly for about 1 minute until tender; do not overcook. Remove to the lined tray, using a slotted spoon.

Return the bacon to the pan and add the onions. Heat through then stir through the dandelion leaves and squid. Once the leaves have wilted, stir in the summer savory and season with salt and pepper to taste. Remove from the heat.

To assemble & serve

Herb sauce (see page 402)

Divide the dandelion and bacon salad between warmed plates, lay the rabbit legs on top and spoon over the herb sauce. Finish with the filo crisps and serve.

Venison & maple-roast squash

with game sausage & spiced crispy chickpeas

—— SERVES 4 ——

This is really two dishes for the price of one! Done fully, it's a proper plate of textures and flavours, but you can also create an amazing starter if you serve the game sausage on its own.

The recipe evolved about three or four years ago as we came out of the summer game season and hit autumn. We typically work with grouse in August and September, before moving on to other game meats like venison throughout autumn and winter.

An incredibly warm and satisfying dish, it combines modern and traditional cooking techniques. We start the venison loin off in a water-bath, but then finish it the classic way – in a pan with foaming butter. It's the best of both worlds: fantastically soft meat with a really lovely caramelised outside.

The garnishes, game sausage included, are deeply flavoured. For the roasted squash, we choose Crown Prince, as it gives off an incredible natural sweetness, and we enhance that with a maple syrup glaze to draw out the flavour even more. Roasted, spiced chickpeas add a crunchy texture, which works beautifully with the softness of the venison and the squash. And the game sausage, made from minced venison and pork belly, makes a spectacular accompaniment to the dish.

I just love the final version. It's the perfect blend of seasonality; the perfect balance of sweetness, spice, texture and crunch.

Lime pickle

5 limes
7g Maldon sea salt
A little vegetable oil for cooking
20g yellow mustard seeds
2 garlic cloves, peeled and grated
25g root ginger, peeled and grated
20g ground cumin
20g ground coriander
80ml water
80g soft dark brown sugar
25ml white wine vinegar

Slice the rind from the limes and cut it into 3mm dice. Roughly dice the lime flesh, discarding the pips, and combine with the diced rind in a bowl. Add the salt and toss to mix. Cover with cling film and leave to stand for 24 hours.

The next day, heat a tiny splash of oil in a frying pan. Add the mustard seeds and toast until they pop. Add the garlic and ginger and sweat for a few minutes, then add the ground spices and cook for 5 minutes.

Add the diced limes, water, brown sugar and wine vinegar. Bring to the boil, then lower the heat and simmer gently for 15–20 minutes until reduced to a chutney consistency.

Allow to cool, then pack into a couple of small sterilised jars or vacuum-pack bags (you will have more than you need for this recipe). Seal and leave in the fridge to mature for at least a week before eating.

Game sausage

300g venison mince
100g pork belly, minced
50g pork fat, minced
4g cracked black pepper
1g ground black pepper
9g table salt
2g curing salt
16g yellow mustard seeds
16g toasted cumin seeds

In a large bowl, mix all of the ingredients together thoroughly until evenly combined. To test the seasoning, take 1 tbsp of the mixture, shape into a small patty and fry in a lightly oiled pan until cooked, then taste for seasoning. Adjust the seasoning of the sausage mixture accordingly, adding more salt and/ or pepper if needed.

On a sheet of cling film, roll the game sausage mixture into a thick ballotine, wrapping it in the cling film. Tie the ends to seal, then place in a large vacuum-pack bag and vacuum-seal. Immerse the bag in a water-bath at 70°C and poach for 30 minutes.

Remove the bag from the water-bath and plunge into iced water or place in the blast chiller to cool the sausage quickly, then refrigerate until ready to serve.

Shortly before serving, remove the game sausage from the bag and cut into 1cm thick slices, ready to fry.

Butternut squash purée

50g unsalted butter, diced
1kg butternut squash, peeled, deseeded and diced
3g ground mixed spice
Sea salt and freshly ground pepper

Melt the butter in a heavy-based saucepan and heat until foaming. Add the diced squash and mixed spice, stir, then cover and cook over a low heat for 1 hour until the squash is soft.

Transfer the squash to a jug blender and purée until smooth. Season with salt and pepper to taste.

Pass the purée through a fine chinois into a bowl and leave to cool. Cover and refrigerate until needed.

Prickly ash

20g Szechuan peppercorns
20g flaky sea salt

Toast the peppercorns and salt together in a dry frying pan until the pepper releases its aroma. Tip onto a plate and leave to cool.

Once cooled, lightly crush the mix to create a coarse, aromatic seasoning. Store in a small airtight container.

Baked chickpeas

400g tin chickpeas, drained
60ml olive oil
Sea salt

Preheat the oven to 190°C/Fan 170°C/Gas 5. Toss the chickpeas with the olive oil and a good pinch of salt, then tip onto a baking sheet. Bake in the oven for 25 minutes until crisp. Remove from the oven and leave to cool. Reheat to serve.

To prepare the venison

400g loin of venison

Trim the venison of all sinew and any fat, then roll in cling film and cut into 4 portions. Place individually in vacuum-pack bags and vacuum-seal. Immerse in a water-bath at 65°C and cook for 8 minutes. Lift out and set aside until ready to serve.

Maple-roast squash

60ml vegetable oil
1 small Crown Prince squash, cut
  into wedges, seeds removed
100g unsalted butter, diced
100ml maple syrup
10ml malt vinegar
Sea salt

Heat a large heavy-based frying pan over a medium-high heat and add the oil. When hot, add the squash wedges and colour on both sides until evenly golden brown.

Add the butter and, as it melts, use it to baste the squash. Season with a little salt. Cover and steam-cook the squash until almost cooked.

Mix the maple syrup with the vinegar, add to the pan and allow to bubble and caramelise, basting the squash wedges with the liquor as it reduces, to glaze them. Serve hot.

To assemble & serve

25g unsalted butter, plus a knob
  for the squash purée if required
2 tbsp vegetable oil
50g Sosa Airbag Granet dehydrated
  pork skin, deep-fried
2 tsp chopped chives
4 curry leaves, deep-fried
60ml venison sauce (see page 401)
Sea salt and freshly ground pepper

Warm the butternut squash purée through, adding a small knob of butter for a glossy finish if required. When ready to serve, heat 1 tbsp oil in a heavy-based frying pan and fry the sausage slices for 1½–2 minutes until crisp and golden on both sides.

Remove the venison loins from the vacuum-pack bags and season them with salt and pepper. Heat a heavy-based frying pan over a medium-high heat. Add the butter and 1 tbsp oil and heat until foaming. Add the venison portions and sear for about 2 minutes, turning as necessary, until browned all over. Remove from the pan, cut each portion into 3 slices and season with prickly ash.

Spoon the butternut squash purée onto warmed plates and swipe across. Arrange the seared venison slices on the plates with a wedge of glazed squash and a slice of fried game sausage alongside. Spoon the crispy chickpeas onto the sausage slices then top with the deep-fried pork skin and chopped chives.

Add a teaspoon quenelle of lime pickle to each plate and top with a deep-fried curry leaf. Finish with the venison sauce and serve.

Fillet of beef

with Hand & Flowers chips & béarnaise sauce

SERVES 4

Don't get me wrong. I love steak and chips. It's an amazing dish; one of the best things ever. But if I'm going to serve steak and chips, I want to make sure it's 100% right. Perfect chips, perfect steak, perfect onion rings with a proper batter. Plus, a little bit of café de Paris butter, red wine sauce, béarnaise sauce. Lovely. So, although this is, essentially, a simple steak and chips, it's got three wonderful sauces that lift it above the ordinary.

And so, to the perfect steak. For me, this has to be cooked in a pan with butter, to order. Just like any Beefeater restaurant, we'll cook your steak whichever way you want it; medium, medium-rare, blue, well done. We're not going to impose our own preference on you at The Hand & Flowers. We just want you to have the Rolls-Royce of steak and chips. We want it to be perfect. To be memorable.

In the early days we used rump steak but eventually we ended up moving to fillet because it's a premium product, and it's a premium product for a reason. Texturally, it's amazing. Enjoy!

To prepare the beef

1kg centre-cut fillet of beef
(we use Stokes Marsh Farm)

Place the fillet of beef on a sheet of cling film and roll tightly in the film to hold the shape. Refrigerate until ready to cook.

Café de Paris butter

110g unsalted butter, softened
½ bay leaf, ground to a powder
¼ tsp chopped thyme leaves
1 tsp chopped chives
1 tsp chopped tarragon leaves
1 tsp chopped chervil leaves
1 tbsp chopped flat-leaf parsley
½ tsp mild curry powder
1 tbsp finely diced gherkin
  (or cornichon)
½ tbsp baby capers, finely chopped
1 small garlic clove, peeled and
  finely grated
1 tbsp finely diced banana shallot
1 medium free-range egg yolk
Sea salt and cayenne pepper

Put the softened butter into a bowl and add all the herbs, curry powder, gherkin, capers, garlic, shallot and egg yolk. Beat with a spatula until evenly combined, then season lightly with salt and cayenne to taste.

Spoon the flavoured butter into a piping bag fitted with a 1cm plain nozzle and pipe onto a sheet of cling film, to form a small log. Wrap in the cling film and roll into a small, smooth cylinder. Tie the ends of the cling film to seal and submerge the parcel in iced water to firm up.

When set, slice the butter into 5mm thick discs and remove the cling film. Cover and store in the fridge until needed. (Any leftover butter can be frozen for future use.)

Fried onion rings

1 medium-large brown onion, peeled
50ml milk
100ml self-raising flour
35g Trisol (wheat starch)
65ml sparkling water
Vegetable oil for deep-frying
30g plain flour, for dusting
Sea salt and freshly ground pepper

Slice off the sides of the onion then cut 8 slices from the middle, each 4mm thick. Press out the middles, to leave 8 perfect onion rings.

Place the onion rings in a container and pour on the milk to cover. Leave to soak in the fridge overnight to draw out the raw onion flavour.

To make the batter, in a bowl, mix the flour and Trisol together then whisk in the sparkling water to make a smooth batter. Cover and leave to stand in the fridge for about an hour before using.

When ready to serve, remove the onions from the milk. You will need to fry the onion rings in batches. Heat the oil in a deep-fryer to 180°C. Season the flour with salt and pepper.

Dip the onion rings in the seasoned flour and turn to coat all over; shake off any excess. Now dip them into the batter, carefully add to the hot oil and deep-fry for 2–3 minutes until crisp and golden.

Remove the onion rings from the pan and drain on kitchen paper. Season with salt and serve.

Triple-cooked chips

10 large chipping potatoes, peeled
Vegetable oil for deep-frying
Sea salt
A little very finely chopped parsley

Cut a slice from the top and bottom of each potato, then press an apple corer through from top to bottom to make round cylinder chips. Put the cut chips into a colander under cold running water to wash of some of the starches.

Now lay the chips on a steamer tray and season them with salt. Steam for 30 minutes until cooked, then place in the blast chiller to cool quickly and draw out excess moisture, or place in a cool, dry place.

Once the chips are cool, heat the oil in a deep-fryer to 140°C. Lower the chips into the hot oil in a wire basket and deep-fry for 10 minutes. Remove the chips from the fryer, drain and leave to cool until needed.

When ready to serve, heat the oil to 180°C and deep-fry the chips for about 6–7 minutes until golden and very crispy. Remove the chips from the fryer and drain on kitchen paper. Season with salt and sprinkle with chopped parsley.

To cook the steaks

100g unsalted butter
50ml vegetable oil
Juice of ½ lemon
Salt

Heat up a large heavy-based frying pan over a medium heat. Cut the fillet of beef through the cling film into 4 steaks (each 250g). Season the top and bottom of each steak heavily with table salt.

Add the butter to the hot pan. Once it is melted and foaming, add the fillet steaks, with the outside still wrapped in cling film. Brown the steaks on both sides to a dark fully roasted colour. This will take about 6–8 minutes.

Lift the steaks out of the pan, remove the cling film and season the sides with salt. Return the steaks to the pan and colour them evenly all around their sides until they have a dark crust.

Once the fillet steaks are cooked medium-rare (or to your taste), lift them out of the pan and set aside on a warm plate in an oven warming drawer to rest for 10 minutes.

Return the pan to the hob and add the lemon juice, stirring and scraping to deglaze, then pour the liquor over the resting steaks.

Béarnaise sauce

15g tarragon leaves, very finely
*   chopped*
100g warm hollandaise sauce
*   (see page 403)*

Just before you serve the dish, stir the chopped tarragon through the warm hollandaise. Spoon into individual serving dishes.

To serve

350ml red wine sauce (see page 402)

Once the fillet steaks are well rested, flash them under a hot salamander or grill briefly to warm.

Place a steak in the middle of each warmed plate and spoon over a little red wine sauce. Top each steak with a disc of the café de Paris butter and a couple of crispy onion rings.

Serve the chips and béarnaise sauce on the side.

Tenderloin of pork

with pommes dauphine, pickled cabbage
& mustard mayonnaise

The inspiration for this dish is, incredibly, a hot dog! It's uncomplicated at its root, and has those recognisable flavours we all love from a street food favourite. I treasure simplicity at the heart of our food.

When I think of something like a hot dog, I automatically break down the various elements in my head. What constitutes a hot dog? Well, a hot dog is a piece of pork that's got mustard on it – lovely; and some people like to have them with roasted onions – delicious. I love the smell that radiates from the hot dog vendors' vans at football matches. A smell of almost burnt, caramelised onions. And often there's some pickled cabbage if you want it (almost like sauerkraut pickles); and a bun.

So how do the deconstructed flavours of a hot dog translate to this dish? The soft richness of a hot dog bun, well that's the pomme dauphine; the tenderloin is the porky component; and the sweet mustard mayonnaise is similar to an American-style mustard. It's a complex dish with several great elements, but those core 'hot dog' flavours absolutely shine through!

Pickled Chinese cabbage

1 Chinese cabbage, trimmed and
  separated into leaves
500ml cider vinegar
230g demerara sugar
25g table salt
2 garlic cloves, peeled and crushed
1.5g ground turmeric
4 sprigs of dill

Rinse the Chinese cabbage leaves and spin-dry in a salad spinner; set aside.

Put the cider vinegar, sugar, salt, garlic and turmeric into a saucepan and bring to the boil, then remove from the heat add the dill sprigs. Set aside to infuse and cool.

Pass the cooled pickling liquor through a fine chinois into a jug.

Place the cabbage in a large vacuum-pack bag, pour in the cold pickling liquor and vacuum-seal to remove all the air. Leave to pickle in the fridge for 3 weeks before serving.

Bring back to room temperature and drain the cabbage to serve.

Mustard mayonnaise

25g liquid free-range egg yolk
35g English mustard
10g caster sugar
2 tsp white wine vinegar
50ml lemon juice
325ml vegetable oil
Sea salt and freshly ground pepper

Put the egg yolk, mustard, sugar, wine vinegar and lemon juice into a blender and blend briefly to combine.

With the motor running, slowly pour in the oil and blend until emulsified to a thick, glossy mayonnaise. Season with salt and pepper to taste.

Transfer the mustard mayonnaise to a bowl, cover and refrigerate until ready to serve.

Dauphine dough

120ml water
50g unsalted butter
2.5g caster sugar
5g table salt
110g 'T45' plain flour, sifted
1 medium free-range egg, beaten
About 200g dry mashed cooked
  potato, put through a potato ricer

Put the water, butter, sugar and salt into a saucepan. Heat to melt the butter and bring to the boil. Add the flour, beat thoroughly and cook out to make a smooth, glossy dough.

Remove from the heat and transfer the choux paste to a mixer fitted with the paddle attachment. Beat on a low speed until the mixture is just warm. Now, with the motor running, add the egg a little at a time, mixing until it is fully incorporated.

Once the choux is cooled, weigh it and mix with the same quantity of dry mashed potato. Place in the fridge to set and rest.

Malted pig's cheek

*1 whole pig's cheek (or jowl),
about 1kg, any hair removed
with a cook's blowtorch, then
soaked in cold water overnight
to remove any blood*
100g runny honey
35ml soy sauce
30g malt extract
100ml chicken stock (see page 400)
Sea salt

Put the pig's cheek into a vacuum-pack bag and vacuum-seal. Immerse in a water-bath at 88.2°C and poach for 8 hours until tender.

Once the pig's cheek is cooked, transfer it to a colander to drain off any excess fat.

To make the glaze, bring the honey to the boil in a heavy-based pan and cook to a dark caramel. Carefully add the soy sauce and malt extract, simmer for a few minutes to dissolve, then stir in the chicken stock.

Flake the pig's cheek (you will end up with about 500g pulled cheek) and put the meat into a heavy-based saucepan. Pour on the glaze and allow this to reduce gently until thickened enough to bind the pork. Keep a close eye, as it is liable to catch as the sugars intensify and the liquid evaporates.

Once the pork mixture is reduced, there will be a heavy layer of fat on the surface. Pour off the excess fat, leaving just a thin layer. Leave to cool slightly.

Beat the cooled mixture with a spatula to emulsify the residual fat then season with a good pinch of salt, to taste. Cover and chill fully. (You won't need all of the mixture for this recipe; freeze the excess for another occasion.)

To make the pork fritters

*80g malted pig's cheek mixture
    (see page 247)*
*1 quantity dauphine dough
    (see 246)*
Vegetable oil for deep-frying
Smoked paprika, to taste
Sea salt

Divide and shape the pig's cheek mixture into 20g pork balls, making them as perfectly round as possible. Press any strands of meat that are sticking out back into the ball, or remove them.

Divide and shape the dauphine dough into 23g balls. One portion at a time, flatten the dough in the palm of your hand and work it with your thumb until it is large enough to wrap three-quarters of the pork ball.

Next, place a pork ball in the middle of the dough and work the dough with your fingers around the meat to enclose it completely and seal. Give one final roll in the palm of your hand to ensure an even finish. Place on a tray lined with baking paper and set aside. Repeat to shape the rest of the pork dough balls. Chill for an hour or so until needed.

When ready to serve, heat the oil in a deep-fryer to 180°C. Add the pork dough balls and deep-fry for 4 minutes until golden brown.

Lift out the pork fritters with a draining spoon, drain on kitchen paper and season with salt and smoked paprika. Serve at once.

Garlic sausage

*200g shoulder of pork,
    coarsely minced*
25g back fat, coarsely minced
*60g unsmoked gammon,
    coarsely minced*
1g curing salt
1g cracked black pepper
2.5g freshly grated garlic
¼ tsp freshly grated nutmeg
1.5g table salt

Put all of the ingredients into a large bowl and mix together thoroughly until evenly combined. To test the seasoning, take 1 tbsp of the mixture, shape into a small patty and fry in a lightly oiled pan until cooked, then taste it for seasoning. Adjust the seasoning of the sausage mix accordingly, adding more salt and/ or pepper if needed.

On a sheet of cling film roll the game sausage mixture into a thick ballotine, wrapping it in the cling film; tie the end to seal. Place in a large vacuum-pack bag and vacuum-seal. Immerse in a water-bath at 70°C and poach for 1 hour.

Remove the bag from the water-bath and place in the blast chiller to cool quickly (or plunge into iced water).

When ready to serve, remove the sausage from the bag and cut into 1cm thick slices. Heat a little oil in a heavy-based frying pan and fry the garlic sausage slices on both sides until crisp and golden. Serve hot.

To prepare the tenderloins

*2 pork tenderloins, trimmed
    of fat and sinew*

Place the pork tenderloins in individual vacuum-pack bags and vacuum-seal. Immerse the bags in a water-bath at 65°C and poach the tenderloins for 15 minutes. Remove and set aside until ready to serve.

Roasted onions

2 medium brown onions (unpeeled)
25ml vegetable oil
4 sprigs of thyme
100g unsalted butter, diced
Sea salt

Preheat the oven to 180°C/Fan 160°C/Gas 4. Cut the onions across in half through the equator. Heat a plancha or non-stick heavy-based frying pan over a high heat and add the oil. Place the onions, cut side down, on the hot plancha or pan and caramelise heavily.

Once they have taken on the desired colour, transfer the onions, cut side down, to a small baking tray. Scatter over the thyme sprigs.

In a separate pan, heat the butter until melted and browned to a beurre noisette. Pour the nutty butter over the onions and season with salt.

Cover the tray with foil and bake for 25–30 minutes until the onions are soft. Remove the skins from the onions. Keep hot.

To finish the pork & serve

1 tbsp vegetable oil
25g unsalted butter
2 tbsp English mustard
4 tbsp yellow mustard seeds,
*   toasted and coarsely ground*
4 tbsp Sosa Airbag Granet
*   dehydrated pork skin, deep-fried*
2 tsp chopped chives
4 tbsp pork sauce (see page 401)
Sea salt and freshly ground pepper

Remove the pork tenderloins from the vacuum-pack bags and season them with salt and pepper.

Heat a heavy-based frying pan over a medium-high heat. Add the oil and butter and heat until foaming. Add the pork tenderloins and sear the outside, until evenly coloured. (Deep-fry the pork fritters and fry the garlic sausage slices at this point.)

Remove the seared tenderloins from the pan and rest for a minute or so. Brush them with English mustard and dust with the ground toasted mustard seeds.

Top the roasted onion halves with the deep-fried pork skin and chopped chives. Lay a wedge of pickled Chinese cabbage across the middle of each warmed plate and place a roasted onion half to one side. Lay a slice of crispy garlic sausage diagonally opposite the onion and top with a crisp pork fritter. Pipe a mound of mustard mayo alongside.

Slice each mustard-crusted pork tenderloin in half and position a portion on each plate. Finish with the pork sauce and serve at once.

Essex lamb bun

SERVES 4

Despite its name, this dish is not a bread bun and the lamb's not from Essex! It is, in fact, a series of layered ingredients wrapped in pastry with lamb at its heart. But when I created the dish originally, the lamb came from a supplier in Essex – hence that name – and the original concept used a brioche dough. No two batches of bread are ever the same, and that upset me because it meant consistency was difficult to achieve. So, the brioche bit the dust and we progressed to pastry instead.

The concept of the dish as a whole was to present, visually, just one thing on the plate. I love that idea: a single thing, layered; with each ingredient encompassing another. What you've got in your 'bun', then, is a big, fat lamb cutlet wrapped in a 'farce' made of lamb breast and sweetbreads; that's then wrapped in cabbage, then crépinette, and finally pastry. So, you've got everything – meat, veg, carb – in this one amazing bundle.

A super-smooth salsa verde (frozen and put through a Pacojet) is the finishing touch to the dish: it has an amazing depth of flavour and really cuts through the richness of everything else.

It's a dish I love. Visually, it's very special. Flavour-wise, it's exceptional. And it's become a Hand & Flowers icon. But it was quite a brave move to put out a dish with only one thing on a plate, particularly in a pub. We still get comments from people saying, 'Is that it?' Yep!

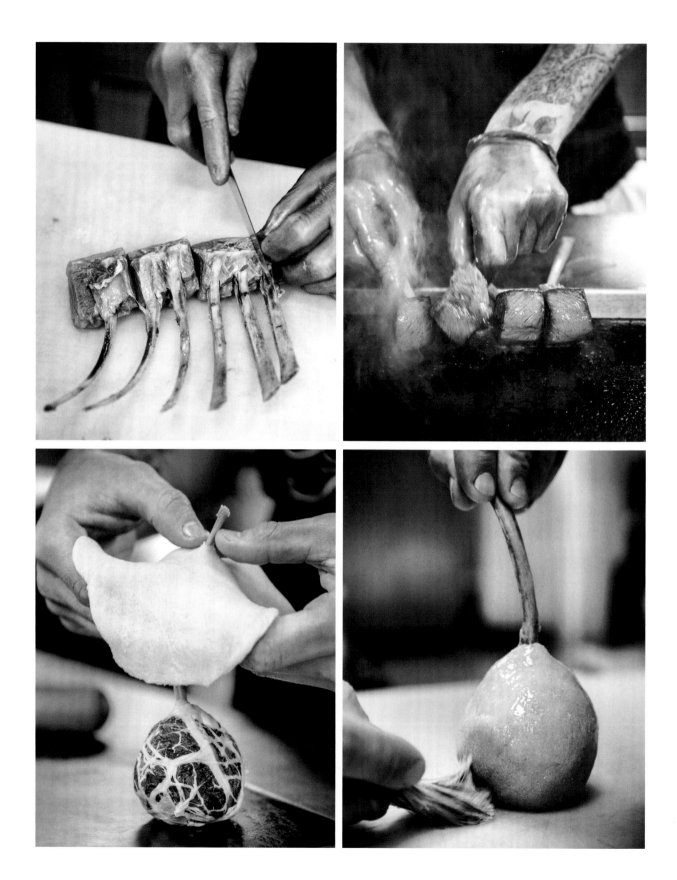

ESSEX LAMB BUN

To prepare the cutlets

1 large French-trimmed rack of lamb
Vegetable oil for frying
Sea salt

Remove all the fat and sinew from the rack of lamb and scrape each bone clean with the back of a knife. Place the rack in a vacuum-pack bag, vacuum-seal on full pressure and cook in a water-bath at 58°C for 30 minutes.

Lift the sous-vide bag out of the water-bath and immerse in a bowl of iced water to chill for 1 hour.

Remove the lamb from the sous-vide bag and portion into 4 cutlets.

Heat a frying pan over a high heat and add a splash of oil. Season the cutlets with salt, place in the hot pan and sear quickly on each side, then remove. Once all the cutlets are seared, chill them in the fridge.

Lamb farce

1 lamb breast (bone-in)
Vegetable oil for frying
200ml chicken stock (see page 400)
75g lamb sweetbreads
Plain flour, for dusting
100g veal bone marrow, soaked
  in cold water overnight
70ml lamb sauce (see page 401)
Sea salt and freshly ground
  black pepper

Cut the lamb breast into 3 pieces down through the rib bones. Heat a little oil in a large frying pan over a high heat. Carefully place the lamb pieces in the pan, skin side down, and sear until the skin is golden brown. Remove from the pan and allow to cool, then chill.

Place the lamb breast pieces in a vacuum-pack bag with the chicken stock. Vacuum-seal on full pressure, then cook in a water-bath at 90°C for 8 hours.

Remove the bag from the water-bath and take out the lamb breast; discard the stock. When cool enough to handle, flake the meat away from the bone, discarding all the fat and sinew. Keep warm.

To prepare the sweetbreads, remove the outer membrane then wash them. Pat the sweetbreads dry and place in a sous-vide bag. Vacuum at full pressure then cook in a water-bath at 65°C for 30 minutes. Lift the sous-vide bag out of the water-bath and immerse in a bowl of iced water to chill.

Once chilled, cut the sweetbreads into 2cm dice and dust with flour.

Heat a little oil in a frying pan over a medium heat. Add the sweetbreads and fry, turning, until crispy. Lift out of the pan onto a tray and refrigerate to cool quickly.

Once cooled, add the sweetbreads to the lamb breast meat.

Put the veal bone marrow into a blender. Heat the lamb sauce in a small pan until boiling, pour onto the marrow and blend to emulsify.

Pour the marrow sauce onto the lamb breast and sweetbreads and mix together well. Season with salt and pepper and refrigerate until needed.

To assemble the filling

10 outer (darker) Savoy cabbage
  leaves, blanched
150g pig's caul, soaked in
  water overnight

Take 75g of the lamb farce. Mould this evenly around one of the lamb cutlets, then wrap in a blanched Savoy cabbage leaf to enclose.

Finally, wrap the parcel in a single layer of pig's caul. Repeat with the other lamb cutlets and place in the fridge until needed.

Salsa verde

100g flat-leaf parsley, blanched
*   and chopped*
30 salted anchovy fillets
*   (we use Ortiz)*
12 garlic cloves, peeled and
*   roughly chopped*
30 capers
1 shallot, diced
Finely grated zest of 1 lemon
50ml olive oil
1 tsp sea salt
½ tsp cayenne pepper

Put all the ingredients into a food processor and blend until very finely chopped and combined. Transfer to a Pacojet beaker and freeze.

Once frozen, churn the salsa verde again and hold, ready for serving.

Glaze

3 medium free-range egg yolks
5g dextrose
2 tsp whole milk

Whisk the egg yolks and dextrose together to combine, then stir in the milk. Leave the glaze to rest for an hour before use.

Pastry

250g 'T45' plain flour
50g polenta
½ tsp bicarbonate of soda
½ tsp sea salt
90ml water
75g rendered lamb fat, diced

Mix the flour, polenta, salt and bicarbonate of soda together in a bowl and make a well in the centre.

Put the water and fat into a saucepan and bring to the boil over a medium heat. Pour this liquid into the flour well and mix with a spoon to a smooth dough.

Divide the pastry into 4 equal portions, shape each into a ball and flatten slightly. Wrap in cling film and use while still warm.

To bake the buns & serve

Plain flour, for dusting
400ml lamb sauce (see page 401)

Preheat the oven to 205°C/Fan 185°C/Gas 6–7.

To wrap the lamb in pastry, roll out a portion of the warm pastry to a round and pierce a hole in the centre. Position the pastry centrally over a lamb parcel and thread the cutlet bone through the hole. Carefully mould the pastry around the caul-wrapped parcel, discarding any excess pastry. Repeat to wrap the other lamb parcels.

Brush the pastry with the egg glaze and bake in the oven for 6 minutes, then rotate the tray of buns to ensure even cooking and bake for a further 6 minutes. Remove from the oven and leave to rest for 5 minutes. Meanwhile, heat up the lamb sauce.

Serve the lamb buns with the lamb sauce and salsa verde on the side.

Cured belly of pork

with cauliflower purée & pickled cockle dressing

SERVES 8

It's crucial, for this recipe, to get the skin nice and crispy on the pork belly. To ensure that, you have to start preparing the meat a day in advance, and the care you take in prep means you get a perfect result.

The flavour combinations in this dish evolved from a couple of ingredient pairings that were popular 10 or 12 years ago: scallops and cauliflower. We took the idea of those two ingredients, and their affinity with each other, and ran with it, replacing the scallops with a pickled cockle dressing. I'm passionate about pork, as you know, so adding the pork was a very natural progression for me.

Even though pork belly has become a staple on menus in recent years, it's generally thought of as a cheap part of the pig. But for me, it's a premium cut because it has the perfect balance of meat and fat, which brings great flavour and a brilliant crispness to any dish you use it in. Those two attributes help to build a wonderful harmony in the dish as a whole; together with the fantastic salty, iodine flavour that you get from the shellfish. The earthy taste and lightness of the cauliflower purée and the touch of acidity from the apples in the pickle add more layers of flavour and give each bite a subtle sophistication.

Cured belly pork

1.3kg belly of pork, skin and rib
*   cage left on*
170g sea salt
55g caster sugar
1 cinnamon stick
1½ tsp crushed juniper berries
1 clove
3 tsp black peppercorns
1 tbsp paprika
1 tsp fresh thyme leaves
1 tsp dried sage
1 tsp dried marjoram
1 litre melted duck fat

Burn any hairs off the pork belly with a cook's blowtorch. Put the salt, sugar, spices and herbs into a spice grinder and grind to a fine powder.

Spread half of the spice mix in a tray (which will hold the pork fairly snugly) then lay the pork belly skin side down on the mix. Spread the remaining cure over the top of the meat. Wrap the tray tightly in cling film and place in the fridge to cure for 8 hours.

Brush off the spice mix and lay the pork belly, skin side down, in a clean, fairly deep tray. Preheat the oven to 90°C/Fan 80°C/lowest Gas.

Pour the duck fat over the pork to cover it completely, then cover the tray with baking parchment and seal with a layer of foil. Place in the oven and confit for 8 hours.

Remove the tray from the oven and leave the pork belly to cool slightly in the duck fat.

When it is cool enough to handle, carefully lift the pork out onto a tray lined with baking parchment and pull the rib cage bones and sinew from the meat. Lay a sheet of parchment on the meat and place another tray on top. Put some heavy weights on the tray to press the pork and leave in the fridge overnight.

Once pressed, transfer the pork belly to a board, square off the edges and cut into even-sized rectangles, each 120–140g. Wrap in cling film and place in the fridge until needed.

Cauliflower purée

500g cauliflower, broken into florets
10g salt
150ml double cream
100ml whole milk

Put the cauliflower and salt into a large vacuum-pack bag and vacuum-seal. Steam for 15 minutes, then take the cauliflower out of the bag and drain in a chinois.

Pour the cream and milk into a saucepan and bring to a simmer. Add the cooked cauliflower, then transfer the mixture to a high-powered blender (Vitamix). Blitz to a smooth purée, then pass through a sieve into a bowl. Cover and chill until needed.

Pickled cauliflower & cockle dressing

1 small cauliflower, broken into small florets
1 tsp salt
250ml white wine vinegar
60g demerara sugar
½ cinnamon stick
1 star anise
3 banana shallots, peeled and finely diced
150ml Chablis (or similar white wine)
500g cockles in shells, thoroughly washed to remove any grit
150ml medium-dry cider
100ml extra-virgin olive oil (we use Leblanc)
2 tsp lemon thyme leaves
2 Granny Smith apples, peeled and diced to the same size as the cauliflower florets

Put the cauliflower into a colander set over a bowl. Sprinkle the florets with the salt and toss together. Leave to stand for 20 minutes, then rinse under cold water.

Meanwhile, put the wine vinegar, sugar and spices into a small pan. Heat to dissolve the sugar and bring to the boil. Remove from the heat and leave to infuse for 20 minutes. Strain the pickling liquor through a fine chinois into a bowl to remove the spices.

Add the cauliflower florets to the pickling liquor. Cover and keep in the fridge until needed.

Heat the shallots and wine in another small pan and let bubble to reduce until almost all of the liquid has evaporated. Set aside to cool.

For the cockles, heat a large heavy-based pan (that has a tight-fitting lid) over a medium-high heat. When hot, add the cockles and cider, put the lid on and steam for 3 minutes until the shells open.

Tip the cockles into a colander set over a bowl to save the liquor and leave until cool enough to handle. Discard any cockles that have not opened. Pass the liquor through a muslin-lined sieve into a bowl. Pick out the cockle meat and add to the cooled cooking liquor.

When ready to serve, heat the olive oil in a saucepan, then add the Chablis shallots and warm through. Add some of the cockle liquor and some of the cauliflower pickling liquor to make a dressing, adjusting the quantities to suit your taste.

Drain the pickled cauliflowers florets and fold through the dressing together with the cockles. Warm through gently and stir in the lemon thyme leaves and diced apple.

To finish the pork & serve

A little vegetable oil for cooking
8 slices of boudin noir, 1cm thick, sliced on an angle
8 tbsp pork sauce (see page 401)

When ready to serve, preheat the oven to 205°C/Fan 185°C/Gas 6–7.

Lay the pork belly portions, skin side down, in an ovenproof frying pan over a medium heat and place an upturned pan on top of them to keep them flat. Place over a low heat so the fat renders slowly and the skin turns golden and crisp. Once you have a crispy crackling skin, transfer to the oven for 4–5 minutes.

Meanwhile, heat a little oil in a frying pan, add the boudin noir slices and fry for about 1½–2 minutes until crispy on both sides. Gently reheat the cauliflower purée and heat up the pork sauce. (Finish the dressing at this stage, too see left.)

Place a portion of pork belly on each warmed plate with a crispy slice of boudin noir and a quenelle of cauliflower purée alongside. Spoon the cauliflower and cockle dressing around the plate and finish with the pork sauce.

Braised shin of beef

with roasted bone marrow, parsnip purée & carrot

SERVES 4

This is a rich and hearty dish. Everything about it is generous. I don't mean in terms of its size (although it's a proper portion); rather, generous in terms of flavour. That's the key to its success.

It's also got the much-loved Hand & Flowers carrot in its DNA, because it's the dish in which it made its first ever appearance – and now that carrot has become genuinely famous. It turns up in dishes at all of our restaurants and it's even popped up on television; I literally get stopped in the street by people wanting to tell me about how they cook this carrot at Christmas.

For me, this is a go-to dish for understanding where flavours should be in our food at The Hand & Flowers. The parsnip purée, which I serve instead of mashed potato, is the richest, most silky parsnip purée you'll taste. The shin of beef is super-flavoursome, it's delightful. The tender, glazed carrot is infused with star anise. The whole dish embraces you.

The key to any good restaurant or restaurateur is generosity. People need to feel that they get more than just food on a plate when they eat in your dining room. Diners want to feel your passion, warmth and enthusiasm in the food that they're eating; it should physically lift their spirits. That's what hospitality should be about. Sheer enjoyment at the table, and this dish sums up that approach.

Braised shin of beef

4 pieces of shin of beef, 225g each
75cl bottle red wine
Vegetable oil for cooking
200g onions, peeled and cut
   into chunks
150g carrots, peeled and cut
   into chunks
150g celery, peeled and cut into
   chunks
2 litres chicken stock
   (see page 400)
5 bay leaves
1 clove
1 tbsp white peppercorns
A bunch of thyme
2 tsp salt

Put the shin of beef pieces into a bowl, pour on the red wine and leave to marinate for 24 hours.

Drain the shin pieces, reserving the wine marinade, and pat dry. Bring the marinade to the boil in a pan and skim off any impurities that come to the surface. Set aside.

Preheat the oven to 160°C/Fan 140°C/Gas 3. Heat a splash of oil in a large flameproof casserole dish or cooking pot, add the onions, carrots and celery and sweat over a medium heat until the mirepoix is softened and browned.

Heat a little oil in a heavy-based frying pan, add the shin pieces and sear until well browned all over. Drain in a colander to get rid of any excess cooking fat, then place the shins on the top of the mirepoix.

Pour on the red wine marinade and chicken stock. Add the bay leaves, clove, white peppercorns, thyme and salt. Bring to a simmer and put the lid on. Place in the oven and braise for 2½ hours. Remove from the oven and leave the shins to cool down in the stock.

Lift the shins out of the casserole and strain the stock through a fine chinois into a pan. Skim off any fat from the surface then reduce by half to 1 litre, skimming frequently. Pour half of the reduced stock into a jug and reserve this 500ml for the sauce.

Reduce the other 500ml further until thickened to a glaze, to use for the bone marrow parcels.

Parsley oil

300ml vegetable oil
250g parsley leaves

Heat the oil in a Thermomix to 70°C and add the parsley leaves. Blend for 1 minute at 70°C, then pass the oil through a fine chinois into a bowl and leave to cool.

Parsley emulsion

65g free-range liquid egg yolk
4g salt
300ml parsley oil (see above)

Put the egg yolk and salt into a high-powered food processor (Robot Coupe) and briefly blend on a slow speed to combine. Slowly add the oil, blending until fully emulsified.

Transfer the parsley emulsion to a piping bag fitted with a 1cm plain nozzle and keep in the fridge until ready to serve.

Braised shin & bone marrow parcels

Braised shin of beef (see page 263)
100g Lyonnaise onions (see page 404)
200g bone marrow fat, diced,
*   soaked in cold water overnight*
500ml reduced shin of beef stock
*   (see page 263)*
4 marrow bone canoes, each
*   12cm long*
4 medium potatoes, peeled
200g caul fat, soaked in cold water
*   for 30 minutes*
50g unsalted butter, diced
400ml chicken stock (see page 400)
Sea salt and freshly cracked
*   black pepper*

Flake the braised shin into a bowl and add the Lyonnaise onions.

Drain the bone marrow fat, put into a blender with the thickened stock and blend to emulsify. Pour onto the flaked shin of beef and onions. Mix together thoroughly and season with salt and cracked pepper to taste. Cover and chill.

Heat the oven to 205°C/Fan 185°C/ Gas 6–7. Lay the bone marrow canoes on a baking sheet and roast in the oven for 15 minutes. Allow to cool, then scrape away any meat or cartilage. Fill the canoes with the beef shin mix, pressing it into the cavities and mounding it up. Chill.

Press a 3cm fondant cutter through the potatoes, then finely slice the potato cylinders, using a mandoline. Lay the potato slices on top of the shin to cover the top. Wrap tightly in caul fat.

Lay the shin marrow parcels in a small baking tray lined with a sheet of baking parchment. Add the butter and chicken stock. Braise in the oven for 15–20 minutes to render the caul fat, basting every 5 minutes or so to glaze the potatoes and caul. Keep warm until ready to serve.

Parsnip purée

4 parsnips, peeled and woody
*   core removed*
150ml milk
150g unsalted butter, diced
Sea salt and freshly ground pepper

Cut the parsnips into 3cm pieces and cook in salted boiling water for about 20 minutes until tender.

Put the milk and butter into another pan, heat to melt the butter and bring to the boil.

Drain the cooked parsnips, then add them to the buttery milk. Transfer to a blender and purée until smooth. Season with salt and pepper to taste.

Pass the parsnip purée through a fine chinois into a bowl, cover and keep warm until ready to serve.

Hand & Flowers carrots

4 medium carrots, topped and tailed
(tops reserved for the garnish)
250g unsalted butter, diced
400ml water
150g caster sugar
4 star anise
1 tsp sea salt, or to taste

Peel the carrots and rub them with an abrasive scourer to remove the peel marks.

Put the butter, water, sugar, salt and star anise into a heavy-based saucepan and bring to the boil.

Add the carrots and simmer for 40 minutes until soft and coated in the buttery glaze.

Beef shin sauce

500ml beef shin braising stock
(see page 263)
250g unsalted butter, diced

Pour the stock into a heavy-based pan and add the butter. Bring to the boil and reduce until the sauce starts to look like bubbling toffee.

Pass through a fine chinois and keep warm over a low heat.

To serve

Carrot tops, to garnish

Warm the beef shin marrow parcels through in a covering of shin stock, if necessary.

Lay the beef shin parcels on warmed serving plates and glaze with the rich beef shin sauce. Add the glazed carrots and garnish with carrot tops. Pipe a mound of parsley emulsion onto each plate and serve the parsnip purée on the side.

Blanquette of veal

with roasted red onions & beetroot linguine

—— SERVES 8 ——

As a chef, you often draw inspiration from your suppliers. And this dish was inspired by one of mine saying that he had started getting bobby calves through. Bobby calves are male calves from dairy herds, and because they won't grow up to produce milk, many of them are slaughtered incredibly young. However, they can be used for veal rather than going to waste – so, we started to think about how we could utilise the meat.

None of the cuts are very big, but after a bit of trial and error, we decided to use the breast meat. Knowing that our supplier was sourcing English rose veal – from farmers who looked after the calves properly – made us feel better about using veal as a product too.

I love a blanquette (classically, white meat with a white sauce) and the idea of braising the veal breast and serving it with a creamy sauce enriched with egg yolk – it was just so enticing!

Roasted and caramelised red onions and beetroot linguine transform the recipe into a kind of fantastic carbonara-style dish (but without the cheese and bacon). There's a bit of confit lemon for acidity, to cut through that lovely richness and lift the dish out of the ordinary. It's beautiful, very simple but very lovely.

To prepare the veal

2.5kg breast of rose veal
3 litres brine (10% solution)
300g caul fat, soaked in cold water
  for 30 minutes
Vegetable oil for cooking
2 white onions, peeled and
  roughly chopped
3 celery stalks, peeled and
  roughly chopped
4 garlic bulbs, cut across in half,
  through the equator
150ml white wine
3 litres chicken stock (see page 400)
4 cardamom pods, lightly bashed

Immerse the veal breast in the brine for 12 hours, then remove and place in the fridge overnight to dry.

The next day, take the veal out of the fridge and start to separate and seam-butcher the muscle by working the tip of a butcher's knife in between the fat and sinew. You will end up with lots of mini fillets; remove all the sinew from each one.

You'll need to make 2 or 3 ballotines. Lay 2 or 3 sheets of cling film side by side. Assemble the ballotines on the cling film, laying the veal pieces on top of one other, then wrap tightly in cling film. Place in the fridge overnight to firm up and set slightly.

The next day, divide the caul fat into 2 or 3 pieces (depending on the number of ballotines assembled) and lay out on a large board. Place the veal ballotines in the middle. Carefully remove the cling film and then wrap the veal ballotines in the caul fat. Tie with butcher's twine to secure.

Preheat the oven to 160°C/Fan 140°C/Gas 3. Heat a splash of oil in a non-stick frying pan over a medium-high heat and sear the veal ballotines one at a time until fully caramelised all over. Remove from the pan and place them all in a braising dish.

Add the onions, celery and garlic to the oil remaining in the frying pan and cook over a medium heat until softened and caramelised. Drain off any excess fat and then add the veg to the veal.

Add the white wine, stock and cardamom pods to the pan and bring to the boil. Pour over the veal, then skim off any impurities from the surface. Cover and braise in the oven for 2 hours until the veal is tender.

Remove from the oven and leave the veal to cool slightly in the liquor.

When it is cool enough to handle, carefully remove the braised veal ballotines from the pan and wrap each tightly in cling film. Place in the fridge to firm up.

Pass the stock through a fine chinois into a jug or bowl and save for the blanquette sauce, and to warm through the veal before serving.

Cardamom salt

8 cardamom pods, lightly bashed
100g sea salt

Toast the cardamom pods in a dry frying pan for a minute or so until they start to release their aroma. Add the salt and warm together. Tip onto a plate and leave to cool.

Put the salt mix into a spice grinder and blitz to a fine powder. Pass through a sieve and keep in a dry container until needed.

Confit lemon zest

2 unwaxed lemons
50ml lemon juice
100g icing sugar

Finely pare the zest from the lemons
and cut into julienne. Bring a small
pan of water to the boil. Add the
lemon zest julienne and blanch for
1 minute, then drain and refresh
in iced water.

Put the lemon juice into a small
saucepan with the icing sugar. Heat
to dissolve the sugar and bring to a
simmer. Stir the blanched lemon zest
through this lemon syrup.

Caramelised red onions

4 even-sized red onions
Vegetable oil for cooking
100g unsalted butter, diced
6 sprigs of thyme
6 cardamom pods, lightly crushed
150ml chicken stock (see page 400)

Preheat the oven to 180°C/Fan
160°C/Gas 4. Cut the onions across
in half through the equator. Heat a
large heavy-based frying pan over
a medium-high heat and add a good
splash of oil. Lay the onion halves,
cut side down, in the hot pan and
caramelise to a rich, dark colour.

Once they have taken on the desired
colour, transfer the onions to a small
baking tray, placing them cut side
down again. Scatter over the butter,
thyme sprigs and cardamom, then
add a quarter of the stock.

Cover the tray with foil and braise
for 25–30 minutes until the onions
are soft and glazed, adding a little
more stock to stop the butter from
burning if necessary. Keep warm.

When ready to serve, lift the onions
from the braising liquor and pop
them out of their skins. Trim a thin
slice off the bases so they'll sit cleanly
on the plates.

To serve, heat the onions through
in a clean pan with a little of their
braising liquor.

Beetroot purée

500g cooked beetroot, peeled
80g unsalted butter
50g redcurrant jelly
20ml red wine vinegar
250ml red wine
Sea salt and cayenne pepper

Finely slice the cooked beetroot and
place in a heavy-based pan with the
butter, redcurrant jelly, wine vinegar
and red wine. Bring to the boil and
reduce until the liquor has almost
totally evaporated.

Transfer to a jug blender and blitz
until smooth. Pass the purée through
a fine chinois into a bowl and season
with cayenne pepper and salt to taste.

Cover the bowl and place in the
fridge until required.

Beetroot linguine

3 medium free-range eggs
3 medium free-range egg yolks
110g beetroot purée (see opposite)
1 tbsp olive oil
300g semolina flour
300g 'oo' pasta flour, plus extra
  for dusting

Using an electric mixer fitted with a dough hook, mix all the ingredients together to form a smooth dough. Knead for about 5 minutes, to stretch the gluten in the flours.

Transfer the pasta dough to a lightly floured surface and knead well for another 5 minutes.

Divide the dough into 4 portions, wrap each in cling film and rest in the fridge for 1 hour.

To shape the linguine, unwrap one portion of dough and roll it through the pasta machine repeatedly, progressively narrowing the rollers a notch at a time, until you reach the narrowest setting. Lay the pasta back on the floured surface. Repeat with the other portions of dough.

Attach the linguine or spaghetti attachment to the pasta machine.

Trim and square off the ends of the pasta, then run the sheets through the pasta cutter.

Hang your linguine on a pasta dryer, so the strands don't stick together, for about 30 minutes before cooking.

Blanquette sauce

5 banana shallots, peeled and sliced
2 large garlic cloves, peeled
  and grated
5 cardamom pods, crushed
5 bay leaves
1 large sprig of rosemary
1 large sprig of thyme
1.5 litres veal braising stock
  (see page 269) or chicken stock
  (see page 400)
600ml double cream
Juice of 2 lemons
4 egg yolks
Sea salt and cayenne pepper

Put the shallots, garlic, cardamom pods, bay leaves and herb sprigs into a large saucepan. Add the stock and bring to the boil, then lower the heat to a simmer. Reduce the stock slowly until it thickens to a glaze.

Pour in the cream, bring to the boil and then lower the heat. Simmer until reduced to 400ml and starting to thicken. Season with the lemon juice, salt and cayenne pepper.

Pass the sauce through a fine chinois into a container, pressing to extract all of the flavour. Cover and set aside until needed.

When ready to serve, gently bring the sauce to a low simmer. Remove from the heat and whisk in the egg yolks; they will cook in the residual heat. Use the sauce straight away.

To finish the veal & serve

Extra-virgin olive oil (we use
  Leblanc), to dress the pasta
A knob of unsalted butter
2 tsp thyme leaves
24 small sprigs of thyme

When ready to serve, carve the veal ballotines, allowing 3 or 4 slices per person. (Finish the caramelised onions at this point.)

Bring a large pan of salted water to the boil. Add the linguine and blanch for 30 seconds until *al dente*. Drain the pasta, dress with good olive oil and season with cardamom salt and confit lemon. Add the thyme leaves.

Gently warm the veal slices in a pan of the reserved veal braising liquor with a little knob of butter, then arrange on warmed plates.

Add the caramelised onion halves and top with a scattering of thyme sprigs. Pour the warm blanquette sauce around the veal and onion.

Serve the linguine in copper pans or warmed bowls alongside, topped with the confit lemon zest.

Treacle-cured chateaubriand

with beef fat brioche & Marmite butter

Every pub in the country has steak on the menu and The Hand & Flowers is no exception. We do steak and chips, naturally, but we also put out a chateaubriand for two – lifting the taste by curing the beef cuts first. However, you have to come on a Sunday or Monday to get it!

The reason for that is the cure – a treacle and red wine mix – is put on the beef every Saturday and not only gives the chateaubriand cuts a greater depth of flavour, but also means that any steaks we don't use for Sunday lunch are perfect for the next day.

The steak comes with a Portobello mushroom stuffed with a brisket ragout that has been smoked in a drum smoker. This is a really nice bit of kit to use (we burn charcoal at the bottom of the drum and the smoke slowly cooks the meat before escaping out of a vent at the top).

A vibrant herb emulsion, made from parsley, tarragon and chives, enhances the dish and the beef-fat brioche is there to help you soak up the sauce. It's a dish that says The Hand & Flowers in capital letters – classic dish, honest flavours and a few surprises!

Cured chateaubriand

1 chateaubriand, about 650g
A little meat glue transglutaminase
powder (if needed)
100ml red wine sauce (see page 402)
200g black treacle

Lay the chateaubriand on a board
and remove any sinew. If necessary,
open the meat up to remove any
embedded sinew, then dust the
middle of the opening with a little
meat glue and seal the meat.

Mix the red wine sauce and treacle
together. Place the chateaubriand in
a vacuum-pack bag and pour in the
marinade. Vacuum-seal and place
in the fridge for 24 hours.

Crispy beef fat

500g beef cod fat, minced
Sea salt and freshly ground pepper

Put the cod fat into a large saucepan
over a low heat. As it starts to render
give it a whisk to separate the grains.
Keep frying over a low heat so the fat
crisps up.

Once you have brown crispy beef fat
crumb, drain in a sieve then tip onto
a small tray lined with a J-cloth.
Season with salt and pepper and
leave to cool.

Beef fat brioche

235g 'T45' plain flour, plus extra
for dusting
5g salt
50ml tepid whole milk
7g fresh yeast
15g caster sugar
100g beaten eggs
(about 2 medium free-range)
185g unsalted butter, diced
and slightly softened
5g diced salted anchovies
(we use Ortiz)
10g capers in brine, drained
7g Marmite
Finely grated zest of ½ lemon
1 tsp rendered beef fat
50g crispy beef fat (see left),
for the glaze
Sea salt

Put the flour and salt into a mixer
fitted with the dough hook and
mix briefly.

Pour the warm milk into a jug,
crumble in the yeast, add the sugar
and stir until the yeast is dissolved.
Add the yeast liquid to the mixer,
followed by the beaten eggs and mix
on a low speed for 4 minutes; the
dough will be very firm, glossy and
pale yellow in colour.

Keeping the mixer on a low speed,
add the butter pieces, one by one, at
3–4 second intervals, so each piece is
incorporated into the dough before
the next is added – you may find this
takes a while. Add the anchovies,
capers, Marmite and lemon zest,
and continue to mix until these
flavourings are evenly distributed.

Scrape the dough into a floured bowl
and cover with cling film. Place in
the fridge to rise slowly overnight.

The next day, take out of the fridge
and tip the dough onto a lightly
floured surface. Knock back, then
roll into a ball. Divide and shape into
100g balls. Place in lined individual
moulds or muffin tins and cover with
cling film. Leave to prove in a warm
place for about 20 minutes.

Preheat the oven to 200°C/Fan
180°C/Gas 6. Brush the top of the
brioche with rendered beef fat and
sprinkle with crispy beef fat and sea
salt. Bake for 10 minutes or until a
fine skewer, inserted into the middle,
comes out clean. Serve warm. (You
will have more than you need; freeze
the extra for another occasion.)

Smoked brisket ragout

500g beef brisket, brined in a
  10% solution for 5 days
Vegetable oil for cooking
½ Spanish onion, peeled and diced
1 garlic clove, peeled and grated
1 litre chicken stock (see page 400)
1 litre beer
500g beef mince
Sea salt and cracked black pepper

Smoke the brisket in a drum smoker at 110°C for 2 hours.

Preheat the oven to 160°C/Fan 140°C/Gas 3. Heat a little oil in a flameproof casserole or ovenproof cooking pot over a medium-high heat. Add the onion and fry until softened and caramelised. Add the garlic and sweat for 2–3 minutes.

Add the smoked brisket, then pour in the chicken stock and beer and bring to a simmer. Cover and braise in the oven for 4 hours.

Lift out the brisket onto a plate and leave to cool, then cut into 8mm dice. Pass the braising liquor through a fine chinois into a clean pan and simmer to reduce to a glaze.

Heat a splash of oil in a large heavy-based frying pan over a medium-high heat. Add the beef mince and pan-roast heavily until well browned and crispy (it should resemble coffee grains).

Drain off the excess fat, then combine the mince with the reduced brisket stock and diced brisket. Season with salt and cracked black pepper to taste. Chill until you need to build the mushroom.

Marmite butter

125g unsalted butter, at room
  temperature
25g Marmite
2.5g sea salt

Beat the ingredients together in a bowl until smoothly combined. Place in a Pacojet beaker and freeze.

Churn before serving. Shape the Marmite butter into quenelles for a neat presentation.

Herb oil

*200g mixed fresh herbs (flat-leaf
  parsley leaves, tarragon leaves,
  chopped chives)*
400ml vegetable oil

Put the fresh herbs and oil into a
Thermomix and set to 70°C, speed 6
for 4 minutes, then turn up to full
speed to blitz thoroughly.

Pass the oil through a muslin-lined
sieve into a container, cover and chill.
(You will have more herb oil than
you need; refrigerate any you're not
using straight away.)

Herb emulsion

*70g pasteurised liquid free-range
  egg yolk*
4g salt
300ml chilled herb oil (see above)

Put the eggs and salt into a high-
powered food processor (Robot
Coupe) and blitz briefly. With the
motor running, slowly pour in the
herb oil.

Once all of the oil has been added
and it is fully emulsified and thick,
transfer to a piping bag and place
in the fridge until ready to serve.

Ragout-stuffed Portobello mushroom

1 large Portobello mushroom
60g blue Stilton
*120g smoked brisket ragout
  (see page 275)*
*100g caul fat, soaked in cold
  water for 30 minutes*
60g unsalted butter, diced
175ml chicken stock (see page 400)
1 tbsp chopped chives

Preheat the oven to 190°C/Fan
170°C/Gas 5. Peel the mushroom
cap and remove the stem.

Pack the gilled side of the mushroom
cap with an even layer of blue cheese.
Cover completely with the smoked
brisket ragout, then wrap the stuffed
mushroom in caul fat.

Sit the wrapped stuffed mushroom
in a small baking tray, dot with the
butter and pour the chicken stock
into the tray. Braise in the oven for
25 minutes to cook the mushroom
and caul fat and reheat the filling,
basting every 5 minutes to glaze.

Remove from the oven and leave to
rest for 5 minutes before serving.
Sprinkle with the chopped chives
and cut the stuffed mushroom in half
to serve.

Fried pickled onion rings

1 medium-large brown onion, peeled
50ml pickling liquor (see page 404)
100ml self-raising flour
35g Trisol (wheat starch)
65ml sparkling water
Vegetable oil for deep-frying
30g plain flour, for dusting
Sea salt and freshly ground pepper

Slice off the sides of the onion then cut 8 slices from the middle, each 4mm thick. Press out the middles, to leave 8 perfect onion rings.

Place the onion rings in a container and pour on the pickling liquor to cover. Leave to soak in the fridge overnight to draw out the raw flavour of the onion.

To make the batter, mix the flour and Trisol together in a bowl and whisk in the sparkling water to make a smooth batter. Cover and leave to stand in the fridge for an hour before using.

When you are ready to serve, remove the onions from the pickling liquor. You will need to fry the onion rings in batches. Heat the oil in a deep-fryer to 180°C. Season the flour with salt and pepper.

Dip the onion rings into the seasoned flour and turn to coat all over; shake off any excess. Now dip the onion rings into the batter, then carefully add to the hot oil and deep-fry for 2–3 minutes until crisp and golden. Remove and drain on kitchen paper. Season the fried onion rings with salt and serve hot.

To cook the beef & serve

40g unsalted butter
100ml red wine sauce (see page 402)
2 portions of triple-cooked chips
(see page 243)
Salt

Immerse the chateaubriand in its vacuum-pack bag in a water-bath at 58°C and cook for 1 hour.

Lift out of the water-bath and remove the chateaubriand from the bag. Pour the treacle marinade into a pan and reduce to a sticky glaze.

When ready to serve, heat the butter in a heavy-based frying pan until melted and foaming. Season the beef with table salt, then add to the foaming butter and caramelise to brown well all over.

Transfer the beef to a warm plate and rest in a warm place for 10 minutes.

Glaze the chateaubriand with the warm treacle glaze, then carve. Serve at once, with the stuffed mushroom, chips, onion rings, herb emulsion, Marmite butter, beef fat brioche and hot red wine sauce.

Loin of venison

with toasted dhal purée, venison ragù
& dehydrated carrot cake

SERVES 4

I'm a big fan of venison; well, game in general. There's always a game dish on the menu, be it partridge, venison (we use farmed in the summer), or grouse. And the lovely thing about game these days is it isn't hung for as long as it used to be, so the flavour isn't overpowering.

You used to get game that had been shot and hung outside until it went green, then cooked until it went pink. It's no wonder that people didn't like it. I mean, that's almost rotten meat! Why *would* you like it? Anyway, these days you can get venison that is mild in flavour all-year-round. It's low in fat, so that works well for a lot of diners, plus it can also hold spices; a dhal purée sits very nicely with it.

The purée brings flavours like cinnamon, ginger and turmeric to the fore but, of course, it doesn't provide crunch or texture to the dish. So, we developed a savoury carrot cake, which we bake, slice and dehydrate to get that texture. And, because it contains lentils, curry powder, cumin and cayenne, the cake ties in beautifully with the dhal purée.

Part of the joy when you eat a curry are the extras: the poppadums and dips, although lime pickle can be a tricky one. Our recipe brings the pickle power and acidity, but doesn't overpower everything. I guess you could say that, essentially, this dish is a venison curry, but it's done, very much, in our own way.

Toasted dhal purée

160g red split lentils
30g unsalted butter, diced
1 small shallot, peeled and sliced
1 garlic clove, peeled and grated
6g root ginger, peeled and grated
¼ tsp ground turmeric
½ tsp ground coriander
1 star anise
½ cinnamon stick
375ml water
Sea salt and freshly ground pepper

Preheat the oven to 205°C/Fan 185°C/Gas 6–7. Scatter the lentils on a baking tray and place in the oven for 30–40 minutes until toasted and dark. Remove and set aside.

Melt the butter in a heavy-based saucepan over a medium-low heat, add the shallot and cook for about 15 minutes until soft. Add the garlic and ginger and sweat for a further 5 minutes.

Add the spices, stir to mix, then add the toasted lentils. Stir to ensure the lentils are fully coated in the buttery spice mix, then add the water. Bring to the boil, lower the heat and simmer for 2 hours or until soft.

Transfer the mixture to a high-powered jug blender (Vitamix) and blend to a purée. Season with salt and pepper to taste.

Pass the purée through a fine chinois into a bowl. Cover the surface with baking parchment to prevent a skin forming and refrigerate until needed.

Savoury carrot cake

3 medium free-range eggs
250ml non-scented oil
*   (such as grapeseed or sunflower)*
200g self-raising flour, sifted
1 tsp salt
1 tsp bicarbonate of soda
1 tbsp ground cumin
1 tbsp curry powder
1 tsp cayenne pepper
1 tbsp caster sugar
200g grated carrot
50g toasted red lentils (prepare
*   as for the dhal purée, left)*

Preheat the oven to 180°C/Fan 160°C/Gas 4. Line a 33 x 26cm baking tin with baking parchment.

Using an electric mixer fitted with the whisk attachment, whisk the eggs and oil together to emulsify. Remove the bowl from the mixer.

Sift the flour, salt, bicarbonate of soda and spices together over the egg mix and add the sugar, grated carrot and toasted lentils. Fold together, using a spatula or large metal spoon until evenly combined.

Spread the mixture in the prepared baking tin and bake for 30 minutes, or until a skewer inserted into the centre comes out clean. Remove the cake from the tin and place on a wire rack to cool.

Once cooled, slice the carrot cake lengthways into 5mm thin slices, reserving the crumbs. Bake the cake slices at 180°C/Fan 160°C/Gas 4 for 20–25 minutes until crisp. You will need 4 slices (the rest can be frozen for another occasion).

Scatter the crumbs on a dehydrator tray and place in the dehydrator at 80°C for a couple of hours until crisp and dry. Reserve for serving.

Venison ragù

Vegetable oil for frying
150g venison mince
2.5g cracked black pepper
5g cumin seeds, toasted and ground
½ tsp salt
50g Milano salami, cut into
  5mm dice
100ml venison sauce (see page 401)

Heat a heavy-based frying pan over a medium-high heat and add a little splash of oil. Add the venison mince and roast until well browned. Drain off the fat.

Add the spices, salt, diced salami and venison sauce. Stir to combine, then simmer to reduce until the liquor is rich and unctuous. Keep hot.

To prepare the venison

400g loin of venison

Trim the venison of all sinew and any fat, then roll in cling film and cut into 4 portions.

Place individually in vacuum-pack bags and vacuum-seal. Immerse in a water-bath at 60°C for 15 minutes. Lift out the bags and set aside until ready to serve.

To finish the venison & serve

Vegetable oil for cooking
4 slices of boudin noir, 1cm thick,
  sliced on an angle
25g unsalted butter, plus an
  extra knob for the dhal purée
4 tsp crème fraîche
1–2 tbsp finely chopped chives
4 Hand & Flowers carrots
  (see page 265)
4 carrot tops
4 thyme sprigs
4 tsp lime pickle (see page 238)
8 curry leaves, deep-fried
100ml venison sauce (see page 401)
Sea salt and freshly ground pepper

Heat a little oil in a frying pan and fry the boudin noir slices for 1½–2 minutes until crispy on both sides, then remove and keep hot.

Reheat the dhal purée, adding a little butter to give it a rich gloss and taste to check the seasoning.

Take the venison loins out of the vacuum-pack bags, remove the cling film and season with salt and pepper.

Heat a heavy-based frying pan over a medium-high heat. Add a splash of oil and the butter and heat until melted and foaming.

Add the venison portions and sear for about 2 minutes, turning as necessary, until browned all over.

Meanwhile, divide the hot venison ragù between warmed individual serving pots, spread a spoonful of crème fraîche on top and sprinkle generously with chopped chives.

Remove the venison loin portions from the pan, cut each into 4 slices and season with sea salt.

Swipe a generous portion of the toasted dhal purée across each warmed plate. Arrange the venison slices on top with the glazed carrot.

Top each serving with a dehydrated carrot cake slice and garnish with a carrot top and a thyme sprig. Add a crispy slice of boudin noir and a teaspoon quenelle of lime pickle to each plate and top both of these with a deep-fried curry leaf. Finish with the venison sauce and serve at once.

Roast hog

with Gem lettuce, crispy bacon & Bramley apple sauce

A sack of potatoes and a pig. That's what you need for this recipe! Let me explain. It's a dish from my second year on Great British Menu, in 2011, for a banquet that would ultimately take place at Leadenhall Market in the City. I'd cooked the main course for the competition's televised final the previous year, and won, so the pressure was on!

I wasn't quite sure what to cook, but as the theme was sharing and communities – food that encouraged people to come together and enjoy eating – I wanted to create a dish that was more of a serving platter than a plate for one person. I took a strategic decision to do pork because I knew nobody had won a main course in the competition with pork.

Of course, I wanted to make the roast pork taste amazing; and I wanted to utilise the whole animal. In the end, I decided to serve pig's head fritters, pork belly and pig's trotter sausage. That way, I used almost all of the more humble cuts of the pig and also referenced traditional British cooking.

When it came to the potatoes, I wanted to do something quite different. Hence, baking them in a salt crust and tying them up like a sack of potatoes! Visually, it looks really special, and the flavour is absolutely delicious, too, as the potatoes steam in their own juices and take on a lovely seasoning from the pastry.

I was very pleased with the dish. It took humble, honest ingredients to a higher level, admittedly with an immense amount of work because we weren't just roasting a pork belly, but boning and stuffing trotters, and braising pigs' heads! But it was worth it because the roast hog is brilliant.

When we went on to serve the dish in the pub, it created a great atmosphere because it's such a social dish. Sharing dishes create an energy in a dining room: a noise. I hate a quiet dining room. What's the appeal in that?

To prepare the pork belly

1 sheet of pork skin rind
½ pork belly, boned and skinned

Put the sheet of pork skin rind into a vacuum-pack bag and seal. Immerse in a water-bath at 70°C and cook for 24 hours. Lift out and cool in iced water, then chill.

Cut the boned pork belly in half horizontally. Roll each piece and wrap tightly in cling film to create a cylinder. Place in separate vacuum-pack bags and seal. Cook in a water-bath at 70°C for 8 hours.

Once cooked, remove the pork belly from the bags and rewrap each, very tightly, in fresh cling film, to form a firm cylinder. Immerse the cylinders in iced water to chill, then lift out and refrigerate for 6 hours.

Remove the pork skin from the bag and cut it in half. Remove the cling film from the pork belly rolls and wrap each tightly in pork skin. Wrap tightly in cling film. Vacuum-pack each roll, seal and leave in the fridge for 24 hours to allow the skin to set around the pork.

An hour before cooking, take the pork belly rolls out of their bags and remove the cling film. Tie the pork quite tightly with kitchen string so the skin stays in place.

Glazed pig's trotter

1 long pig's trotter
145g minced pork shoulder
125g minced bacon
60g minced pig's liver
35g fresh breadcrumbs
5 sage leaves, chopped
60g cooked, diced onion
3g salt
2.5g cracked black pepper
75g caster sugar
1 tbsp water
1 tbsp soy sauce
5g Marmite

Burn the hairs off the pig's trotter with a cook's blowtorch.

In a bowl, mix together the minced pork shoulder, bacon and liver. Add the breadcrumbs, chopped sage, cooked onion, salt and cracked pepper and mix thoroughly. Put the mixture into a piping bag fitted with a large plain nozzle.

Bone the trotter out, being careful not to split the skin. Scrape the sinew and gristle out of the empty trotter. Pipe in the stuffing mixture and reshape the trotter. Roll tightly in cling film, then in foil and finally place in a vacuum-pack bag.

Immerse in a water-bath at 70°C and cook for 9 hours. Remove the bag and immerse in iced water to chill. Lift the bag out and refrigerate for 6 hours.

Remove all the packaging from the pig's trotter and clean off all the jelly. Set aside.

Put the sugar into a heavy-based saucepan and melt over a medium heat, then increase the heat and cook to a dark caramel. Carefully add the water and soy sauce, stirring to combine, then whisk in the Marmite. Leave to cool.

Brush the pig's trotter with the cooled caramel and place in a clean vacuum-pack bag. Seal and refrigerate until needed.

When ready to serve, immerse the pig's trotter bag in a water-bath at 70°C for at least 30 minutes to reheat.

Deep-fried braised pig's head

½ pig's head
200ml white wine vinegar
1 onion, roughly chopped
1 celery stick, roughly chopped
2 carrots, roughly chopped
A bunch of thyme sprigs
A bunch of rosemary sprigs
2 tbsp salt
2 tbsp black peppercorns
2 tbsp coriander seeds
6 tbsp English mustard
75g plain flour, for dusting
4 medium free-range eggs, beaten
100g panko breadcrumbs
Vegetable oil for deep-frying
Sea salt and freshly ground pepper

Preheat the oven to 150°C/Fan 130°C/Gas 2. Burn the hairs off the half pig's head with a cook's blowtorch then place in a large ovenproof pan or cooking pot. Pour on enough cold water to cover and bring to the boil, then drain off the water. Cover again with cold water and repeat the process twice more.

Pour on fresh cold water and add the wine vinegar, vegetables, herbs, salt and the spices, tied together in a muslin bag. Bring to the boil and cover with foil. Place the pan in the oven for 6–8 hours until the pig's head is cooked.

When cool enough to handle, lift the head out of the liquor and place on a board. Flake all the meat and skin, tongue and brain and place in a bowl. Mash it all together with your hands, then add the mustard and mix well. Season with salt and pepper to taste.

Line a small tray with cling film. Transfer the meat mixture to the tray and spread evenly, pressing the mixture firmly to compact it. Leave in the fridge for 12 hours to set.

Remove the set mixture from the tray and cut into 3cm cubes. Roll each cube in flour to dust all over, then dip into the beaten eggs and finally into the breadcrumbs to coat fully. Set aside until ready to serve.

When ready to serve, heat the oil in a deep-fryer to 180°C. Deep-fry the pig's head cubes for 4–5 minutes, then drain on kitchen paper and season with salt and pepper to taste.

Potato sack

500g plain flour
150g table salt
2 medium free-range egg whites
About 105ml water
8–10 medium-small baking potatoes

Using an electric mixer fitted with the dough hook, mix the flour and salt together. Add the egg whites and then slowly add the water until the mixture comes together to form a dough; you may not need all of the water. Continue to knead the dough in the mixer for about 5 minutes, then remove and wrap in cling film. Leave to rest for 2 hours.

Preheat the oven to 210°C/Fan 190°C/Gas 6–7. Roll out the dough into a circle, about 5mm thick. Place the potatoes in the middle and draw the edges up over the potatoes to enclose them in a sack of dough. Tie with cotton rope to secure. Bake for 2 hours until the salt-crust potatoes are cooked.

Garlic butter

*250g salted butter, at room
temperature*
3 garlic cloves, peeled and grated
3 tbsp finely chopped flat-leaf parsley
*4 deep-fried flat-leaf parsley leaves,
to garnish*

Beat the butter, garlic and chopped
parsley together in a bowl.

Spoon the flavoured butter onto
a sheet of cling film, to form a log,
about 3cm in diameter. Wrap in
the cling film and roll into a small,
smooth cylinder. Tie the ends of the
cling film to seal and submerge the
parcel in iced water to firm up.

When set, slice the butter into 6mm
thick discs and remove the cling film.
Cover and store in the fridge until
needed. (Any leftover butter can be
frozen for future use.)

Serve the garlic butter discs topped
with the deep-fried parsley leaves.

Apple purée

4 Bramley apples
300ml water
100g caster sugar
15g Sosa Antioxidant Gel Powder
Juice of 1 lemon

Peel, halve, core and roughly slice the
Bramley apples. Put the water, sugar,
antioxidant and lemon juice into a
small saucepan and bring to the boil.
Add the sliced apples and cook for
about 15 minutes until soft.

Transfer to a jug blender and purée
until smooth. Pass through a sieve
into a bowl, cover and keep in the
fridge until needed. Reheat to serve.

Salad cream

1 tbsp plain flour
4 tbsp caster sugar
2 medium free-range eggs
1 tbsp English mustard powder
100ml white wine vinegar
150ml double cream
A squeeze of lemon juice
Sea salt and cayenne pepper

Put the flour, sugar, eggs, mustard
powder and wine vinegar into a large
heatproof bowl. Whisk over a pan
of simmering water until thick and
increased in volume to form a thick
sabayon, and to cook out the flour.
Remove the bowl from the heat and
leave to cool.

In a separate bowl, whisk the cream
to soft peaks. Once the sabayon is
cooled, fold in the cream and season
with the lemon juice, cayenne pepper
and salt to taste.

To assemble & serve

100g piece of smoked bacon
Vegetable oil for cooking
4 Gem lettuces, divided into leaves
120ml pork sauce (see page 401)

Preheat the oven to 240°C/Fan 220°C/Gas 9. Place the pork belly rolls in a roasting tin and cook in the oven for 30 minutes or until the skin is crispy. Remove from the oven and leave to rest in a warm place for 30 minutes before serving. (Reheat the trotter at this stage.)

Meanwhile, cut the bacon into small dice. Heat a little oil in a frying pan, add the bacon and fry until crispy. Remove and drain on kitchen paper. (At this stage, deep-fry the pig's head cubes and warm through the apple purée in a small pan.)

Dress the lettuce leaves with salad cream, arrange in serving bowls and scatter over the crispy bacon. Bring the pork sauce to the boil and pour into a warmed jug.

Place the pork belly, pig's trotter and crisp pig's head cubes on a board with the pork sauce and apple purée. Place the potato parcel on a board with a toffee hammer to crack it open and the garlic butter on the side. Serve at once, with the salad.

Interior design & atmosphere

Interior design is how you begin to create a vibe, an atmosphere, a feeling in a pub or restaurant. When we took over The Hand & Flowers, Beth and I asked ourselves: 'How do we make it special? How do we make it nice, bearing in mind we have no money?' That's where the artistic (and, I'll be honest, the practical) skill-set of Beth and her family came into play. And that's why we ended up with a table made of scaffolding boards in the pub! It makes me smile every time I think of it: Beth built a table out of scaff boards, and we achieved two Michelin stars with people eating from it.

When we first walked into the pub, it was most definitely showing wear and tear, and it really felt quite dark; the decor just needed to be modernised, made fresh. We didn't want to lose the feel of a pub, but we wanted it to be comfy and welcoming. So we went for a lot of leather because it works so well in British pubs and it's one of those great tactile materials that is also hard-wearing. It's got a softness about it, too.

Beth, her dad and her brother put in some bulkhead seating. The benches were made from MDF with foam seating, which was then wrapped in leather (by us) and they're still there now – well, the framework is. As far as tables went, we bought a few and then, because we were short of funds, Beth built our scaffolding board one. We've now redone the seats bit by bit (we take them out and redo them overnight when the pub's empty), but today's interior is essentially the same as the original concept that Beth, her brother and her father came up with and built in 2005.

We went through a period where I was unhappy with our level of service – not in terms of its professionalism or slickness, but the atmosphere wasn't quite warm enough. When we first opened, Beth always talked about giving customers a hug, sometimes literally, making them feel warm and welcome. Offering a bed for a night helped the team to develop that missing ingredient. The team now look after customers when they arrive, show them their rooms and carry their luggage. Some of the rooms are in town, so they pick guests up and bring them to The Hand & Flowers for dinner, then drive them back to their room afterwards. Then they will see the guests all over again for breakfast. The team view those customers as house guests.

This has driven The Hand & Flowers to become very warm and very special, because every guest – whether they are staying overnight or just dining with us – is treated the same, even if they're only with us for a quick lunch of fish and chips. We get amazing compliments from people about how wonderful our staff are. And that's because they have become this all-encapsulating, warm, huggy group of nice people!

The rooms are, of course, good for business because room revenue is great, but more importantly they have been exceptional for building character. Nowadays the fittings and decor of the pub are watched over by Beth and her sister, Eve Cullen-Cornes, who is an interior designer, and we are still continuing the work. Everything stems from Beth's warmth and Eve's ability to find the knick-knacks and make the contacts at the leather companies or with the people who build everything. Between the two of them they do an exceptional job at maintaining that special feel we've established at The Hand & Flowers and its 15 bedrooms.

Onion tarte tatin

with onion soubise, onion marmalade & vin jaune

SERVES 4

This is a dish that lets onions shine in a rich, caramelised tarte tatin surrounded by a stunning white onion soubise – made by cooking white onions gently to a soft purée.

You start the dish off by making a caramel with onion stock, in which you then gently roast the baby onions. The onions are removed and the sauce reduced back down to a caramel. This goes into individual pans to form the base of each tart and the baby onions are fanned out in the caramel then cloaked with puff pastry, in the classic style for a tarte tatin. The tarts are then ready to bake to order.

Lovely toasted hazelnuts, fresh thyme, a little quenelle of red onion and mustard seed chutney, plus white onion gravy with a splash of vin jaune give our tarte tatin a lovely balance and depth of flavour. Rochers of the white onion soubise finish the dish off beautifully.

The recipe owes its origin to Rikki Hughes, our junior sous chef; he's been influential over the past few years at the restaurant, coming up with meat garnishes and delicious vegetarian dishes. Rikki is a brilliant cook and he's been with us for about five years, but when he first joined the team, he was a party-hard sort of chef! We've given him an increased amount of responsibility over the years and he's now an exceptional member of the brigade whose personal journey illustrates that the more you ask of a chef and allow them to grow, the more they reward you by coming up with incredibly creative dishes.

You only have to look at this tarte tatin to see how that management style works in practice. It's lovely to eat, it's a really popular dish, and it's totally in tune with the rest of the cuisine at at The Hand & Flowers.

Onion stock

600g Spanish onions,
  peeled and sliced
600ml water

Put the sliced onions into a large vacuum-pack bag, add the water and vacuum-seal at full pressure. Steam at 100°C for 2 hours.

Open the bag and strain the stock through a fine chinois, discarding the onions. Leave the stock to cool.

Poached baby onions

100g caster sugar
30g unsalted butter, diced
½ garlic clove, peeled and crushed
300ml onion stock (see above)
2 sprigs of thyme
100 baby onions, peeled

Melt the sugar in a heavy-based saucepan over a medium-low heat, bring to the boil and cook to a dark golden caramel. Immediately take off the heat and whisk in the butter pieces and garlic.

Pour in the onion stock, add the thyme and bring to the boil. Add the baby onions and simmer for about 5 minutes until just tender. Using a slotted spoon, transfer the onions to a bowl, cover and leave to cool, then refrigerate until needed.

Reduce the cooking liquor until thick and glossy. Pass this onion caramel glaze through a chinois into a container and set aside.

Onion marmalade

A splash of vegetable oil
7 red onions, peeled and finely sliced
100g soft dark brown sugar
65ml cider vinegar
65ml balsamic vinegar
35g toasted mustard seeds

Heat the oil in a saucepan, add the sliced onions and sweat over a low heat for 15–20 minutes until soft, without colouring.

Add the sugar, stir to dissolve, then add both vinegars, stirring to deglaze. Simmer for 15–20 minutes to reduce to a chutney consistency. Stir in the mustard seeds. Transfer to a bowl, let cool then cover and refrigerate.

Onion soubise

250g unsalted butter
8 Spanish onions, peeled and sliced
130ml maple syrup
130ml cider vinegar
Sea salt and freshly ground pepper

Melt the butter in a saucepan, add the onions and sweat over a low heat for 10–15 minutes until soft, without colouring. Drain off the excess butter.

Add the maple syrup and cook for 1 minute. Deglaze with the vinegar.

Transfer to a Thermomix and cook at 80°C for 10–15 minutes. Blend until smooth, then season. Pass through a chinois into a bowl, cover and refrigerate until ready to serve.

Vin jaune onion sauce

A splash of vegetable oil
300g Spanish onions, peeled
  and sliced
300ml onion stock (see left)
A splash of vin jaune, to taste
Sea salt and freshly ground pepper

Heat the oil in a large pan, add the sliced onions and sweat over a medium-low heat for 10–15 minutes until golden brown. Add the onion stock and reduce by one-third.

Transfer to a high-powered jug blender (Vitamix) and blend until smooth. Season the sauce with salt and pepper to taste.

When ready to serve, warm the sauce and add a splash of vin jaune to taste. Pour into individual jugs to serve. (Any leftover sauce can be frozen for future use.)

Onion tatins

600g puff pastry (see page 405),
or 2 x 320g ready-rolled all-butter
puff pastry sheets
6 tbsp onion caramel glaze (from the
poached baby onions, see opposite)
100 poached baby onions (see
opposite)

Have ready 4 individual tatin tins or individual omelette pans, 10–12cm in diameter. Roll out the puff pastry to a 5mm thickness and cut out 4 discs, a little larger than your tatin tins or pans. Cover with cling film and place in the fridge to rest for 30 minutes.

Warm the onion caramel in a small saucepan. Divide evenly between the individual pans (about 1½ tbsp caramel per pan). Leave to cool.

Pack the poached baby onions into the pans as tightly as possible; you should be able to fit 25 onions into each pan.

Lay the puff pastry discs over the filling and use a spoon to tuck the pastry down around the edges and under the onions to form a lip.

Dock the top of the pastry with the tip of a small knife in 6 places to allow steam to escape. Place in the fridge until needed.

When ready to cook and serve, preheat the oven to 205°C/Fan 185°C/Gas 6–7. Place the tatin tins on a baking sheet and bake on the middle shelf of the oven for 20–25 minutes until dark golden. Leave the onion tatins to rest for 3 minutes before serving.

To finish & serve

16 hazelnuts, toasted and halved
4 thyme sprigs, deep-fried

While the onion tatins are in the oven, warm the onion marmalade and the onion soubise; warm and finish the vin jaune onion sauce (see opposite).

Carefully turn out the onion tatins and place one on each serving plate. Top with a rocher of warm onion marmalade and garnish with the hazelnuts and thyme. Surround with rochers of the onion soubise and serve at once.

Mushroom Wellington

with mushroom & truffle purée & mushroom chutney

No apologies, this dish is an absolute mushroom fest. Wellington, chutney, gravy, purée: every part celebrates a different kind. And you don't have to be vegetarian to fall in love with it!

The Wellington stuffing is built around king oyster mushrooms, which haven't really been around that long because they're a cultivated variety. They've probably only been used in cooking for the past decade but they have got a robust 'meaty' texture, a bit like a cep (although with nowhere near the same intense flavour), so they give plenty of chew and fantastic texture to the dish. Texture continues through the pastry, which has our secret ingredient: a touch of polenta which gives a lovely feel in the mouth.

At The Hand & Flowers, we're fans of wrapping things in pastry and we serve a few Wellington-inspired dishes. But the creation of this dish was all about presenting something tasty and super-delicious for our non-meat-eating guests – a substantial and satisfying main course with layers of earthy flavour that's on a par with the menu's meat dishes.

It's important to me that all our dishes sit well alongside one another – that they are all strong and powerful in flavour – and this dish absolutely delivers on that score.

Mushroom ketchup

750g Paris brown mushrooms
5g sea salt
100g white wine vinegar
40g caster sugar
25ml dark soy sauce
3g gellan gum powder type F
Sea salt and freshly ground pepper

Blitz the mushrooms with the salt in a blender to a finely chopped texture. Place in a muslin cloth, tie and hang over a bowl to catch the mushroom juice overnight. You will need 300ml.

Put the wine vinegar, sugar and soy sauce into a saucepan over a medium heat to dissolve the sugar, and bring to the boil. Remove from the heat and allow this gastrique to cool.

Pour the 300ml mushroom juice into a Thermomix and add the gellan powder. Heat to 95°C and blend on level 4. Once it reaches 95°C, hold at this temperature for 2 minutes then transfer the jug to the fridge and leave to set.

Once, set place the jug back on the base, add the gastrique and blend to combine. Season with salt and pepper to taste and spoon into a small bowl. Place the bowl in the vacuum-pack machine and close the lid. The vacuum will draw the air bubbles out of the ketchup. Store in a small container until needed.

Mushroom chutney

250g button mushrooms
2 Bramley apples, peeled,
*   cored and diced*
1 Spanish onion, peeled and diced
50g raisins
50g ginger, peeled and finely grated
250g dark brown sugar
¼ tsp ground cloves
¼ tsp ground cinnamon
½ tsp freshly grated nutmeg
170ml malt vinegar
1 tsp table salt

Briefly blitz the button mushrooms in a blender to a coarse texture.

Transfer the blitzed mushrooms to a saucepan, add the rest of the ingredients and bring to the boil. Lower the heat to a steady simmer and cook for about 25 minutes until the liquid is reduced down and you have a rich chutney.

Remove from the heat and allow to cool. Cover and refrigerate until ready to serve.

Mushroom gravy

125g unsalted butter
50ml vegetable oil
200g shallots, peeled and sliced
15g garlic cloves, peeled and grated
10g tarragon leaves
7g thyme leaves
350g button mushrooms, sliced
350g Paris brown mushrooms, sliced
350g Portobello mushrooms, sliced
50ml port
50ml Madeira
500ml parsley nage (see page 54)
Sea salt and freshly ground pepper

Heat the butter and oil in a wide-based saucepan over a medium-low heat. Add the shallots and garlic and sweat for 10–15 minutes to soften.

Add the tarragon and thyme and cook for a further 5 minutes. Add all the mushrooms, stir and cook for a further 10 minutes.

Pour in the port and Madeira and reduce to a glaze, then add the parsley nage. Cover and simmer for a further 10 minutes.

Transfer the mixture to a high-powered blender (Vitamix) and blitz to a smooth sauce. Pass through a chinois and season with salt and pepper to taste. Cover and refrigerate until ready to serve.

Mushroom duxelles

1kg Portobello mushrooms,
*   peeled*
100ml port
100ml Madeira
50ml double cream
20ml truffle oil
Sea salt

Briefly blitz the mushrooms in a blender to a coarse texture. Transfer to a large saucepan and place over a very low heat to slowly dehydrate, about 30 minutes.

Once the mushrooms are dry and almost resemble a mushroom tobacco, add the port and Madeira and reduce until totally evaporated.

Add the cream and truffle oil and simmer for 5 minutes or until reduced and thickened. Season with salt to taste. Allow to cool, cover and refrigerate until needed.

King oyster mushrooms

160g unsalted butter,
*   at room temperature*
8g truffle oil
6g sea salt
8 king oyster mushrooms

In a bowl, beat the butter, truffle oil and salt together to make a truffle butter. Put an oyster mushroom and 20g of the truffle butter into each of 8 small vacuum-pack bags.

Vacuum-seal the bags on full pressure and steam at 100°C for 30 minutes. Allow to cool and refrigerate until needed.

Mushroom boudins

Mushroom duxelles (see left)
Poached king oyster mushrooms
*   (see above)*

Divide the mushroom duxelles into 8 portions. Lightly roll out each portion on cling film until it is just large enough to wrap around a poached mushroom.

Place each oyster mushroom in the middle of a portion of duxelles and wrap the duxelles around it to form a thick mushroom boudin, then wrap the whole parcel in the cling film. Place in the fridge to firm up for 20 minutes.

Mushroom & truffle purée

160g button mushrooms, sliced
¼ tsp sea salt
Juice of ¼ lemon
125ml double cream
3.5g Sosa Antioxidant Gel Powder
10g black truffle paste
Sea salt and freshly ground pepper

Put the sliced mushrooms into a bowl, add the salt and lemon juice, toss to mix and leave to macerate for 30 minutes.

Tip the mushrooms into a clean towel and squeeze out the excess moisture.

Pour the cream into a saucepan, add the antioxidant and bring to the boil. Add the mushrooms and bring back to the boil.

Transfer to a high-powered jug blender (Vitamix) and blend until smooth. Season with salt and pepper to taste and pass through a fine chinois into a bowl. Cover and refrigerate until needed.

When ready to serve, warm through and stir in the truffle paste.

Egg glaze

3 medium free-range egg yolks
5g dextrose
2 tsp whole milk

Whisk the egg yolks and dextrose together to combine, then stir in the milk. Leave to rest for an hour before use.

Pastry

250g plain flour
50g polenta
½ tsp bicarbonate of soda
½ tsp sea salt
75g unsalted butter
95ml water

Put the flour, polenta, bicarbonate of soda and salt into a mixer fitted with the paddle attachment.

Melt the butter with the water in a saucepan over a medium heat and bring to the boil. Immediately pour onto the dry ingredients and mix on a low speed to form a smooth dough.

Remove the dough from the bowl and knead lightly with your hands, just to bring it together to form a ball. Divide the pastry into 80g balls and wrap individually in cling film. Use while still warm.

Mushroom Wellingtons

One at a time, roll out each pastry ball to an oval, large enough to wrap around the boudin. Unwrap the mushroom boudin, place on the pastry and wrap the pastry around it, pressing the edges together to seal. Place in the fridge to rest for 1 hour.

When ready to cook and serve, preheat the oven to 205°C/Fan 185°C/Gas 6–7. Brush the parcels evenly with egg glaze and bake for 12 minutes, turning them halfway through cooking.

Remove from the oven and set aside to rest for 3 minutes before serving.

To finish & serve

1 autumn black truffle, grated
4 deep-fried tarragon sprigs

While the mushroom Wellingtons are in the oven, gently warm up the mushroom chutney, mushroom ketchup and mushroom and truffle purée. Reheat the gravy and pour it into a warm jug.

Place a rocher each of chutney, ketchup and mushroom and truffle purée on one side of each warmed serving plate.

Sprinkle the tops of the baked mushroom Wellingtons with grated truffle and place one on each plate. Finish with a deep-fried tarragon sprig and serve immediately.

DESSERTS

In the early days at The Hand & Flowers, we never really had a pastry chef, as such. Pastry chefs have to work in an extremely structured way and there's very little room for error. If you've forgotten to cook a steak, you can rectify the mistake and get one cooked relatively quickly – but you can't just knock up a quick ice cream. All of which means that a true pastry chef has a different mindset from everyone else.

But not having an out-and-out pastry chef to create the first menus proved to be a huge bonus, because it meant the same people were creating the starters, mains and desserts – so there was real continuity between each course. Perhaps our chefs were more interested in flavour than sweetness, whereas a pastry chef would usually make techniques and sugars a priority. So that gave our desserts their own signature. And if we wanted to try different types of tuile or experiment with sugar work, we had to do the research ourselves.

Developing and making desserts is an on-going, slow process. Some dishes take two, three, four days to pull together by the time you've reduced an element down or set it in the freezer. About three years after we opened, Jolyon d'Angibau joined us at The Hand & Flowers to head the pastry section and develop our dessert menu. Jolyon is pretty much self-taught. He studied graphic design at college, which gives him an edge; he makes things look so lovely. I'll often say to him, 'I want something that looks like this, and works like that, can you make it?' and he's got the skill to piece the concept together.

We also brought in pastry chef and chocolatier Damian Allsop as a pastry consultant for a while, to help us progress to the next level with our desserts. Damian's pastry skills are incredible and his understanding of technique goes beyond sugar and flour. There are lots of variables when working with fruit, for example, and Damian gave us some real insights into that. Critically, he understood what we were about as a kitchen, and was able to help build on the approach we had established at the start.

So I'm very proud of our desserts. As for all the dishes at The Hand & Flowers, our mantra is: keep them simple and make them the best that they can possibly be.

Lime bavarois

in a white chocolate shell with dark chocolate sorbet

SERVES 6

This luxurious dessert looks amazing and delivers a beautiful surprise when you eat it. It originally came about because I liked the idea of having a mousse on the menu and I started thinking about stunning, classically French, free-style desserts that are just a single thing on a plate.

That led me to the concept of a satin-smooth chocolate sphere filled with flavour – and mousse – but I didn't want customers to be able to tell what was in the middle of the sphere until they cracked it open.

It was one of the times when I had a vision that our pastry chef, Jolyon d'Angibau, translated brilliantly into reality. We perfected tempered white chocolate spheres and developed a recipe for the bavarois (the mousse, in other words). We ended up with a lovely, rich sphere encasing a beautiful limey mousse and gorgeously bitter dark chocolate sorbet.

We've got a great crunch in there, too, with a tuile that runs through the middle of the sphere between the sorbet and the mousse; plus an almost croûton-like, dehydrated hazelnut sponge, which sits as a layer between the mousse and the tuile. For a touch of decadence, the sphere's topped with gold leaf and lime sugar.

Visually, it's stunning. Then you break through the sphere and get the most incredible flavours.

White chocolate spheres

300g white chocolate, in pieces

Polish 12 half-dome moulds, 7.5cm in diameter and 3.5cm deep, with cotton wool.

Gently melt the white chocolate in a heatproof bowl over a bain-marie and warm to 40°C. Set the bowl over a larger bowl of iced water to cool the melted chocolate to 25°C, stirring as it cools.

Return the bowl to the bain-marie and warm the chocolate to 30°C, then remove the bowl from the heat. Flood the half-dome moulds with the chocolate and pour off the excess. Leave to set then clean around the edges of the moulds.

Brush another two layers of white chocolate into the moulds, allowing each layer to set completely before applying the next. Leave to set at room temperature.

Lime sugar

*Finely grated zest of 5 limes
   (use a fine Microplane grater)
100g caster sugar*

Mix the lime zest and sugar together and lay on a dehydrator tray. Place in the dehydrator for 1 hour to remove all moisture.

Once fully dry, blitz the mixture in a spice grinder to make lime sugar.

Lime bavarois

*2 sheets of bronze leaf gelatine
500ml freshly squeezed lime juice
140g free-range liquid egg white
200g caster sugar
400ml double cream*

Soak the gelatine in a shallow dish of cold water for 5–10 minutes to soften. Heat the lime juice in a saucepan and simmer steadily to reduce by half, to 250ml.

Whisk the egg white in a very clean bowl using an electric whisk until stiff. Gradually whisk in the sugar in stages until fully incorporated and you have a thick, glossy meringue.

In a separate bowl, whip the cream to soft peaks.

Bring the reduced lime juice to a simmer, then take off the heat. Squeeze the gelatine to remove the excess water, then add it to the hot lime juice and stir until fully melted.

Working quickly, fold the cream and meringue together, then fold in the lime syrup. Spoon into one or two piping bags and place in the fridge to firm up.

Dark chocolate sorbet

*2 sheets of bronze leaf gelatine
240g dark chocolate (70% cocoa
   solids), finely chopped
750ml water
240ml milk
60g caster sugar
60g trimoline or liquid glucose
100g cocoa powder*

Soak the gelatine in a shallow dish of cold water for 5–10 minutes to soften. Put the chopped chocolate into a bowl.

Combine the water, milk, sugar and trimoline or glucose in a medium saucepan. Heat to dissolve the sugar and bring to the boil. Add the cocoa powder and simmer, stirring for 5 minutes.

Pour the hot cocoa mixture onto the chocolate and whisk until melted.

Squeeze out the excess water from the gelatine, then add it to the chocolate mixture, stirring until fully melted.

Pass the mixture through a fine chinois, pour into a Pacojet beaker and freeze overnight.

Before serving, churn the sorbet for 2 hours and place back in the freezer, ready to serve.

White chocolate tuiles

180g fondant icing sugar
80g liquid glucose
80g white chocolate, in pieces
30g dark chocolate (80% cocoa
*   solids), for grating*

Heat the fondant icing sugar and liquid glucose in a medium pan to 155°C (use a digital probe to check the temperature). Remove from the heat and leave to cool slightly, for 2 minutes.

Add the white chocolate and stir until melted to make a paste. Spread the mixture out on a silicone mat and leave to cool and set.

Once cool and brittle, blitz the white chocolate mixture to a fine powder. Preheat the oven to 200°C/Fan 180°C/Gas 6. Line a large baking sheet with a silicone mat.

Using a 10cm disc stencil, sift the chocolate powder inside the template to create a white chocolate disc on the silicone mat. Repeat to create 6 discs in total. Grate over the dark chocolate and bake for 8 minutes.

Remove from the oven and leave to cool. Store the tuiles in an airtight container interleaved with baking parchment until ready to serve.

Hazelnut sponge

160g praline paste
240g free-range liquid egg white
160g liquid free-range egg yolk
160g caster sugar
50g plain flour, sifted

Have ready 6 small plastic cups, each perforated around the sides with 3 pin-holes.

Put all of the ingredients into a large bowl and beat together to make a smooth batter. Pour the mix into an ISI cream whipper, charge with one charge and shake well.

Squirt the batter into the plastic cups to one-third fill them. Microwave on full power for 25 seconds.

Now place the cups on a dehydrator tray in the dehydrator for 6 hours until crisp and brittle.

To assemble & serve

A piece of gold leaf

Half-fill 6 white chocolate half-dome shells with the lime bavarois, then fill with the dehydrated cake, carefully pressing it in.

Carefully position the tuile on top and then add a rocher of the dark chocolate sorbet. Carefully place a white chocolate half-dome lid over the sorbet.

Pipe decorative lines of melted chocolate on the plate and put a little extra in the centre of the plate (to hold the sphere in place).

Carefully lift the sphere and position in the centre of the plate. Finish with the lime sugar and gold leaf.

Apple tarte fine

with meadowsweet ice cream

—————— SERVES 8 ——————

I've got many happy memories of walking through the streets of Paris and admiring the beautiful fruit tarts on display in pâtisserie shop windows. They really are a thing of beauty; so striking, so well made, perfect spacing between each piece of fruit. And this recipe is very much inspired by those magnificent works of art.

While many chefs like to bake tartes fines individually, I thought it would be fun to create my own version of a Parisian apple tart. So we do it as one big tart with puff pastry and it's a kind of combination of traditional tarte fine, tarte tatin and frangipane tart. It has just the right amount of sugar dusted on top to caramelise when we flip it over and cook it. The end result is a slice of apple tart cooked to perfection and served with a quenelle of ice cream on an orange tuile.

The tart is so simple in appearance, with thin layers of everything, but it really showcases our pastry chef Jolyon d'Angibau's amazing skills because the amount of work involved in creating this kind of pared-back beauty is huge. Cooked and caramelised, the tart looks incredibly neat and appealing. Even better, it's absolutely delicious!

We've used lovely, aromatic meadowsweet in the ice cream and that brings another layer of flavour to the dish; I just love using English foraged plants on the menu. Vanilla ice cream works equally well, though. You just need to remember that the goal, here, is to work with classic flavours that complement one another brilliantly.

Meadowsweet ice cream

375ml double cream
375ml whole milk
50g glycerine
50g meadowsweet
160g liquid free-range egg yolk
100g caster sugar

Pour the cream, milk and glycerine into a saucepan. Bring to the boil, remove from the heat and add the meadowsweet. Leave to infuse for 5 minutes.

Strain the liquid through a fine chinois into a clean pan and slowly bring back to the boil. Meanwhile, in a bowl, whisk the egg yolk and sugar together to combine. Pour on the hot infused creamy milk, whisking as you do so.

Return the mixture to the saucepan and cook over a medium-low heat, stirring constantly, until the crème anglaise reaches 82°C (check the temperature with a digital probe).

Pass the cooked crème anglaise through a fine chinois into a container, cover the surface closely with baking parchment to prevent a skin forming and leave to cool.

Once cooled, pour into a Pacojet beaker and freeze overnight.

Before serving, churn the ice cream for 2 hours and place back in the freezer, ready to serve.

Orange tuiles

35g unsalted butter, softened
100g caster sugar
Finely grated zest and juice of
½ orange
35g plain flour

Cream the butter and sugar together in a bowl until pale and smoothly combined. Stir in the orange zest and juice, then add the flour and stir to bring the mixture together.

Wrap the tuile mixture in cling film and rest in the fridge for 1 hour.

Preheat the oven to 190°C/Fan 170°C/Gas 5. Line a baking sheet with a silicone mat.

Spread the tuile mixture very thinly and evenly on the silicone mat to a 3mm thickness. Bake for 15 minutes, then remove and cut into perfect 4cm squares while still hot.

Leave the tuiles to cool and set, then carefully break into the squares.

Frangipane

70g unsalted butter, softened
70g icing sugar
1 medium free-range egg, beaten
70g ground almonds

Using an electric mixer, cream the butter and icing sugar together until light and aerated. Beat in the egg, then fold in the ground almonds using a spatula. Cover and rest in the fridge until needed.

Remove the frangipane from the fridge and bring back to room temperature before using.

To assemble & bake the tart

400g puff pastry (see page 405)
100g frangipane (see opposite)
8 Braeburn apples, peeled and cored
100g icing sugar, for dusting

Line a baking tray with baking parchment. On a lightly floured surface, roll out the puff pastry to a 5mm thickness and prick the surface all over with a fork.

Using a plate as a guide, cut out a 23cm round from the pastry. Using a rolling pin, lift the pastry round onto the prepared tray and place in the fridge to rest for 1 hour.

Meanwhile, using a sharp knife, shape the apples into perfect barrels and remove the cores with an apple corer. Using a mandoline, thinly slice the apple barrels.

Preheat the oven to 240°C/Fan 220°C/Gas 9. Remove the tray from the fridge and spoon the frangipane into the middle of the puff pastry disc. Spread it evenly over the pastry, leaving a 2.5cm clear margin around the edge.

Arrange the apple slices neatly on top, overlapping them slightly, to cover the frangipane completely. Fold the excess pastry around the edge up to form the edge of the tart and crimp it decoratively. Dust liberally all over with icing sugar.

Bake the tart in the hot oven for 10 minutes, then lower the oven setting to 190°C/Fan 170°C/Gas 5 and bake for a further 8 minutes.

Lower the oven setting to 180°C/Fan 160°C/Gas 4. Take the tart out of the oven and invert a baking tray lined with baking parchment over the top, then flip the trays and tart over so that the apple is now face down. Lift off the top tray.

Bake for a further 20 minutes to fully cook the puff pastry and caramelise the apple. Remove from the oven and allow to cool. Once cooled, flip the tart over onto a board.

When ready to serve, slice the tart into portions and warm through in the oven at 205°C/Fan 185°C/Gas 6–7 for 4–5 minutes.

Dust the apple with a little extra icing sugar. Protecting the pastry crust with a metal tray, re-caramelise the apple with a cook's blowtorch.

Serve at once, with an orange tuile on the side, topped with a quenelle of meadowsweet ice cream.

Warm pistachio sponge

with melon sorbet & marzipan

I love Battenberg – both the way that it looks and those magical marzipan flavours! But, of course, in recreating something well-known like this, you have to ask yourself, 'How do I make it unique?' I decided to incorporate pistachio paste (instead of marzipan) because I love the flavour: it's quite intense, it's lovely, and it still gives off an almond-y flavour.

The result was a nice, warm, pistachio cake (as a substitute for the pink squares in a traditional cake), which I serve with a cold sorbet contrast: I can't think of anything better than cool and divine melon sorbet.

The wonderful thing about melon is that it's not overpowering. It has a beautiful fresh, subtle flavour profile. It's also quite almond-y and it sits perfectly alongside the pistachio cake.

Building melon pieces to mimic the chequerboard effect of a classic Battenberg just seemed the obvious thing to do! By compressing the melons, we squeeze out all the juice and intensify the flavour of the fruit, which we essentially cure in the squeezed-out juice so it becomes nice and firm. We then use a gelling agent to glue the melon pieces together.

The dish takes a lot of work, especially piecing everything together. But it's super-striking and it tastes utterly gorgeous.

Melonberg

1 watermelon, skin removed,
deseeded and cut into neat bars,
12 x 12mm and 8cm long
3 Cantaloupe melons, skin removed,
deseeded and cut into neat bars,
12 x 12mm and 8cm long
50g Sosa Gelburger

Put the watermelon and Canteloupe bars into separate vacuum-pack bags and seal under full pressure to compress the melon. Place in the fridge for 8 hours.

Assemble the watermelon and Canteloupe melon bars in alternate layers like a Battenberg, dusting each layer with Gelburger; it should measure 5 x 3cm. Once built, wrap tightly in cling film and place in the fridge to set for 2 hours.

Once set, remove the melonberg from the fridge and square off any imperfect edges. Re-wrap in cling film and refrigerate until needed.

When ready to serve, carefully cut the melonburger into 5mm thin slices.

Pistachio sponge

100g unsalted butter, softened
150g caster sugar
2 medium free-range eggs, beaten
1 medium free-range egg yolk
50g pistachio paste
7g green food colouring
200g self-raising flour

Using an electric mixer, cream the butter and sugar together. Gradually beat in the eggs and extra yolk, then incorporate the pistachio paste and food colouring. Carefully fold in the flour, using a spatula.

Scrape the mixture into a large piping bag and keep in the fridge until needed.

Preheat the oven to 200°C/Fan 180°C/Gas 6. Pipe the mixture into a silicone tray of 8 rectangular mini-loaf cake moulds, dividing it equally. Bake in the oven for 12 minutes or until a skewer inserted into the centre comes out clean.

Leave to cool slightly in the tins for 5 minutes, then turn out onto a wire rack to finish cooling.

Melon sorbet

2 Charentais melons, peeled,
deseeded and roughly chopped
100ml water
100g caster sugar
100g liquid glucose
100g Pro Sorbet

Put the melon flesh into a high-powered jug blender (Vitamix) and blend to a smooth purée; you will need 1 litre. Pass the melon purée through a chinois into a bowl.

Put the water, sugar and liquid glucose into a heavy-based saucepan and heat to dissolve the sugar then bring to the boil. Take off the heat and leave to cool.

Once cooled, mix the sugar syrup with the melon purée, then add the Pro Sorbet and stir to combine.

Pass the mixture through a fine chinois, pour into a Pacojet beaker and freeze overnight.

Before serving, churn the sorbet for 2 hours and place back in the freezer, ready to serve.

Pistachio glass

200g Isomalt
10g pistachio paste
5g green food colouring

Melt the Isomalt in a saucepan and heat to 120°C (check the temperature with a digital probe). Whisk in the pistachio paste and food colouring until evenly combined. Pour onto a silicone mat and spread thinly and evenly with a palette knife.

Leave the pistachio glass to cool and then break into shards.

Pistachio crumb

100g skinned Iranian pistachio nuts

Blitz the pistachios in a spice grinder to a fine powder. Put into an airtight container and set aside until ready to plate up.

Marzipan sticks

100g marzipan

Preheat the oven to 140°C (no fan)/ Gas 1. Line a baking tray with a silicone mat.

Roll out the marzipan on the silicone mat to a 3mm thickness and cut into long, thin strips. Place in the oven for 10 minutes, then remove and leave to cool on the tray.

Pistachio glaze

50g caster sugar
100ml water
20g pistachio paste
3g green food colouring

Put the sugar and water into a small saucepan and heat to dissolve the sugar, then bring to the boil. Remove from the heat and leave to cool.

Once cooled, add the pistachio paste and food colouring and mix until well combined. Set aside until ready to serve.

To assemble & serve

40g skinned Iranian pistachio nuts

When ready to serve, warm the pistachio sponges through in the oven at 205°C/Fan 185°C/Gas 6–7 for 4 minutes.

Square off the top of the pistachio sponges and drizzle with the pistachio glaze. Place a sponge on one side of each serving plate. Top with pistachio nuts and brush with more glaze. Stand the pistachio glass shards on top of the sponge.

Lay a slice of melonberg alongside the sponge. On one end of the melonberg, sprinkle a teaspoonful of the pistachio crumb evenly into a 3cm round cutter (this will stop the sorbet sliding around). Lift off the cutter and place a scoop of melon sorbet on the pistachio crumb disc.

Finish with a marzipan stick and serve at once.

Chocolate ale cake

with salted caramel & muscovado ice cream

——————— SERVES 12 ———————

The Hand & Flowers is a pub. Pubs serve ale. We always needed an ale cake! So that's the idea behind this particular recipe, which grew out of my first book and TV series, *Proper Pub Food*, where I taught people how to cook the simpler pub classics at home.

It was 2011 and there were loads of chocolate and Guinness cake recipes out there; in fact, we use Guinness as well as ale in this cake.

Over time, the dessert has evolved from a relatively typical chocolate cake into a beautiful dark chocolate torte recipe, which I picked up from an amazing pastry chef I worked with at The Capital in Knightsbridge. For The Hand & Flowers version, I reduce Guinness and dark ale, and the new injection of ingredients works perfectly.

From start to finish – to end up with one brown cube of cake on the plate – it takes three days! Cooking the sponge, making the torte, setting the sponge in the torte and then spraying it so that it has a perfect finish.

Some people will look at this and think it's just a lovely chocolate pudding, and that's absolutely fine – but, for me, there's more to it than that. Personally, I just adore the whole process of getting to the finished dish. I love the reality that we have worked hard on it from, say, Thursday to Saturday; that hard graft is what makes each cake perfect.

CHOCOLATE ALE CAKE

Muscovado ice cream

250ml milk
250ml double cream
100g soft dark brown sugar
105g liquid free-range egg yolk
25g glycerine

Pour the milk and cream into a saucepan, add the brown sugar, heat to dissolve the sugar and bring to the boil. Meanwhile, whisk the egg yolk in a bowl. Pour on the hot creamy milk, whisking as you do so.

Return the mixture to the saucepan and cook over a medium-low heat, stirring constantly, until the crème anglaise reaches 82°C (check the temperature with a digital probe).

Pass the cooked crème anglaise through a fine chinois into a container, cover the surface closely with baking parchment to prevent a skin forming and leave to cool.

Once cooled, stir in the glycerine. Pour the crème anglaise into a Pacojet beaker and freeze overnight.

Before serving, churn the ice cream for 2 hours and place back in the freezer, ready to serve.

Frosted pecans

100g pecan nuts
125g caster sugar
30ml water

Preheat the oven to 180°C/Fan 160°C/Gas 4.

Scatter the pecan nuts on a tray lined with baking parchment and toast in the oven for 10–12 minutes until golden brown and fragrant. Let cool.

Put the sugar and water into a heavy-based pan over a medium heat to melt the sugar and continue to heat until the sugar syrup just begins to colour. Add the toasted pecans and stir until the sugar crystallises and covers the nuts.

Tip the frosted pecans onto a baking tray and set aside to cool.

Salted caramel

100g caster sugar
40ml water
3.5g sea salt

Melt the sugar in a heavy-based saucepan over a medium-low heat and cook to a light caramel, 155°C (check the temperature with a digital probe). Immediately and carefully stir in the water and salt.

Allow the salted caramel to cool, then pour into a squeezable plastic bottle ready for serving.

Chocolate ale sponge

350g plain flour
½ tsp baking powder
2 tsp bicarbonate of soda
400ml dark ale
100g cocoa powder
220g unsalted butter, softened
550g soft dark brown sugar
4 large free-range eggs

Preheat the oven to 200°C/Fan 180°C/Gas 6. Line a 33 x 26cm deep baking tin with baking parchment.

Sift the flour, baking powder and bicarbonate of soda together; set aside. In a small bowl, slowly mix the dark ale into the cocoa powder to form a paste.

In a large bowl, cream together the butter and brown sugar until smoothly blended, then beat in the eggs, one at a time. Fold in the cocoa paste and flour mixture alternately, a little at a time.

Spread the mixture in the prepared baking tin and bake for 20 minutes, or until a skewer inserted into the centre comes out clean. Remove the sponge from the tin and place on a wire rack to cool.

Once cooled, cut the chocolate sponge into 2cm cubes and put to one side.

Chocolate ale torte

1 litre dark ale
1 litre Guinness
550g dark chocolate (70% cocoa solids), in pieces
75g liquid free-range egg yolk
50g caster sugar
675ml double cream
100g liquid glucose
Chocolate ale sponge cubes (see left)

In a large saucepan, bring the ale and Guinness to the boil and simmer to reduce to 200ml. Set aside to cool.

Melt the chocolate in a heatproof bowl over a bain-marie.

Over a second bain-marie, whisk the egg yolk and sugar together to make a pale, thick sabayon.

In a large saucepan, gently warm 350ml of the cream with the liquid glucose and ale reduction, stirring to combine. Transfer to a large bowl and stir in the melted chocolate.

Whip the remaining 325ml cream in a separate bowl until soft peaks form. Carefully fold the sabayon into the chocolate and ale mixture, then fold in the whipped cream until smoothly combined.

Line a tray with acetate and place 12 metal 4cm square moulds on the tray. Flood the base of each mould with the torte mixture, then press in the diced ale cake. Fill with the torte mixture and level off with a palette knife. Place in the fridge to set for 6 hours. (You will have more torte mix than you need but you can freeze the rest for another occasion.)

To finish the cakes

400g dark chocolate (70% cocoa solids), in pieces, melted
400ml cocoa butter, melted

Carefully turn the square chocolate cakes over, so the smooth-edged base is now uppermost. Using an apple corer, cut a hole in the centre of each cake, down to the sponge layer (this will hold the salted caramel later). Return to the fridge for 30 minutes.

Take the cakes from the fridge and carefully warm the sides of the metal moulds using a cook's blowtorch, to release the cakes from them. Remove the moulds to leave perfectly square ale cakes. Place them in the freezer to fully firm up.

Mix the melted dark chocolate and cocoa butter together in a bowl, then pour into a chocolate spray gun.

Set up a chocolate spray box and lay the frozen cakes on a surface lined with cling film inside. Spray the cakes evenly all over, then carefully lift them, using a palette knife, onto a tray. Place in the fridge until needed.

Remove the cakes from the fridge an hour before serving to allow them to come up to room temperature.

Sablé paste

400g unsalted butter
100g caster sugar
4g sea salt
500g plain flour
120g ground almonds

Preheat the oven to 195°C/Fan 175°C/Gas 5. Line a baking tray with a silicone mat.

Using an electric mixer, cream together the butter and sugar until pale. Add the salt, flour and ground almonds and mix to combine.

Roll out the sablé paste on the silicone mat to a 1cm thickness and bake for 20 minutes. Remove from the oven and leave to cool.

Once cool, chop the sablé mixture into a fine crumb.

Sablé tuiles

200g caster sugar
200g chopped sablé paste
(see left)

Melt the sugar in a heavy-based saucepan over a low heat, then bring to the boil and continue to cook the sugar syrup until it forms a golden caramel. Add the chopped sablé paste and cook, stirring, for a minute.

Pour the sablé caramel onto a silicone mat and leave to cool slightly.

When it is cool enough, roll out to a thin sheet. While still warm, press a 4cm cutter into the sheet make sablé discs. Leave until cooled and set then lift the sablé tuiles off the mat.

To serve

Place a dot of caramel in the centre of each plate and position a sablé disc on top (the caramel will stop the disc sliding about). Place the cake directly on to the disc and then fill the hole in the top with salted caramel. Top with a rocher of muscovado ice cream and finish with a frosted pecan.

Apple crumble soufflé

with Cox's apple sorbet & crème anglaise

There's something special about desserts like soufflés because, quite often, they're the things that people won't make at home. I understand that: ordering and eating something you don't cook at home makes it seem super-indulgent.

We've had a soufflé on the menu at The Hand & Flowers pretty much since we moved into the new kitchen, about two years after we opened. I've always worked in restaurants that had a soufflé on the menu but they were difficult to do in our original gas oven, which was heated from the bottom. Suddenly, there was this lovely Rational convection oven staring at me, begging for one to be cooked in it! So, I thought, 'let's get a soufflé on!'

There is a certain skill set involved in making a soufflé. And each soufflé is different, depending on its central ingredient. Different fruits have different acidity levels, which govern how they work with the egg white, for instance, or with sugar. You need to understand the science of how to get a perfect soufflé; what ingredients need, or bring to it more stability. It's crucial, for example, that you fold the fruit panade and crème pâtissière together evenly to form the base of the soufflé, before blending in the meringue mix and the diced apple.

Obviously, being The Hand & Flowers and a pub, we wanted our soufflés to be something that reflects what we're about; familiar, but with a surprise element that lifts them to a higher level. So, the first one was always going to be an apple soufflé – topped with crumble, and served with an apple sorbet for good measure. It delivers the flavours that everyone knows and loves, with a layer or two of sophistication.

Cox's apple sorbet

*1 litre cloudy Cox's apple juice
  (we use Copella)*
300ml water
200g caster sugar
100g liquid glucose

Pour the apple juice into a bowl. Put the water, sugar and liquid glucose into a saucepan, heat to dissolve the sugar and bring to the boil.

Whisk the sugar syrup into the apple juice, then pass through a fine chinois. Pour the mixture into Pacojet beakers and freeze overnight.

Before serving, churn the sorbet for 2 hours and place back in the freezer, ready to serve.

Crumble mix

150g plain flour
125g caster sugar
65g unsalted butter, diced

Preheat the oven to 180°C/Fan 160°C/Gas 4.

Combine the flour and sugar in a large bowl and rub in the butter until the mixture resembles crumbs.

Scatter the crumble on a baking tray and bake in the oven for about 15 minutes until golden, stirring every 5 minutes until golden.

Allow to cool, then blitz the crumble briefly in a blender to fairly fine, even crumbs. Set aside until ready to assemble.

Apple panade

500ml Cox's apple purée (Boiron)
75g caster sugar
*20g cornflour, mixed to a paste
  with 2 tbsp cold water*

In a bowl, whisk the apple purée and sugar together, then transfer to a saucepan and heat to dissolve the sugar. Continue to cook over a medium heat until the mixture has reduced by half.

Stir in the cornflour paste and cook, stirring constantly, over a high heat for 5–8 minutes until thickened.

Once thickened, transfer the apple mixture to a high-powered jug blender (Vitamix) and blend thoroughly. Pass through a fine sieve into a bowl and leave to cool.

Crème pâtissière

300ml whole milk
½ vanilla pod, split and seeds scraped
2 medium free-range eggs
60g caster sugar
25g plain flour, sifted
10g cornflour

Pour the milk into a heavy-based saucepan, add the vanilla pod and seeds, and slowly bring to the boil.

Meanwhile, whisk the eggs and sugar together in a bowl until smoothly combined, then whisk in the flour, followed by the cornflour.

Put the hot milk onto the whisked mixture, whisking as you do so to keep the mixture smooth. Return the mixture to the pan and cook, stirring, over a medium-high heat for 5–8 minutes until thickened.

Pass the crème pâtissière through a fine chinois into a bowl. Cover the surface closely with baking parchment to prevent a skin forming and allow to cool.

Crème anglaise

250ml whole milk
250ml double cream
120ml liquid free-range egg yolk
120g caster sugar

Pour the milk and cream into a heavy-based saucepan and bring to the boil.

Meanwhile, whisk the egg yolk and sugar together in a bowl to combine. Pour on the hot creamy milk mix, whisking as you do so.

Return the mixture to the saucepan and cook over a medium-low heat, stirring constantly, until the crème anglaise reaches 82°C (check the temperature with a digital probe).

Pass the cooked crème anglaise through a fine chinois into a container, cover the surface closely with baking parchment to prevent a skin forming and set aside to cool.

Heat the crème anglaise through gently before serving.

Apple crumble soufflé

40g unsalted butter, melted, for greasing
40g caster sugar, plus extra for dusting
160g apple panade (see opposite)
120g crème pâtissière (see left)
370g free-range liquid egg white
4 tbsp crumble mix (see opposite)

Preheat the oven to 205°C/Fan 185°C/Gas 6–7. Brush the base and sides of 8 individual copper pans or individual soufflé dishes, 250ml capacity, with melted butter and place in the fridge to set. Butter the dishes again, then dust with caster sugar, shaking out any excess. Return to the fridge.

Using a spatula, fold the apple panade and crème pâtissière together until evenly combined to make the soufflé base.

In a large, clean bowl, whisk the egg white to stiff peaks, then gradually whisk in the 40g sugar to make a glossy meringue.

Using a spatula, gently fold half of the meringue mixture into the soufflé base, then carefully fold in the rest of the meringue.

Spoon the mixture into the buttered and sugared moulds, sprinkle the crumble mix evenly on top of the soufflés and bake in the oven for 10 minutes until well risen and light golden.

Serve with a jug of warm crème anglaise and a scoop of Cox's apple sorbet in a bowl on the side.

Tonka bean panna cotta

with poached rhubarb & ginger wine jelly

SERVES 6

If you've not had it before, tonka bean tastes like a cross between vanilla and coffee and it's just lovely. It's a great substitute for vanilla in creamy, smooth panna cotta.

It's deceptively simple, panna cotta, but you have to get it absolutely right. You have to do all its simple elements perfectly: for that you need exactly the right amount of cream, milk, gelatine, sugar and infusion of flavour (in this case, tonka bean). If you get all that spot on, you're home and dry!

Panna cotta is normally infused with vanilla, but the problem with that is, unless you set the panna cotta slowly over ice, to suspend the vanilla, it ends up sinking to the bottom. Using tonka bean is a way of getting a beautiful vanilla flavour without that risk.

You do have to watch how the panna cotta sets, though. If it is set too hard, it's like something that has only just been defrosted; if it's too loose, it's soupy. You have to aim for that incredible texture that's firm enough but wobbly, too.

To make the panna cotta a bit special, we have created several layers of texture and flavour. Crunchy meringue and honeycomb for a snap of sweetness, ginger wine jelly and a sorbet for acidity and flavour-depth.

And, of course, we've got rhubarb to cut through the rich creaminess of the panna cotta. Its sharpness works beautifully. You can change the fruit seasonally; strawberries or cherries are perfect. If you think about it, you're just putting fruit and cream (in a posh, Italian way) on the plate!

Tonka bean panna cotta

425ml double cream
140ml whole milk
55g caster sugar
6g tonka beans, chopped
1¼ sheets of bronze leaf gelatine

Pour the cream and milk into a saucepan and add the sugar and tonka beans. Heat to dissolve the sugar and slowly bring to the boil. Remove from the heat and leave to infuse for 30 minutes.

Meanwhile, soak the gelatine in a shallow dish of cold water to soften for 5–10 minutes.

Bring the infused creamy milk back to a low simmer, then remove from the heat. Squeeze the gelatine to remove the excess water, then add it to the creamy milk, stirring until fully melted.

Pass the mixture through a fine chinois into a container and place in the fridge for about 4 hours to set.

Once set, gently warm the mixture to a pourable consistency, but not completely liquid (this will prevent a skin forming on the panna cottas).

Pour the panna cotta mix into individual dishes and carefully cover the dishes with cling film. Place back in the fridge to set.

Rhubarb purée

100g caster sugar
100ml water
500g rhubarb stalks
30ml grenadine

Heat the sugar and water in a saucepan over a medium heat to dissolve the sugar and bring to the boil. Add the rhubarb and grenadine and bring back to a simmer. Cook gently for 15 minutes until soft.

Transfer the rhubarb and syrup to a jug blender and blitz until smooth. Pass through a fine chinois into a bowl, cover and place in the fridge to chill.

Rhubarb sorbet

100ml water
100g liquid glucose
50g caster sugar
50g dextrose
500ml rhubarb purée (see above)
80g Pro Sorbet

Put the water, liquid glucose and caster sugar into a saucepan, heat to dissolve the sugar and bring to the boil. Remove from the heat and add the dextrose, rhubarb purée and Pro Sorbet. Stir to combine and then leave to cool.

Pour the mixture into a Pacojet beaker and freeze overnight.

Before serving, churn the sorbet for 2 hours and place back in the freezer, ready to serve.

Ginger meringues

30ml water
12g liquid glucose
150g caster sugar
75g free-range egg white
½ tsp ground ginger

Put the water, liquid glucose and sugar into a heavy-based pan, heat to dissolve the sugar and bring to the boil. Continue to cook until the syrup reaches 119°C (use a digital probe to check the temperature).

Meanwhile, using an electric mixer or hand-held electric whisk, whisk the egg white until starting to form soft peaks.

As soon as the sugar syrup reaches 119°C, pour it onto the egg white, continuing to whisk as you do. Turn the mixer speed up to high and continue to whisk until the cooked meringue is cooled. Whisk in the ground ginger.

Spoon the meringue into a piping bag fitted with a 1cm plain nozzle. Pipe small drop meringues onto a dehydrator tray lined with cling film. Place in the dehydrator to dry for about 5 hours.

Once dry, remove the meringues from the tray and store in an airtight container, with silica gel to keep them crisp and dry.

Ginger wine jelly

1¼ sheets of bronze leaf gelatine
140ml Stone's ginger wine

Soak the gelatine in a dish of cold water to soften for 5–10 minutes.

Bring 40ml of the ginger wine to the boil in a pan, then take off the heat. Squeeze the gelatine to remove the excess water, then add it to the hot ginger wine and stir until melted. Stir in the rest of the ginger wine.

Pass through a fine chinois into a shallow container and allow to cool. Cover and chill for 2 hours to set.

Once set, dice the ginger jelly into 1cm cubes; you need 5 per portion.

Honeycomb

165g caster sugar
25g runny honey
65g liquid glucose
30ml water
7g bicarbonate of soda

Line a small baking tray with baking parchment. Put the sugar, honey, glucose and water into a heavy-based pan, heat gently to dissolve the sugar and then bring to the boil. Cook to a pale caramel (registering 151°C on a digital probe). Immediately take of the heat and whisk in the bicarbonate of soda. Pour onto the prepared tray and leave to cool and harden.

Break the honeycomb into chunks before serving.

Poached rhubarb

100g caster sugar
250ml water
25ml grenadine
½ vanilla pod
150g rhubarb stalks, trimmed

Put the sugar, water, grenadine and vanilla pod into a large saucepan, heat to dissolve the sugar and bring to the boil.

Meanwhile, cut the sticks of rhubarb into shorter lengths that will comfortably fit into the saucepan.

Once the sugar syrup reaches the boil, add the rhubarb, bring back to a simmer and remove from the heat. Cover the pan with a tight-fitting lid and leave the rhubarb to cook in the residual heat and cool down.

Once cooled, drain the rhubarb, reserving the liquor, and cut into 2cm slices. Place in a bowl and pour on enough of the reserved poaching liquor to cover. Set aside.

To assemble & serve

Sprigs of atsina cress, to finish

Arrange the poached rhubarb, ginger wine jelly cubes and honeycomb pieces on the panna cotta and position the ginger meringues around the edge of the dish.

Place a rocher of rhubarb sorbet in the centre and finish with a few sprigs of atsina cress.

Vanilla crème brûlée

Vanilla crème brûlée is one of those classic desserts that everyone knows about and loves. And it's been on the menu at The Hand & Flowers right from the very start.

As far as I'm concerned, the key to a properly perfect brûlée is to have three distinct flavours that you taste – vanilla, eggs and caramel – so that it's not just a sweet, creamy dessert. And I've got Alex Bentley to thank for teaching me that. This is 100% the brûlée recipe I was cooking as a young chef at Monsieur Max, where he was head chef.

I think Alex was given or inherited the recipe from Max Renzland, the restaurant's chef-patron. Apparently, it was an old Elizabeth David recipe; she must have learnt it during her travels in France, so goodness knows how old it really is. Until Alex taught this recipe to me, most crème brûlée recipes I'd come across were sweet and made only with egg yolks. This one uses whole eggs and just a small amount of sugar. It was a game changer for me. I suddenly knew how to make a magical crème brûlée.

The technique that really brings the dessert to life is its caramelisation on top. Instead of just melting the sugar, Alex taught me to caramelise it really heavily. At Monsieur Max, customers sometimes complained that the sugar was burnt, but that's the whole point. It's supposed to be; the caramelisation makes it taste toasty and nutty. You end up with a smooth, vanilla dessert that's creamy with a bittersweet crunchy topping.

We match it at The Hand & Flowers with an Innis & Gunn craft beer rather than a dessert wine. The beer's aged in old whiskey barrels so it has this really rich toffee, creamy flavour, which harmonises beautifully with the crème brûlée.

Vanilla crème

750ml double cream
1 vanilla pod
4 medium free-range eggs
30g caster sugar

Put the cream and vanilla pod into a heavy-based saucepan and bring to the boil over a medium heat. Remove from the heat and leave to infuse for 30 minutes.

Beat the eggs and sugar together in a bowl until smoothly blended. Bring the vanilla-infused cream back to the boil, then slowly pour onto the beaten egg mixture, whisking as you do so to combine.

Pour the mixture back into the pan and cook, stirring constantly, over a medium-low heat until the custard thickens and reaches 88°C (check the temperature with a digital probe). Immediately remove from the heat and pass through a fine chinois into a clean bowl.

Press a layer of cling film onto the surface to prevent a skin forming and leave to cool for 20 minutes or until the custard is at room temperature.

Pour the custard into a high-powered jug blender (Vitamix) and blitz for 30 seconds; this will lighten it slightly.

Now pour the custard into crème brûlée dishes or ramekins, dividing it equally (about 125ml per dish). Cover each dish with cling film, leaving a small gap on one side, to allow any moisture to evaporate. Stand the dishes on a tray and place in the fridge to set; this will take about 3 hours.

Caramel glaze

200g demerara sugar

When ready to serve, sprinkle a generous, even layer of demerara sugar over the surface of each set custard. Wipe the edge of the dish with a clean cloth.

Using a cook's blowtorch, caramelise the sugar, starting from the edges and working towards the centre. Take the caramel to a dark brown – this dish is all about balancing the rich creamy egg custard with the slightly bitter caramel flavour.

Leave to cool for about 5 minutes before serving.

Sweet malt gâteau

with malted milk ice cream, tuiles & butterscotch sauce

—————— SERVES 8 ——————

I love the flavour of malt extract; Maltesers; malted milk ice cream. Delicious. The stickiness that malt gives you is utterly unique and this recipe came about because I wanted that in a drop-dead-gorgeous dessert.

It began with a trip to our local Rebellion brewery in Marlow when I came away with some malt (of course I did!) and we set about thinking how to use it to make a really rich, gooey, sticky, lovely malt cake: a little bit of a play on Soreen Original Malt Loaf, if you like.

That's when I thought of my good friend, chef Paul Ainsworth (of No 6 in Padstow), and a pistachio cake he did on Great British Menu made with olive oil. We experimented with Paul's recipe, using oils and brioche breadcrumbs, plus the malt extract and malted barley from the brewery.

We ended up with a beautiful, gooey cake, which we then refined and combined with gorgeous delights like butterscotch sauce, the amazing Malteser-like malted milk ice cream; and a tuile filled with crème fraîche shot through with lemon (almost like a brandy snap).

I wanted to give a nod to the brewing industry, too, so as a final touch we did a simple yeast tuile and added a few toasted, frosted malts made with the chocolate malts from the brewery process. Mission accomplished.

Sweet malt gâteau

75g brewer's malted barley grains,
   50% chocolate malt, 50% golden
   malt (we get ours from the
   Rebellion brewery)
50g sesame oil
100g rapeseed oil
4 medium free-range eggs
200g caster sugar
400g malt extract
90g brioche crumbs
50g ground almonds
160g plain flour
1 tsp baking powder

Preheat the oven to 160°C/Fan 140°C/Gas 3. Line a 33 x 26cm deep baking tin with baking parchment.

Blitz the malted barley grains in a spice grinder, to break them down (but not to a fine powder).

Using an electric mixer, whisk the sesame and rapeseed oils together with the eggs to emulsify. Add the sugar, malt extract, blitzed malts, brioche crumbs and ground almonds and mix well.

Sift the flour and baking powder together over the mixture and carefully fold in, using a spatula, until smoothly combined. Spread the mixture evenly in the tin and bake in the oven for 1 hour.

Leave in the tin for 5 minutes, then turn the cake out and place on a wire rack to cool.

Malted milk ice cream

190ml milk
190ml double cream
6 medium free-range egg yolks
40g caster sugar
75g malt extract

Pour the milk and cream into a saucepan and bring to the boil.

Meanwhile, whisk the egg yolks, sugar and malt extract together in a bowl to combine. Pour on the hot creamy milk, whisking as you do so.

Return the mixture to the saucepan and cook over a medium-low heat, stirring constantly, until the crème anglaise reaches 82°C (check the temperature with a digital probe).

Pass the cooked crème anglaise through a fine chinois into a container, cover the surface closely with baking parchment to prevent a skin forming and leave to cool.

Once cooled, pour into a Pacojet beaker and freeze overnight.

Before serving, churn the ice cream for 2 hours and place back in the freezer, ready to serve.

Butterscotch sauce

250g caster sugar
75ml water
75g unsalted butter, diced
1 vanilla pod, split and seeds scraped

Put the sugar and water into a heavy-based pan over a medium-low heat to dissolve the sugar and bring to the boil. Cook to a dark golden caramel, then gradually whisk in the butter and add the vanilla pod and seeds. Set aside to cool and infuse.

Pass the sauce through a fine chinois before serving to remove the vanilla.

Yeast tuiles

300g sweetened condensed milk
30g plain flour
30g dark muscovado sugar
30g fresh yeast

In a bowl, whisk the condensed milk and flour together until smoothly combined. Cover and leave to rest for 3 hours.

Preheat the oven to 160°C (no fan)/ Gas 3. Line a baking sheet with a silicone mat.

Spread the mixture evenly on the silicone mat and scatter the brown sugar evenly over the surface. Using a Microplane, finely grate the yeast on top, distributing it evenly.

Bake in the oven for 10 minutes until golden. Leave to cool, then break into random pieces.

Orange tuiles

140g unsalted butter, softened
400g caster sugar
Finely grated zest and juice
of 2 oranges
140g plain flour

Cream the butter and sugar together in a bowl until pale and smoothly combined. Stir in the orange zest and juice, then add the flour and stir to bring the mixture together. Wrap in cling film and rest in the fridge for 2 hours.

Preheat the oven to 190°C/Fan 170°C/Gas 5. Line a baking sheet with a silicone mat.

Spread the tuile mixture very thinly and evenly on the silicone mat to a 3mm thickness. Bake for 15 minutes until dark golden.

Remove from the oven and, while still warm, cut the tuile sheet into 12 x 8cm rectangles (long and wide enough to wrap around a cannoli tube). Immediately roll each one around a cannoli tube to make a cylindrical tuile. Leave to set, then carefully slide the tuile off the tube.

Store the tuiles in a shallow airtight container, with a little silica gel to keep them dry and crisp.

Malt tuiles

25g brewer's malted barley grains,
50% chocolate malt, 50% golden
malt
100g fondant icing sugar
65g liquid glucose

Blitz the barley grains in a spice grinder, to break them down (but not to a fine powder).

Heat the fondant icing sugar and liquid glucose in a medium pan to 160°C (use a digital probe to check the temperature). Remove from the heat and stir in the blitzed malts.

Spread out as thinly as possible on a silicone mat (to about a 2mm thickness). Let cool slightly. While the tuile sheet is still warm, break into random shapes. Leave to cool.

Frosted malts

100g caster sugar
25ml water
50g chocolate malts

Put the sugar and water into a small heavy-based pan over a medium-low heat to dissolve the sugar and bring to the boil. Cook until the sugar syrup reaches 150°C (use a digital probe to check the temperature).

Over a medium heat, stir in the malts and agitate to crystallise the sugar on them. Once a white crust forms on the malts, remove from the heat and pour the mixture onto a silicone mat. Leave to cool.

Lemon crème fraîche

100g thick crème fraîche
Finely grated zest of 1 lemon

Whip the crème fraîche and lemon zest together in a bowl. Spoon into a piping bag and keep in the fridge until ready to serve.

To assemble & serve

Square off the edges of the cake and portion into 8 equal squares. Place on a baking tray and warm though in the oven at 205°C/Fan 185°C/Gas 6–7 for 5 minutes.

Meanwhile, warm the butterscotch sauce. Pipe the lemon crème fraîche into the tuile tubes to fill them.

Remove the cake from the oven and place a portion on each serving plate. Pour on some butterscotch sauce and balance a crème fraîche filled tuile at one end with a yeast tuile.

Place a scoop of malted milk ice cream on top of the cake and finish with frosted malts and a malt tuile. Serve at once.

Choux à la crème

I love the old French classics: things like crème brûlée, parfait, soufflés and choux buns – in all guises. And this one reminds me of childhood Saturdays in town with my mum, going past the bakers and getting a crème choux bun as a treat. It seems like everyone is doing choux buns now, but we introduced them a long time ago at The Hand & Flowers.

We are famous in the UK for our indulgent comfort desserts, like sticky toffee, bread and butter, and steamed sponge puddings. But, because of my training, I'm more inclined to look to the French pastry tradition if I want to make an extra special dessert. I mean, when you get a perfect Paris-Brest (a classic praline-filled choux gâteau) or a flawless chocolate éclair it's just amazing.

This dessert evolved because I liked the idea of creating a special choux bun. If you get that choux pastry right, you can then concentrate on what you're going to fill it with. Here, it's rhubarb that plays a starring role alongside ginger, and this layering of flavour and texture elevates the dessert into something spectacular.

Sablé

100g unsalted butter
120g plain flour
120g demerara sugar

Put all of the ingredients into an electric mixer fitted with the paddle attachment and mix to combine and form a smooth dough; this will take about 3 minutes.

Place the dough in a large vacuum-pack bag (30 x 40cm) and seal the bag 3cm from the top. Roll the sablé paste evenly in the bag, right to the edges. Place in the freezer until firm.

Once frozen, remove the pastry from the bags and cut out 8–10 discs, 6cm in diameter, to top off the pre-baked choux pastry buns.

If you're not using the sablé discs straight away, keep them frozen, interleaved with baking parchment.

Choux buns

85ml milk
85ml water
75g unsalted butter
110g plain flour
3g sea salt
10g caster sugar
160g free-range beaten eggs
    (about 3 medium)

Put the milk, water and butter into a saucepan and heat gently until the butter is melted. Add the flour, salt and sugar and beat thoroughly to make a smooth, glossy dough.

Remove from the heat and transfer the choux paste to a mixer fitted with the paddle attachment. Beat on a low speed until the mixture is just warm. Now, with the motor running, add the beaten eggs a little at a time, mixing until fully incorporated. Spoon into a large piping bag.

Preheat the oven to 250°C/Fan 230°C speed 3/Gas 9. Line a sturdy baking sheet with a silicone mat. Snip the end off the piping bag and pipe 60g choux paste rounds on to the silicone mat, spacing them well apart to allow space for them to expand.

Top each choux bun with a sablé. Put the tray in the oven, close the door, turn off the oven and leave to cook in the residual heat for 10 minutes.

Now turn the oven on to 200°C/Fan 180°C/Gas 6 and bake for another 10 minutes.

Then lower the oven setting to 180°C/Fan 160°C/Gas 4 and bake for a further 10 minutes.

Lower the oven setting to 150°C/Fan 130°C/Gas 2 and bake for a final 10 minutes. Remove from the oven.

Place the choux buns on a wire rack to cool. Once cooled, slice off and discard the bottom of the choux buns. If necessary, scoop out some of the inner choux to make space for the filling.

Italian meringue

65ml water
25g liquid glucose
300g caster sugar
150g free-range liquid egg white

Put the water, liquid glucose and sugar into a heavy-based pan, heat to dissolve the sugar and bring to the boil. Continue to cook steadily until the sugar syrup reaches 119°C (use a digital probe to check the temperature).

Meanwhile, using an electric mixer or hand-held electric whisk, whisk the egg white until starting to form soft peaks.

As soon as the sugar syrup reaches 119°C, pour it onto the egg white, continuing to whisk as you do. Turn the mixer speed up to high and continue to whisk until the cooked meringue is cooled.

Crème chiboust

1 quantity Italian meringue
  (see left)
270g thick crème fraîche

Whisk the meringue and crème fraîche together in a bowl until smoothly combined.

Spoon into a large piping bag fitted with a vermicelli nozzle (or you could use a fluted nozzle) and place in the fridge until needed.

Rhubarb purée

100g caster sugar
100ml water
500g rhubarb stalks
30ml grenadine

Put the sugar and water into a medium saucepan over a medium heat to dissolve the sugar and bring to the boil.

Add the rhubarb and grenadine and bring back to a simmer. Cook gently for 15 minutes until soft.

Transfer the rhubarb and syrup to a jug blender and blitz until smooth. Pass the rhubarb purée through a fine chinois into a bowl, then cover and chill.

Rhubarb sorbet

100ml water
100g liquid glucose
50g caster sugar
50g dextrose
500ml rhubarb purée (see page 343)
80g Pro Sorbet

Put the water, liquid glucose and caster sugar into a saucepan, heat to dissolve the sugar and bring to the boil. Remove from the heat and add the dextrose, rhubarb purée and Pro Sorbet. Stir to combine and leave to cool.

Pour the mixture into a Pacojet beaker and freeze overnight.

Before serving, churn the sorbet for 2 hours and place back in the freezer, ready to serve.

Poached rhubarb

8 forced Yorkshire pink
  rhubarb stalks
600ml water
300g caster sugar
Pared zest of 1 lemon
1 vanilla pod, split and seeds scraped
4 star anise
½ cinnamon stick

Cut the rhubarb into 3cm lengths and place in a bowl.

Put the water, sugar, lemon zest, vanilla pod and seeds, star anise and cinnamon into a saucepan, heat to dissolve the sugar and then bring to the boil.

Pour the hot liquor and flavourings over the rhubarb and cover with cling film.

Leave to cook in the residual heat and cool down for 30 minutes; the rhubarb should retain a slight bite.

Once cooled, remove the rhubarb from the syrup with a slotted spoon and transfer to a bowl; cover and reserve for serving. Strain the poaching syrup and reserve (for the rhubarb jelly and rhubarb gel).

Rhubarb crisps

2 rhubarb stalks
50g icing sugar, sifted

Cut the rhubarb into small batons and finely slice these on a mandoline.

Lay the rhubarb slices out on a dehydrator tray and dust with icing sugar. Dry in the dehydrator at 80°C for 2 hours, or until crisp with no colour. Remove and leave to cool.

Once cooled and brittle, store the rhubarb crisps in an airtight container with silica gel in the bottom to help keep them crisp.

Vanilla parfait

165ml whole milk
110g caster sugar
40g liquid free-range egg yolk
25g custard powder
120g unsalted butter, in pieces,
softened
20ml water
15g liquid glucose
35g free-range liquid egg white

First make a crème pâtissière. Put the milk and 35g of the sugar into a medium heavy-based saucepan, heat to dissolve the sugar and slowly bring to the boil. Meanwhile, whisk the egg yolk and custard powder together in a bowl until smoothly combined.

Put the hot milk onto the whisked mixture, whisking as you do so to keep the mixture smooth. Return the mixture to the pan and cook, stirring, over a medium-high heat for 5–8 minutes until thickened.

Remove from the heat and stir in 5g of the butter. Cover the surface closely with baking parchment to prevent a skin from forming and set aside to cool.

Now make an Italian meringue. Put the water, liquid glucose and remaining 75g sugar into a heavy-based pan, heat to dissolve the sugar and bring to the boil. Continue to cook until the sugar syrup reaches 119°C (use a digital probe to check the temperature).

Meanwhile, using an electric mixer or hand-held electric whisk, whisk the egg white until starting to form soft peaks. As soon as the sugar syrup reaches 119°C, pour it onto the egg white, continuing to whisk as you do.

While the meringue is still warm and with the motor running, start to feed the meringue with the remaining 115g butter, a little at a time. The mixture may split a little but it will come back together. Continue until all the butter is incorporated.

Line a chilled marble slab with baking parchment. Fold the crème pâtissière and Italian meringue together until evenly combined and then spread evenly on the lined marble to a 1cm thickness. Freeze until firm.

Once frozen, cut the parfait into 6cm discs. Keep in the freezer until ready to assemble.

Rhubarb jelly

2 sheets of bronze leaf gelatine
250ml reserved rhubarb poaching
syrup (see opposite)
2.5g agar agar

Soak the gelatine in a dish of cold water to soften for 5–10 minutes.

Meanwhile, pour the rhubarb poaching syrup into a saucepan. Sprinkle in the agar agar and slowly bring to the boil, then take off the heat. Squeeze out the excess water from the gelatine, then add it to the hot syrup, stirring until fully melted.

Pass the rhubarb liquid through a fine chinois into a warm jug and flood the base of the serving plates. Chill in the fridge to set the jelly.

Rhubarb fluid gel

200ml reserved rhubarb poaching
 liquor (see page 344)
2g agar agar
10g preserved stem ginger in syrup,
 sliced, plus 1–2 tsp syrup from
 the jar

Pour the rhubarb poaching liquor
and agar agar into a Thermomix,
heat to 100°C and hold at that
temperature for 2 minutes. Pour into
a bowl and allow to cool and set.

Once firm, return the rhubarb gel
to the blender, add the stem ginger
and blend until smooth. Transfer
to a piping bag or squeezable plastic
bottle, ready for serving.

Ginger parkin discs & crumb

80g oats
100g self-raising flour
10g ground ginger
1 tsp ground nutmeg
1 tsp ground mixed spice
175g golden syrup
100g soft dark brown sugar
50g black treacle
100g unsalted butter, in pieces,
 softened
1 medium free-range egg
10ml whole milk

Preheat the oven to 160°C/Fan
140°C/Gas 3. Line a 33 x 26cm deep
baking tin with baking parchment.
Toast the oats in a dry frying pan
over a medium heat for 1–2 minutes
until golden. Tip onto a plate and
allow to cool.

Put the flour, oats and spices into
a mixer fitted with the paddle
attachment and mix briefly. Add the
golden syrup, brown sugar, black
treacle and butter, and mix well.

In a jug, beat the egg with the milk,
then add to the cake mixture and
mix until evenly combined.

Pour the mixture into the prepared
tin and bake for 1 hour or until
a skewer inserted into the centre
comes out clean.

Remove the sponge from the tin and
place on a wire rack to cool. Cut into
6cm discs and set aside; reserve the
trimmings.

For the crumb, slice the trimmings
and spread out on a dehydrator tray.
Place in the dehydrator at 80°C for
3 hours until crisp. Allow to cool,
then blitz the sponge trimmings to
a fine powder in a blender.

Ginger tuiles

*100g preserved stem ginger in syrup,
    drained*
65g unsalted butter
165g icing sugar
55g plain flour

Blitz the stem ginger in a blender
to a purée.

Cream the butter and icing sugar
together in a bowl until pale and
smoothly combined. Stir in the
ginger, then add the flour and stir
to bring the mixture together.

Wrap the tuile mixture in cling film
and rest in the fridge for 1 hour.

Preheat the oven to 200°C/Fan
180°C/Gas 6. Line a baking sheet
with a silicone mat.

Spread the tuile mixture very thinly
and evenly on the silicone mat to a
3mm thickness, using a palette knife.
Bake for 10 minutes until golden,
then remove and cut into discs,
6cm in diameter, while still hot.
Leave the tuiles to cool and set.

To assemble & serve

Finely dice the poached rhubarb; you
need about 8 tbsp. Mix with a little
of the rhubarb gel to bind and make
a compote.

For the base, place a vanilla parfait
disc on each disc of parkin. Cover
with a ginger tuile and then place a
tight ball of rhubarb sorbet on top.

Spoon the rhubarb compote into the
choux buns, then carefully position
over the vanilla parfait assembly.

Place the filled choux on a tray and
pipe over fine strands of the crème
chiboust. Drizzle with rhubarb gel
and sprinkle with the ginger parkin
crumb. Finish with rhubarb crisps,
pressing them into the crème.

Using a stepped palette knife,
carefully lift each choux assembly
and place in the centre of a jellied
plate. Serve at once.

White chocolate parfait

with poached cherries & orange nougat

I owe pastry chef and chocolatier Damian Allsop a debt of gratitude for showing me that you can grill white chocolate (yes, you can!) and providing me with a recipe that I could adapt and transform into this particular dessert.

In 2007, Damian spent some time with us in the kitchen at The Hand & Flowers and that was instrumental in giving the brigade and me a deeper understanding of pâtisserie. So, his knowledge really helped us develop the dessert menu and take the restaurant forward.

Prior to working with Damian, I never knew that you could blister white chocolate under the grill like toasted marshmallows. Amazingly, it doesn't split; it just gets a lovely toasted crust on it.

Once we knew that we could caramelise white chocolate, we were brave enough to try cooking it in an oven. And that worked! The sugars in the chocolate cook quite slowly and you end up with this amazing Caramac-like flavour.

After that it seemed natural to put the blistered chocolate into a parfait and play around with it, trying out some additional ingredients. Cherries, when they're in season, are fantastic – so we added poached black cherries, which sit between layers of chewy, orange nougat squares. Delicious.

Caramelised white chocolate parfait

250g white chocolate
90g liquid free-range egg yolk
25g dextrose
95ml water
200ml double cream
75ml whole milk
A pinch of sea salt

Preheat the oven to 120°C/Fan 110°C/Gas ½. Place the white chocolate in a baking dish and bake in the oven for 1 hour until golden, whisking every 10 minutes, with a spatula. Spoon the caramelised chocolate into a container and leave to cool and set.

Put the egg yolk, dextrose and water into a large heatproof bowl over a simmering bain-marie and whisk until thick and glossy. Remove the bowl from the bain-marie.

Transfer the set caramelised white chocolate to a high-powered food processor (Robot Coupe) and blitz until smooth.

In a separate bowl, whip the cream to soft peaks.

Add the white chocolate purée to the whisked mixture and fold together, then fold in the whipped cream and milk. Add the salt and leave the mixture to settle.

Cut 8 rectangles from a sheet of acetate, each 8 x 5cm, and form each into a tube, 5cm in length and 2.5cm wide, securing them along the length with tape. Place in the freezer for 30 minutes or so.

Cover one end of each tube with cling film to form a base and then fill the tube with the parfait, making sure there are no gaps.

Stand them upright, close together, in a small tray and tap to release any air bubbles. Freeze for 24 hours.

Salted almond ice cream

250g flaked almonds
500ml whole milk
3g table salt
10 medium free-range egg yolks
225g caster sugar
250ml double cream

Preheat the oven to 180°C/Fan 160°C/Gas 4. Lay the flaked almonds on a baking tray and toast in the oven for 10–15 minutes until rich brown in colour.

Meanwhile, slowly bring the milk to the boil in a large saucepan. Add the hot toasted nuts and salt to the hot milk and leave to infuse for 1 hour.

Pass the infused milk through a fine chinois, pressing the almonds to extract as much flavour as possible. You need 300ml almond milk.

In a large bowl, whisk the egg yolks and sugar together until the mixture is light and aerated.

Pour the cream and almond milk into a heavy-based saucepan and slowly bring to the boil. Pour onto the egg and sugar mixture, whisking as you do so.

Return the mixture to the cleaned saucepan and cook over a medium-low heat, stirring constantly, until the crème anglaise reaches 82°C (check the temperature with a digital probe).

Pass the cooked crème anglaise through a fine chinois into a container, cover the surface closely with baking parchment to prevent a skin forming and leave to cool.

Once cooled, pour into a Pacojet beaker and freeze overnight.

Before serving, churn the ice cream for 2 hours and place back in the freezer, ready to serve.

Orange nougat

100ml orange juice
100g liquid glucose
300g dextrose
5g pectin
250g unsalted butter
400g flaked almonds
Finely grated zest of 1 orange

Put the orange juice, liquid glucose, dextrose, pectin and butter into a saucepan and bring to the boil over a medium heat, stirring to combine. Continue to cook the mixture until it reaches 106°C (check the temperature with a digital probe).

Add the almond flakes and orange zest, stir to combine, then bring the mixture up to 110°C.

Pour the mixture onto a silicone mat and roll out thinly and evenly to a 2mm thickness. While still warm, cut the nougat into 3cm squares; you will need 4 per plate, 32 in total.

Orange tuiles

35g unsalted butter, softened
100g caster sugar
Finely grated zest and juice of
 ½ orange
35g plain flour

Cream the butter and sugar together
in a bowl until pale and smoothly
combined. Stir in the orange zest
and juice, then add the flour and stir
to bring the mixture together.

Wrap the mixture in cling film and
rest in the fridge for 1 hour.

Preheat the oven to 190°C/Fan
170°C/Gas 5. Line a baking sheet
with a silicone mat.

Spread the tuile mixture very thinly
and evenly on the silicone mat to a
3mm thickness. Bake for 15 minutes,
then remove and cut into 8 x 1cm
strips while still slightly warm.

Leave the tuiles to cool and set, then
carefully break into the strips.

Poached black cherries

500ml water
140g caster sugar
40g dextrose
1 vanilla pod, split and seeds scraped
25g Sosa Antioxidant Gel Powder
400g black cherries, stones removed

For the poaching liquor, put the
water, sugar, dextrose and vanilla
pod and seeds into a saucepan, heat
to dissolve the sugar and bring to the
boil. Remove from the heat, whisk
in the antioxidant and leave to cool.

Divide the cherries between two
vacuum-pack bags and lightly cover
them with the poaching liquor.
Vacuum-seal the bags and cook
in a steamer at 82°C for 5 minutes.

Remove the vacuum-pack bags from
the steamer and plunge into a bowl
of iced water to stop the cooking.

Before serving, open the bags and
drain the cherries. Pat dry with
kitchen paper.

Caramel-dipped hazelnuts

8 hazelnuts
100g Isomalt

Spear each hazelnut with a wooden
cocktail pick. Heat the Isomalt until
it is a light golden caramel colour.
Dip each hazelnut in the Isomalt
to coat and form a long thread.

Suspend, thread downwards, over
the edge of a surface, securing the
cocktail stick to the surface with
tape. Leave to cool and set.

White chocolate flock

250g white chocolate
250g cocoa butter

Melt the white chocolate with the cocoa butter in a heatproof bowl over a bain-marie of simmering water and heat to 45°C. Hold at this temperature until ready to use.

To use, pour the liquid chocolate into a spray gun.

To assemble & serve

Icing sugar, for dusting

Line a tray with a silicone mat. Carefully remove the plastic tubes from the parfaits and place on the prepared tray. Spray/flock the parfaits to coat them in a fine layer of white chocolate, then return to the freezer to firm up.

Dust 8 nougat squares with icing sugar, to coat half of the surface (as pictured on page 348). On each serving plate, layer 3 plain nougat squares with poached cherries, finishing with a sugar-dusted square.

Sit a white chocolate parfait cylinder on an orange tuile alongside. Place one of the remaining nougat squares on each plate and top with a rocher of salted almond ice cream. Finish with a caramel-dipped hazelnut.

Rum baba

with coconut sorbet, candied lime & Alphonso mango

—— SERVES 12 ——

I just love rum babas. Simple and refined, they're beautiful and a great French dessert, if done well.

The inspiration for this baba recipe comes from legendary French chef Alain Ducasse. His life story is astonishing, he's intelligent and warm, and his understanding of produce is phenomenal. If you eat at one of Alain Ducasse's two- or three-star restaurants in France and rum baba is on the menu, you must have it.

Essentially, baba is a savarin (a yeast-based sponge), soaked in rum and topped with whipped cream. But the way Alain serves it – the ceremony at the table – is just incredible.

For our Hand & Flowers rum baba, the trick is to get the core of the dish right; to get the savarin right. Then, to look at extra flavours that go well with rum. Of course, rum comes from the Caribbean and that got me thinking coconut and mango: both those flavours work so well together, as well as with rum.

Okay, I know our rum baba is topped with Alphonso mango from India, but you're allowed a bit of culinary licence, aren't you? The key thing was to get that beautiful flavour mix of coconut and mango, with a splash of lime to lift it. The dish looks so simple in presentation, but the depth of flavour is exceptional.

Rum babas

250g strong white bread flour
5g sea salt
18g fresh yeast
30g caster sugar
4 medium free-range eggs, beaten
90g unsalted butter, melted

Rum syrup:
300ml water
150g caster sugar
100ml dark rum (100% proof)

Put the flour into a mixer fitted with the dough hook, add the salt to one side and crumble the yeast onto the other side. Add the sugar.

Pour in the beaten eggs and mix on a low speed for 4 minutes. Keeping the speed low, add the melted butter and mix until fully incorporated. The dough should be smooth and silky.

Remove the dough hook, cover the bowl with a damp cloth and leave to rise in a warm place for about an hour until doubled in volume.

Have ready 1 or 2 non-stick silicone tray(s) of individual baba moulds (you need 12 moulds). Knead the dough lightly to knock it back then place in a piping bag fitted with a large plain nozzle. Pipe the dough into the moulds, dividing it evenly.

Leave to prove in a warm place for 30 minutes or until risen almost to the top of the moulds. Preheat the oven to 200°C/Fan 180°C/Gas 6.

Bake the babas in the oven for 12 minutes or until golden. Leave to cool in the tins for 10 minutes then turn out onto a wire rack.

For the rum syrup, heat the water and sugar in a pan to dissolve the sugar. Bring to the boil and add the rum.

Lay the babas in a deep-sided tray and pour on the rum syrup. Cover the tray with cling film and leave the babas to soak for 20 minutes.

Uncover and carefully turn the babas over to become gorged in the rum syrup. Leave until ready to serve.

Coconut sorbet

150ml water
150g caster sugar
50g liquid glucose
500g coconut purée (Boiron)
10ml Malibu
Finely grated zest and juice of 1 lime

Put the water, sugar and liquid glucose into a saucepan, heat to dissolve the sugar and then bring to the boil.

In a large bowl, mix the coconut purée, Malibu and lime zest and juice together. Add the sugar syrup and stir to combine.

Pour the mixture into a Pacojet beaker and freeze overnight.

Before serving, churn the sorbet for 2 hours and place back in the freezer, ready to serve.

Candied lime zest

3 limes
50g caster sugar

Finely pare the zest from the limes and cut into julienne. Halve the fruit, squeeze the juice and set aside.

Bring a small pan of water to the boil. Add the lime zest julienne and boil for 1 minute. Drain and refresh in iced water. Repeat the process twice more, using fresh boiled water each time.

Heat the lime juice and sugar in a small pan to dissolve the sugar and bring to the boil. Add the lime zest and simmer to reduce the syrup until thickened to form a glaze.

Leave the lime zest to cool in the syrupy glaze.

To assemble & serve

2 ripe Alphonso mangoes,
* peeled and diced*
Extra rum, if required
12 dried vanilla sticks

Peel the mangoes, cut the flesh away from the stone and cut into neat dice. Place a baba in each shallow serving bowl. Drizzle with some of the rum syrup, adding an extra kick of rum to each bowl if you like.

Place a scoop of coconut sorbet in the centre of each baba and arrange the mango dice around it. Finish with a few shreds of candied lime zest and a dried vanilla stick.

Apple & custard slice

with Bramley apple sorbet

I grew up with custard slices from our local bakery; and those from a certain Mr Kipling! They satisfied my childhood sweet tooth – I loved them and they massively inspired this dessert.

Of course, we needed to add sophistication to my childhood favourite to transform it into a dessert for our menu. We had to refine it; work out where we would get our acidity, sweetness and crunch from; and how we would bring the elements together to build the slice – or mille-feuille, to give it its posh name.

The custard is critical. Our secret ingredient is Bird's Custard Powder. Yes, we use it – because that childhood taste memory is so important for me. I mean, who doesn't love it? We still make a classic parfait for the slice, with egg white and glucose, but it's got a touch of custard powder in it, too. That's all you need.

As ever, the final dish rests on perfecting each element of it. From the puff pastry to the delicate icing on the top, it's got to be flawless. The last thing you want to do is put a beautiful mille-feuille dessert on the plate and ruin it with the icing!

Our pastry chef, Jolyon d'Angibau, came up with a brilliant way of getting the apple balance and texture of the slice right. We needed the apple to be flavoursome; to give acidity but not to be leaching. Jolyon came up with the idea of making an apple terrine, pressed and baked, so that we could then slice it and layer it with the other elements. The result is something splendid. A worthy custard slice.

Bramley apple purée

7 medium-large Bramley apples
1 litre water
30g Sosa Antioxidant Gel Powder

Peel, quarter and core the apples and place in a saucepan with the water and antioxidant. Bring to a simmer and cook gently for about 15 minutes until soft. Strain off and reserve the excess liquor.

Blitz the cooked apples in a blender until smooth then transfer to a bowl. Leave both the apple purée and reserved cooking liquor to cool.

Bramley apple sorbet

500ml Bramley apple purée, plus
  50ml reserved liquor (see above)
50g liquid glucose
50g caster sugar
50g Pro Sorbet
Finely grated zest of ½ lemon

Put the apple cooking liquor, liquid glucose and sugar into a saucepan and heat to dissolve the sugar. Bring to the boil, then remove from the heat and allow to cool.

Stir the sugar syrup into the apple purée, then add the Pro Sorbet and lemon zest and stir to combine.

Pass the mixture through a fine chinois, pour into a Pacojet beaker and freeze overnight.

Before serving, churn the sorbet for 2 hours and place back in the freezer.

Vanilla parfait

335ml whole milk
225g caster sugar
80g liquid free-range egg yolk
50g custard powder
240g unsalted butter, in pieces, softened
40ml water
35g liquid glucose
75g free-range liquid egg white

First make a crème pâtissière. Put the milk and 75g of the sugar into a medium heavy-based saucepan, heat to dissolve the sugar and slowly bring to the boil. Meanwhile, whisk the egg yolk and custard powder together in a bowl until smoothly combined.

Pour the hot milk onto the whisked mixture, whisking as you do so to keep the mixture smooth. Return the mixture to the pan and cook, stirring, over a medium-high heat for 5–8 minutes until thickened.

Take off the heat and stir in 15g of the butter. Cover the surface closely with baking parchment to prevent a skin forming and allow to cool.

Now make an Italian meringue. Put the water, liquid glucose and remaining 150g sugar into a heavy-based pan, heat to dissolve the sugar and bring to the boil. Continue to cook until the sugar syrup reaches 119°C (use a digital probe to check the temperature).

Using an electric mixer or hand-held electric whisk, whisk the egg white until starting to foam. Slowly pour the hot sugar syrup onto the egg white, continuing to whisk as you do.

While the meringue is still warm and with the motor running, start to feed the meringue with the butter, a little at a time. The mixture may split a little but it will come back together. Continue until all the butter is all incorporated.

Line a chilled marble slab with baking parchment. Fold the crème pâtissière and Italian meringue together until evenly combined and then spread evenly on the lined marble to a 1cm thickness. Freeze until firm.

Once frozen, cut the vanilla parfait into 3 x 8cm rectangles. Keep frozen until needed.

Apple tuiles

150ml apple juice
25g unsalted butter, melted
25g rice flour
50g icing sugar

Pour the apple juice into a small pan, bring to the boil and reduce down to 30ml.

Place all of the ingredients in a mixer fitted with the paddle attachment and mix until smooth. Wrap in cling film and rest in the fridge for 1 hour.

Preheat the oven to 200°C/Fan 180°C/Gas 6. Line a baking sheet with a silicone mat.

Spread the tuile mixture thinly and evenly on the silicone mat to a 3mm thickness. Bake for 12–15 minutes, then remove and, while still slightly warm, cut into 4cm perfect squares. Leave the tuiles to cool and set.

Once cooled, carefully snap the tuiles into squares (to sit the sorbet on).

Apple terrine

10 Bramley apples
300g caster sugar
100g unsalted butter, in pieces

Preheat the oven to 190°C/Fan 170°C/Gas 5. Line a 33 x 26cm deep baking tin with baking parchment.

Peel, quarter and core the apples, then slice thinly, using a mandoline; set aside.

Melt the sugar in a heavy-based saucepan over a low heat, swirling the pan (rather than stirring) to encourage it to melt evenly. Bring to the boil and cook to a golden caramel, then carefully whisk in the butter.

Pour the caramel into your terrine mould. Layer the apples on the caramel to build the terrine. Place a second mould or tray on top, that just fits inside the tin, and add a weight to press the apples into the caramel as they bake. Bake for 45 minutes.

Remove from the oven and leave to cool with the weight still in place.

Puff pastry slices

1 quantity puff pastry (see page 405)
20ml beaten egg yolks or liquid egg yolk, for glazing

Roll out the puff pastry to a rectangle, the thickness of a £1 coin. Brush the pastry twice with egg yolk and rest in the fridge for 1 hour.

Preheat the oven to 200°C/Fan 180°C/Gas 6. Place the pastry on a baking sheet and bake in the oven for 30 minutes.

Lower the oven setting to 190°C/Fan 170°C/Gas 5 and bake for another 15 minutes. Then lower the oven setting to 180°C/Fan 160°C/Gas 4 and bake for a further 25 minutes.

Now lower the oven setting to 170°C/Fan 150°C/Gas 3 and bake for a further 50 minutes. Finally, lower the oven setting to 150°C/Fan 140°C/Gas 2 for 45 minutes until dark golden and crisp. Carefully transfer the puff pastry sheet to a wire rack and leave to cool.

Once cooled, carefully lift the puff pastry onto a board and cut into rectangles, 3 x 8cm. Set aside until ready to assemble.

Icing tops

400g icing sugar
55g free-range liquid egg white
½ tsp lemon juice
30g dark chocolate, melted

Preheat the oven to 140°C/Fan 120°C/Gas 1. Line a large baking tray with a silicone mat.

Beat the icing sugar, egg white and lemon juice together in a bowl to a smooth paste.

Using a stencil to match the size of the puff pastry slices (3 x 8cm), flood the template to create a thin icing rectangle on the silicone mat. Repeat to create 8–10 icing tops in total. Place in the oven for 3 minutes, then remove and leave to cool.

Put the melted chocolate into a small greaseproof paper piping bag, snip off the end and drizzle the icing tops with the chocolate (as you would a mille-feuille).

To assemble & serve

Remove the apple terrine from the mould and cut into rectangles, the same size as the puff pastry, vanilla parfait and icing tops.

Layer up the puff pastry, apple terrine and vanilla parfait. Add another layer of puff pastry and another of vanilla parfait. Top with the decorated icing sheets.

Carefully lift the assembled slices, using a palette knife, and place on individual plates.

Place an apple tuile alongside and top with a rocher of apple sorbet.

Rhubarb crumble tartlet

with lemon verbena ice cream

This recipe is all about making the simplest of things taste delicious, and elevating a pub classic.

I was always keen to get rhubarb crumble on the menu, but the challenge was how to present it neatly. So, I decided to line little tart moulds with sweet almond pastry, bake them until crisp and crunchy, then fill them with a rhubarb and apple compote and top with an almond crumble. It worked a treat.

The lemon verbena ice cream on the side came about by a happy chance. We had a verbena plant at the back of The Hand & Flowers that had gone bananas! It was like when the Roman Empire overran Europe. We had loads of it. So, one year we ripped it out and infused it in a load of ice cream. And it was absolutely delicious. Lemon verbena is such a beautiful herb and works so nicely as an ice cream infusion; plus, it makes a pleasant change from a traditional vanilla scoop.

This recipe marks the time when I first got going with herb-infused ice creams. I think chef Simon Rogan had started doing them by the time I discovered how wonderful they could be; and Heston Blumenthal had already broken the mould by doing bacon and egg ice cream, then flaming sorbet. We thought we were cutting edge when we did verbena ice cream – but eight miles away, Heston was setting fire to sorbet!

I love the simplicity of our rhubarb crumble tartlet, with the surprise of a lemon verbena ice cream. It has an understated feel about it.

Lemon verbena ice cream

285ml milk
285ml double cream
35g lemon verbena leaves
6 medium free-range egg yolks
35g caster sugar
40ml vodka
12ml gin

Pour the milk and cream into a saucepan, add half of the lemon verbena leaves and bring to the boil. Remove from the heat and set aside to infuse for 30 minutes.

Meanwhile, whisk the egg yolks and sugar together in a bowl to combine. Pour on the hot creamy milk, whisking as you do so.

Return the mixture to the saucepan and cook over a medium-low heat, stirring constantly, until the crème anglaise reaches 82°C (check the temperature with a digital probe).

Put the remaining lemon verbena into a bowl. Pass the cooked crème anglaise through a chinois onto the fresh lemon verbena. Stir in the vodka and gin. Cover and leave to infuse again and cool for 1 hour.

Once cooled, pass through a fine chinois to remove the lemon verbena. Pour into a Pacojet beaker and freeze overnight.

Before serving, churn the ice cream for 2 hours and place back in the freezer, ready to serve.

Orange tuiles

35g unsalted butter, softened
100g caster sugar
Finely grated zest and juice
*   of ½ orange*
35g plain flour

Cream the butter and sugar together in a bowl until pale and smoothly combined. Stir in the orange zest and juice, then add the flour and stir to bring the mixture together.

Wrap the mixture in cling film and rest in the fridge for 1 hour.

Preheat the oven to 190°C/Fan 170°C/Gas 5. Line a baking sheet with a silicone mat.

Spread the tuile mixture thinly and evenly on the silicone mat to a 3mm thickness. Bake for 15 minutes, then remove and cut into perfect 4cm squares while still slightly warm.

Leave the tuiles to cool and set, then carefully break into the squares.

Sweet almond pastry

150g unsalted butter
100g icing sugar
A pinch of salt
25g ground almonds
60g free-range beaten egg
*   (about 1 large)*
250g plain flour

Cream the butter, icing sugar and salt together in a large bowl. Add the ground almonds and beaten egg and stir until evenly blended, then mix in the flour.

Bring the almond pastry together in a ball, wrap in cling film and press to flatten slightly. Place in the fridge to rest for 1 hour.

Unwrap the almond pastry, divide it into 8 equal portions and shape into balls. Roll each portion of pastry out thinly. Use to line individual tart rings, 8cm in diameter, placed on a baking sheet, making sure you press the pastry into the corners.

Line the almond tart cases with a disc of baking parchment and fill with baking bean or rice grains. Place in the fridge to rest for a further 1 hour.

Preheat the oven to 190°C/Fan 170°C/Gas 5. Bake the tart cases blind in the oven for 20 minutes. Remove the baking beans or rice and paper and bake the tart cases for a further 5 minutes to dry the tart bases. Transfer to a wire rack to cool.

Once cooled, store the almond tart cases in an airtight container until ready to assemble.

Crumble topping

200g plain flour
100g caster sugar
35g ground almonds
80g unsalted butter, diced, softened
10g flaked almonds
3 or 4 drops of water

Preheat the oven to 190°C/Fan 170°C/Gas 5.

Combine the flour, sugar and ground almonds in a large bowl and rub in the butter until the mixture resembles crumbs. Stir in the flaked almonds and water.

Scatter the crumble on a baking tray and bake in the oven for about 20 minutes until golden, stirring a few times during baking to ensure even colouring. Leave to cool.

Once cooled, store in an airtight container until needed.

Rhubarb compote

100g Bramley apples
300g forced Yorkshire pink
   rhubarb stalks
50g unsalted butter
50g caster sugar
Finely grated zest of 1 orange
1 vanilla pod, split and seeds scraped

Peel, quarter and core the apples then chop into 1cm dice. Cut the rhubarb into similar-sized dice.

Melt the butter in a heavy-based pan and add the sugar and orange zest. Add half the apple and rhubarb, along with the vanilla pod and seeds. Cook for about 15 minutes until soft and reduced to a purée.

Add the remaining diced apple and rhubarb and cook for a further 1–2 minutes only, just to soften them very slightly.

Remove from the heat and tip into a colander to drain off any excess liquid; the diced fruit will continue to cook in the residual heat, yet retain some texture.

To assemble & serve

Icing sugar, for dusting

Preheat the oven to 190°C/Fan 170°C/Gas 5.

Warm the rhubarb compote through gently and spoon into the tart cases, filling them generously. Sprinkle liberally with the crumble topping. Place the tarts in the oven to warm through for about 4 minutes.

Remove the tarts from the oven and dust with icing sugar. Place a tart in the centre of each plate.

Position an orange tuile alongside the tart and place a rocher of the lemon verbena ice cream on top. Serve immediately.

Blackberry soufflé

with blackberry sauce & gingernut biscuit ice cream

Blackberries are a lovely British berry. They taste amazing and deserve to be celebrated, but often they're just used as an extra alongside apples in a traditional crumble. I wanted to change that. As we change our soufflés seasonally, this one is perfect for autumn.

It was just a question of how to make the soufflé work for the blackberries; how to feature them beautifully and make the dessert special. Sometimes that development process leads you to unexpected places, and this recipe's surprise ingredient is banana!

Banana purée goes into the base mixture (the panade) because it works as a stabiliser. The make-up of a banana is very different from that of most fruit; it's not watery, so it helps to hold the texture as you cook the soufflé, plus it ensures that the sides don't split.

We serve this soufflé with a gingernut biscuit ice cream, and I love the way that the ginger gives you that little bit of spice. Ginger is great with autumn and winter British fruits, and not quite so obvious as cinnamon. The result is an elegant dessert that showcases a very humble ingredient.

BLACKBERRY SOUFFLÉ

Gingernut crumb

170g self-raising flour
115g soft dark brown sugar
5g bicarbonate of soda
55g unsalted butter, chilled and diced
5g ground ginger
5g golden syrup
1 medium free-range egg

Preheat the oven to 200°C/Fan 180°C/Gas 6. Line a baking sheet with baking parchment.

Put all of the ingredients except the egg into a mixer fitted with the paddle attachment. Work until the mixture resembles fine crumbs. Add the egg and mix briefly to incorporate and form a stiff dough.

Roll out the dough on the lined baking sheet to a 3mm thickness. Bake in the oven for 15–20 minutes until crisp and browned. Transfer to a board and leave to cool.

Chop the gingernut biscuit into a fine crumb and divide in half. Set aside one half for the soufflé topping. The other half is used for the ice cream base.

Gingernut ice cream

125ml milk
125ml double cream
Gingernut crumb (see left, ½ quantity)
3 medium free-range egg yolks
40g caster sugar
25g glycerine

Pour the milk and cream into a saucepan, add the gingernut crumb and bring to the boil.

Meanwhile, whisk the egg yolks and sugar together in a bowl to combine. Pour on the hot creamy milk, whisking as you do so.

Return the mixture to the saucepan and cook over a medium-low heat, stirring constantly, until the crème anglaise reaches 82°C (check the temperature with a digital probe).

Add the glycerine to the cooked crème anglaise and stir to mix. Pass through a fine chinois into a container, cover the surface closely with baking parchment to prevent a skin forming and leave to cool.

Once cooled, pour into a Pacojet beaker and freeze overnight.

Before serving, churn the ice cream for 2 hours and place back in the freezer, ready to serve.

Blackberry sauce

75g caster sugar
100ml water
200g blackberry purée (Boiron)

Heat the sugar and water in a saucepan over a medium heat to dissolve the sugar and bring to the boil. Remove from the heat and stir in the blackberry purée.

Pass the sauce through a fine chinois into a bowl, cover and keep in the fridge until ready to serve.

Blackberry panade

2 litres blackberry purée (Boiron)
110g banana purée (Boiron)
50g caster sugar
40g cornflour, mixed to a paste
  with 40ml water
1g Sosa blackberry aroma

Put the blackberry purée, banana purée and sugar into a heavy-based saucepan and heat to dissolve the sugar. Bring to a simmer and continue to cook over a medium heat until the mixture has reduced by one-third.

Stir in the cornflour paste and cook, stirring constantly, over a high heat for 5–8 minutes until thickened.

Once thickened, transfer the mix to a high-powered jug blender (Vitamix), add the blackberry aroma and blend thoroughly. Pass through a fine chinois into a bowl, cover with a disc of baking parchment to prevent a skin forming and leave to cool.

Blackberry soufflé

Butter, melted, for greasing
150g caster sugar, plus extra
  for dusting
400g free-range liquid egg white
400g blackberry panade (see left)
Gingernut crumb (see opposite,
  ½ quantity)
8 blackberries

Using a pastry brush, brush the base and sides of 8 individual soufflé dishes, 250ml capacity, with melted butter and place in the fridge to set. Butter them again, then dust with caster sugar, shaking out any excess. Return to the fridge.

In a large, clean bowl, whisk the egg white to stiff peaks, then gradually whisk in the sugar to make a glossy meringue.

Using a spatula, gently fold the meringue into the blackberry panade until evenly combined.

Spoon the mixture into the prepared soufflé dishes and level the surface with a spatula. Place in the fridge until ready to bake and serve.

Preheat the oven to 205°C/Fan 185°C/Gas 6–7. Sprinkle the crumb mix evenly on top of the soufflés. Bake in the oven for 8–10 minutes until fully risen.

To assemble & serve

While the soufflés are in the oven, warm the blackberry sauce through gently and pour into individual jugs. Place a scoop of gingernut ice cream in each of 8 small serving bowls.

Serve the soufflés the moment they are ready, topped with a fresh blackberry. Serve the blackberry sauce in individual jugs and the ice cream in small bowls on the side.

Mango & strawberry lasagne

with violet ice cream

————— SERVES 8 —————

You could call this recipe a modern take on fruit salad. Instead of free-roaming fruit, as it were, it comes to the plate in lasagne-like layers of compressed mango and strawberry!

Let me explain. You layer mango and strawberry into moulds then press and press them for 24 hours and eventually you end up with beautiful layers of fruit, which can then be caramelised on top.

The recipe, like the caramelised white chocolate parfait on page 349, was inspired by pastry chef and chocolatier Damian Allsop. He and I were reminiscing one day about a beautiful compressed tomato cake that I used to make back in the day when I was working in London at Rhodes in the Square. And because it was summer at the time and I wanted something fruity on the dessert menu, Damian suggested trying the same technique with mango and strawberry.

By continuously pressing the fruit, you release its natural starches and sugars, which eventually begin to gel together. After a while, you end up with lovely fruity layers; but it can be a trial and error thing because how well the process works is dependent on how much moisture content there is in the mango or strawberries.

We serve our 'lasagne' with a delicate, floral violet ice cream. The whole dessert is so clean and fresh in the mouth. It's very special and it doesn't make you feel naughty when you eat it, because it's just got natural fruit sugars giving you that sweet hit we all crave in a dessert.

Fruit terrine

4–6 ripe Alphonso mangoes
1kg strawberries, hulled
Demerara sugar, for dusting

Peel the mangoes, slice the flesh away from the stone and cut into thin slices, 2–3mm thick. Slice the strawberries to the same thickness.

Line a 20cm square cake tin with cling film, leaving enough hanging over the sides of the tin to cover the top generously.

Press a layer of mango slices into the base of the lined tin, filling any gaps, then add a layer of strawberries. Repeat these layers until all the fruit is used and the fruit extends above the rim of the tin.

Fold the cling film over the fruit to seal it in and pierce the film in a few places with a sharp knife. Invert another cake tin, the same size, with a loose bottom, on top. Turn both tins over so the first layers of mango and strawberries are now on top.

Place the tin on a larger tray and position a heavy weight on top. Place in the fridge for 24 hours. The fruit juice should drain through the pierced cling film.

Just before serving, remove the fruit terrine from the cling film and slice into portions. Sprinkle the top with demerara sugar and use a cook's blowtorch to caramelise.

Violet ice cream

450ml milk
40g dextrose
45g milk powder
50g Pro Crema (Sosa)
25g caster sugar
50ml double cream
22 drops of Sosa violet flavouring

Put all of the ingredients into a bowl and whisk together, using a handheld electric whisk, to combine.

Pour into a Pacojet beaker and leave to stand for 1 hour, then freeze overnight.

Before serving, churn the ice cream for 2 hours and place back in the freezer, ready to serve.

Strawberry tuiles

100g unsalted butter
100g icing sugar
150g strawberry purée (Boiron)
5g crimson food colouring
75g plain flour

Cream the butter and icing sugar together in a bowl until pale and smoothly combined. Stir in the strawberry purée and food colouring, then add the flour and stir to bring the mixture together.

Wrap the tuile mixture in cling film and rest in the fridge for 1 hour.

Preheat the oven to 180°C/Fan 160°C/Gas 4. Line a baking sheet with a silicone mat.

Spread the tuile mixture thinly and evenly on the silicone mat to a 3mm thickness. Bake for 15 minutes, then remove and cut into perfect 4cm squares while still slightly warm.

Leave the tuiles to cool and set, then carefully break into the squares.

Strawberry purée

200g strawberries, hulled
50g caster sugar

Slice the strawberries and toss in
the sugar to coat. Leave to macerate
for 10 minutes.

Purée the macerated strawberries
in a blender until smooth. Pass the
purée through a fine chinois into a
bowl, cover and set aside until ready
to serve.

To assemble & serve

About 20 edible violets

Carefully lift a portion of the fruit
terrine onto each serving plate. Lay
a strawberry tuile alongside and
place a rocher of violet ice cream on
top. Add a spoonful of strawberry
purée to each plate.

Place an edible violet on top of the
ice cream and decorate the plates
with violet petals. Serve at once.

Tirami Choux

We take what we do incredibly seriously, but dining at The Hand & Flowers is about being comfortable and having fun. We don't believe in the ideology of being a temple of gastronomy.

Our tirami choux is pretty much what-you-see-is-what-you-get. A crisp choux bun filled with coffee and a really nice way of keeping tiramisu on the menu. That, hopefully, makes people smile. It's no secret that I love choux buns (like the choux à la crème on page 341); they're a link to both my childhood and my classical French training as a chef.

After baking our choux buns and cutting them in half, we build up the tiramisu-inspired ingredients, starting with coffee-soaked raisins. The raisins are topped with coffee ice cream, followed by mascarpone mousse and coffee-soaked cake cubes. The buns are then pressed together, dusted with cocoa powder and dressed with a piping of Chantilly cream and a coffee bean.

The bun looks beautiful and simple, but so many delicious flavours are hidden inside it that, texturally, it's fantastic, too. And its name is a bit of silliness, which may have started off as a joke but really does represent our food at The Hand & Flowers. I love that.

Coffee ice cream

185ml whole milk
185ml double cream
25g good-quality instant coffee
25ml coffee essence (Camp)
4 medium free-range egg yolks
35g caster sugar
15ml glycerine

Pour the milk and cream into a saucepan, add the instant coffee and coffee essence and bring to the boil.

Meanwhile, whisk the egg yolks, sugar and glycerine together in a bowl to combine. Pour on the hot creamy milk, whisking as you do so.

Return the mixture to the saucepan and cook over a medium-low heat, stirring constantly, until the crème anglaise reaches 82°C (check the temperature with a digital probe).

Pass through a fine chinois into a container, cover the surface closely with baking parchment to prevent a skin forming and leave to cool.

Once cooled, pour into a Pacojet beaker and freeze overnight.

Before serving, churn the ice cream for 2 hours and place back in the freezer, ready to serve.

Chocolate sablé

100g unsalted butter
120g plain flour
120g demerara sugar
6g cocoa powder

Put all of the ingredients into an electric mixer fitted with the paddle attachment and mix to combine and form a smooth dough; this will take about 3 minutes.

Place the dough in a large vacuum-pack bag (340g capacity) and seal the bag 3cm from the top. Roll the sablé paste evenly in the bag, right to the edges, to a 3mm thickness. Place in the freezer until firm.

When needed, remove the pastry from the bags and cut out enough 6cm discs to top off the choux pastry.

Choux buns

85ml milk
85ml water
75g unsalted butter
110g plain flour
3g sea salt
10g caster sugar
160g free-range beaten eggs
    (about 3 medium)

Put the milk, water and butter into a saucepan and heat gently until the butter is melted. Add the flour, salt and sugar and beat well to make a smooth, glossy dough.

Remove from the heat and transfer the choux paste to a mixer fitted with the paddle attachment. Beat on a low speed until the mixture is just warm. Now, with the motor running, add the egg a little at a time, mixing until it is fully incorporated. Spoon into a large piping bag.

Preheat the oven to 250°C/Fan 230°C speed 3/Gas 9. Line a sturdy baking sheet with a silicone mat. Snip the end off the piping bag and pipe 40g choux paste rounds on to the silicone mat, spacing them well apart to allow space for them to expand.

Top each choux bun with a chocolate sablé disc. Put the tray in the oven, close the door, turn off the oven and leave to cook in the residual heat for 10 minutes.

Now turn the oven on to 200°C/Fan 180°C/Gas 6 and bake for another 10 minutes.

Then lower the oven setting to 180°C/Fan 160°C/Gas 4 and bake for a further 10 minutes.

Finally, lower the oven setting to 150°C/Fan 130°C/Gas 2 for another 10 minutes. Remove from the oven and place on a wire rack to cool.

Slice the cooled buns in half and, if necessary, scoop out some of the inner choux to create a hollow in both halves to hold the filling.

Coffee-soaked raisins

100g raisins
100ml espresso coffee
100ml coffee essence (Camp)
100ml coffee liqueur (such as Tia
    Maria or Kahlua)

Put all of the ingredients into a vacuum-pack bag and vacuum-seal on full pressure. Immerse in a water-bath at 65°C for 8 hours. Lift out the bag and leave to cool.

When ready to serve, remove the raisins and drain, reserving the liquor to soak the cake crumbs (see page 382).

Coffee oil

250ml vegetable oil
125g ground coffee

Put the oil and ground coffee into a vacuum-pack bag and vacuum-seal. Immerse in a water-bath at 88.2°C for 4 hours.

Pass the coffee-infused oil through a muslin-lined sieve into a jug, cover and refrigerate until needed for the cake.

Coffee cake

40 raisins
15ml coffee essence (Camp)
15g espresso coffee
1 medium free-range egg
100g soft light brown sugar
35g marzipan, finely chopped
100ml coffee oil (see page 381)
100g plain flour
1.5g bicarbonate of soda
1.5g baking powder
1g salt
Finely grated zest of ½ lime

Put the raisins into a small bowl, pour on the coffee essence and espresso and leave to soak for 30 minutes.

Preheat the oven to 200°C/Fan 180°C/Gas 6. Line a 33 x 26cm deep baking tin with baking parchment.

Using an electric mixer fitted with the whisk attachment, whisk the egg, brown sugar and marzipan together until smoothly combined. Slowly pour in the coffee oil, whisking constantly to emulsify.

Change the whisk to the paddle attachment and then beat in all of the remaining ingredients, including the raisins and their soaking liquor, until evenly combined.

Spread the mixture in the prepared tin and bake for 25–30 minutes, or until a skewer inserted into the centre comes out clean. Remove the sponge from the tin and place on a wire rack to cool.

Once cooled, cut the coffee cake into 1cm cubes and lay on a dehydrator tray. Place in the dehydrator at 80°C for about 2 hours until crisp. Store in an airtight container until needed.

Before serving, soak the dried cake cubes in the coffee liquor from the raisins (see page 381).

Mascarpone mousse

90g mascarpone cheese
40g cream cheese
35g crème fraîche
25g caster sugar
1 tbsp amaretto liqueur

Put the mascarpone cheese, cream cheese, crème fraîche and caster sugar into a Thermomix and blend briefly to combine. Add the amaretto and blend to incorporate.

Spoon the mascarpone mixture into a piping bag fitted with a 1cm plain nozzle and refrigerate until needed.

Hot chocolate sauce

150g dark chocolate pistoles
(70% cocoa solids)
90ml runny honey
75g unsalted butter, diced
250ml double cream
5g table salt
15g cocoa powder

Place the chocolate pistoles in a heatproof bowl.

Put all the rest of the ingredients into a small heavy-based pan and bring to the boil, stirring to combine.

Pour the hot creamy liquor onto the chocolate, stirring as you do so, to melt the chocolate and bring the sauce together. Keep hot until ready to serve.

Chantilly cream

100ml double cream
25g icing sugar
1 vanilla pod, split and seeds scraped

Whisk the cream, icing sugar and vanilla seeds together in a bowl until thickened enough to form peaks.

Spoon into a piping bag fitted with a small star nozzle.

To assemble & serve

60g cocoa powder, sifted
8 coffee beans

Put 1 tbsp of the soaked raisins into the hollowed-out top of each choux bun, then add a small scoop of the coffee ice cream.

Pipe the mascarpone mousse into the choux bases and add 5 soaked coffee cake cubes to each.

Press the choux halves together, dust generously with cocoa powder and place one on each serving plate. Pipe on the Chantilly cream and finish each with a coffee bean.

Spoon some hot chocolate sauce alongside and serve straight away.

Sesame sponge cake

with matcha tea sorbet

Like the sweet malt gâteau with malted milk ice cream on page 337, this recipe is inspired in large part by my amazing friend Paul Ainsworth and an oil-based cake recipe he did for the Great British Menu television series in 2012.

But it was also partially motivated by a trip to Singapore that I did around the same time with our head chef Jamie May for a food festival. The food scene is just amazing there, and we came across some incredible flavours while doing a big week's worth of cooking ourselves. I wanted to get some of the tastes we had experienced onto the menu at The Hand & Flowers, in a way that sat comfortably with our own style of cooking.

Paul's sponge cake recipe was the link. I thought it might work with the lovely flavour of sesame oil, so we experimented with various techniques to showcase sesame's nutty sweetness in the sponge.

The big Singaporean element comes via a matcha tea sorbet, which we serve with the cake. An orange tuile provides a hint of citrus, which counterbalances its filling of whipped lemon crème fraîche, and a pool of maple syrup lends extra sweetness. The dessert is finished with a fine sesame tuile and a syrup-coated piece of popcorn.

Sesame sponge

90g fresh brioche crumbs
50g ground almonds
1 tsp baking powder
200g caster sugar
50g sesame seeds, toasted
4 medium free-range eggs
100ml rapeseed oil
100ml sesame oil
200g tahini paste

Preheat the oven to 150°C/Fan 130°C/Gas 2. Line a 33 x 26cm deep baking tin with baking parchment.

In a large bowl, mix the brioche crumbs, ground almonds, baking powder, sugar and sesame seeds together. Make a well in the centre.

In another bowl, whisk together the eggs, rapeseed and sesame oils, and the tahini paste. Pour the mixture into the well in the dry ingredients and beat until evenly combined.

Pour the cake batter into the prepared loaf tin and bake in the oven for 45 minutes–1 hour until a skewer inserted into the centre comes out clean.

Leave in the tin for 10 minutes then turn out the sponge and place on a wire rack to cool.

Matcha tea sorbet

500ml water
125g liquid glucose
100g caster sugar
5g good-quality matcha green
  tea powder
Juice of 1 lemon

Put the water, liquid glucose and sugar into a saucepan, heat to dissolve the sugar and bring to the boil. Remove from the heat, whisk in the green tea powder and add the lemon juice. Leave to cool.

Pour the mixture into a Pacojet beaker and freeze overnight.

Before serving, churn the sorbet for 2 hours and place back in the freezer, ready to serve.

Sesame tuiles

100g fondant icing sugar
65g liquid glucose
40g black sesame seeds
40g white sesame seeds

Heat the fondant icing sugar and liquid glucose in a medium pan to 160°C (use a digital probe to check the temperature). Remove from the heat and stir in the sesame seeds.

Spread out evenly on a silicone mat to a 5mm thickness and leave to cool slightly. While the sesame tuile sheet is still slightly warm, cut it into long, thin sticks, 10cm x 5mm. Leave to cool and firm up.

Syrup-coated popcorn

100g Isomalt
8 pieces of popcorn

Line a tray with a silicone mat. Melt the Isomalt in a saucepan and heat to 130°C (check the temperature with a digital probe).

Dip each piece of popcorn into the syrup to coat, then drain and place on the silicone mat. Leave until set.

Orange tuiles

140g unsalted butter, softened
400g caster sugar
Finely grated zest and juice of
  2 oranges
140g plain flour

Cream the butter and sugar together in a bowl until pale and smoothly combined. Stir in the orange zest and juice, then add the flour and stir to bring the mixture together.

Wrap in cling film and rest in the fridge for 2 hours.

Preheat the oven to 190°C/Fan 170°C/Gas 5. Line a baking sheet with a silicone mat.

Spread the tuile mixture very thinly and evenly on the silicone mat to a 3mm thickness. Bake for 15 minutes until dark golden.

Remove from the oven and, while still warm, cut the tuile sheet into 12 x 8cm rectangles (long and wide enough to wrap around a cannoli tube). Immediately roll each one around a cannoli tube to make a cylindrical tuile. Leave to set, then carefully slide the tuile off the tube.

Store in an airtight container with a little silica gel to keep them dry and crisp.

Maple sauce

200g maple syrup
2.5g agar agar

Pour the maple syrup into a saucepan, stir in the agar agar and bring to the boil. Remove from the heat and set aside to cool and set.

Once set, transfer to a blender and blend to a smooth sauce. Pour into a jug and set aside until ready to serve.

Lemon crème fraîche

100g thick crème fraîche
10g caster sugar
Finely grated zest of 1 lemon

In a bowl, whip the crème fraîche with the sugar and lemon zest. Transfer to a piping bag and place in the fridge, ready for serving.

To assemble & serve

Pipe the lemon crème fraîche into the orange tuiles to fill them.

Cut the sesame sponge into portions and place one on each plate, with a pool of maple sauce on the side. Rest a filled orange tuile on one end of the sponge.

Place a scoop of matcha tea sorbet on top of the sesame sponge and finish with a sesame tuile and a nugget of coated popcorn.

Ceramics

Ceramics have a big emotional pull for my wife Beth and me. Beth's from Stoke-on-Trent and her dad's a potter who had his own business at one stage (well, you have to be a potter in Stoke, don't you?), so that means the ceramics at The Hand & Flowers have always been more than just plates and crockery for us.

When we first opened the pub we had to be cost effective and practical, so we served our dishes on white, white and white crockery from back-street pottery places and seconds outlets. But as The Hand & Flowers became increasingly successful, I started to realise that a plate is so much more than a vessel for serving food. The plate is the frame for what's on it; it adds character and helps define a dish.

We shelled out for stunning French stoneware from Montgolfier, which made an impact on the table and is relatively hard-wearing so it's practical, too. But then it started popping up in lots of different places, including on television. It was time to move on!

Over the next few years, we tracked down ceramicists who could make specially commissioned plates just for us. It was a beautiful idea, but it turned out that we shot ourselves in the foot a little. Independent ceramicists work to the beat of their own drum and because they're not in the business of mass production, if you break two or three plates and you need more, it can often take months to get them replaced.

Another idea that seemed great on paper was to have individual plates for each dish on the menu. I loved that concept. But, in reality, it was a nightmare! You're constantly picking out the wrong plate, because in the kitchen you're in a rush all the time. So we ended up going full circle: back to bone china whiteware for almost everything on the menu. These days we're hooked up with William Edwards, a plate design manufacturer based in Stoke-on-Trent, and that feels right, for all sorts of reasons. The company's designed a bespoke print for The Hand & Flowers, a kind of reversible, mottled pattern.

I find ceramicists fascinating to work with. They're baking something in a kiln, and I see that as being similar to what I do as a chef – temperatures have to be controlled, there's a creative process to go through, you have to understand your environment. There's a connection between the two crafts.

And, actually, what I have learnt about ceramics has helped me to understand my own job, in some respects. It's not just about serving great food, but also about the environment people eat it in. The people who create our crockery see that too: they come and visit the pub, and they take in the colours and textures of everything that's here. That way, we build something truly unique, together.

Milk toffee tart

with old English spices & burnt grapefruit sorbet

This tart is inspired by a traditional Kent dessert, gypsy tart; a rich, cooked-out, sugary tart. It's absolutely delicious.

Normally, it's made with evaporated milk and dark muscovado sugar, but for The Hand & Flowers version I liked the idea of using a more unrefined sugar. So, we decided to use grated palm sugar, to give the tart a slightly darker, more rustic taste.

The tart is extremely sweet, so the dusting of an incredible spice mix on top of it counterbalances that. The mix has nutmeg in it; that was an easy one for me. But I wanted another spice to lift the flavour of the tart even further. Cloves seemed a natural choice, as both cloves and nutmeg are old-fashioned spices that have been used in traditional English puddings for centuries. The final element of our spice-dust was star anise, a great favourite of mine.

Our former head chef, Aaron Mulliss, suggested a burnt grapefruit sorbet to help cut through the tart's sweetness in another way; it is created by toasting grapefruits under the grill until they go completely black. This imparts them with an incredible bitterness that underpins the sorbet.

The dessert works because it gives you polar opposites of flavour: intense acidity and intense sweetness. They almost clash but are brought together by a sprinkling of grated orange zest. The tart has proper elegance and, above all, it tastes gorgeous.

Burnt grapefruit sorbet

12 pink grapefruit
9 medium free-range egg yolks
75g dextrose
75g caster sugar

Preheat the grill to high. Halve the grapefruit and place, cut side up, on a baking tray. Grill until caramelised and almost blackened. Set aside until cool enough to handle, then squeeze the juice; you need 500ml.

Pour the pink grapefruit juice into a saucepan and bring to the boil. Meanwhile, whisk the egg yolks, dextrose and sugar together in a bowl to combine. Now pour on the hot grapefruit juice, whisking as you do so.

Return the mixture to the saucepan and cook over a medium-low heat, stirring constantly, until the mixture reaches 82°C (check the temperature with a digital probe).

Pass through a fine chinois into a container, cover the surface closely with baking parchment to prevent a skin forming and leave to cool.

Once cooled, pour into a Pacojet beaker and freeze overnight.

Before serving, churn the sorbet for 2 hours and place back in the freezer, ready to serve.

Orange tuiles

35g unsalted butter, softened
100g caster sugar
35g plain flour
Finely grated zest and juice
of ½ orange

Cream the butter and sugar together in a bowl until pale and smoothly combined. Stir in the orange zest and juice, then add the flour and stir to bring the mixture together.

Wrap in cling film and rest in the fridge for 1 hour.

Preheat the oven to 190°C/Fan 170°C/Gas 5. Line a baking sheet with a silicone mat.

Spread the tuile mixture very thinly and evenly on the silicone mat to a 3mm thickness. Bake for 15 minutes, then remove and cut into perfect 4cm squares while still slightly warm.

Leave the tuiles to cool and set, then carefully break into the squares.

Sweet pastry case

250g plain flour
A pinch of sea salt
100g icing sugar
25g ground almonds
25g feuilletine flakes
150g unsalted butter, chilled
and diced
60g free-range beaten eggs
(about 1½ medium)
2 medium egg yolks, beaten, to seal

Put the flour, salt, icing sugar, ground almonds and feuilletine flakes into a blender and blitz to a fine powder. Add the butter and blitz briefly until the mixture resembles fine crumbs. Pour in the beaten eggs and process briefly to form a smooth dough.

Remove the dough from the blender and wrap in cling film. Flatten slightly and rest in the fridge for 1 hour.

Unwrap the pastry, roll out thinly and use to line a 23cm loose-based tart tin. Leave to rest in the fridge for a further 1 hour.

Preheat the oven to 180°C/Fan 160°C/Gas 4. Line the tart case with a disc of baking parchment and fill with baking bean or rice grains. Bake the tart case blind in the oven for 30 minutes.

Remove the baking beans or rice and paper. Brush the inside of the pastry case with egg yolk to seal it and bake for a further 5 minutes to dry the base. Cool on a wire rack.

Milk toffee filling

1 litre sweetened condensed milk
375g palm sugar, grated
3 sheets of bronze leaf gelatine

Pour the condensed milk into a Thermomix, add the palm sugar and set on 90°C for 35 minutes.

About 10 minutes before the time is up, soak the gelatine in a shallow dish of cold water to soften. With 3 minutes to go, squeeze out the excess water from the gelatine, then add it to the hot sweet milk base.

When the time is up, the filling is ready to use.

Old English spice mix

6 cloves
6 star anise
1 nutmeg, freshly grated
40g icing sugar

Toast the cloves and star anise in a dry frying pan over a medium-low heat for a few minutes until they smell fragrant. Tip onto a plate and leave to cool.

Blitz the toasted spices to a powder in a spice grinder, then tip into a small bowl, add the grated nutmeg and icing sugar and stir to mix. Set aside until ready to serve.

To assemble & serve

A little finely grated orange zest

Using a sieve or dredger, dust the surface of the cooled tart with the Old English spice mix. Cut into slices, place a portion on each plate and top with a little orange zest.

Lay an orange tuile next to the tart slice and top with a rocher of burnt grapefruit sorbet. Serve at once.

To bake the tart

Preheat the oven to 165°C/Fan 145°C speed 2/Gas 3.

Pour the warm milk toffee filling into the tart case. Bake in the oven for 10 minutes, then lower the setting to 135°C, Fan 115°C, Gas 1 and bake for a further 1 hour.

Turn the oven off and leave the tart to finish cooking in the residual heat and cool down.

Raspberry & rose water trifle

with white chocolate cremosa & raspberry sorbet

Trifle is one of those great British desserts that you can easily elevate to a more sophisticated level because it's got so many elements to play around with. For a chef with a restaurant, that's super-enticing!

Raspberries are a great British berry: intense, sweet, delicious. When I was learning my trade at Stephen Bull in London's St Martin's Lane, around 20 years ago, I worked with an Australian couple, Nat and Kev, who were both really good cooks and they had this wonderful recipe for raspberry and rose geranium sorbet. It was absolutely delicious and I remember vividly tasting that fruit and flower combination for the first time; the intense fruitiness of the raspberry shot with that delicate headiness of the rose geranium. The thought of using flowers blew my mind.

Because it was such a pivotal moment for me as a chef, that flavour combination stuck in my memory bank for ages. Eventually I began to think about how to get something close to it into a dessert for The Hand & Flowers. Creating a trifle was a logical way to go.

Naturally, the trifle starts with a raspberry and rose jelly, which is topped with a white chocolate cremosa (this is similar to a crème anglaise), raspberry pulp, toasted brioche crumb, custard and crème fraîche.

Having a white chocolate cremosa as part of the trifle works brilliantly: the chocolate, raspberry and rose water are lovely flavours to bring together, making me think of Turkish delight. Those lush flavours help to elevate what is essentially a traditional trifle into something very special.

Raspberry sorbet

150ml water
50g liquid glucose
100g icing sugar
500g raspberry purée
   (freshly made or Boiron)

Put the water, liquid glucose and icing sugar into a saucepan, heat to dissolve the sugar and bring to the boil. Remove from the heat and pour onto the raspberry purée in a bowl. Stir to combine and leave to cool.

Pour the mixture into a Pacojet beaker and freeze overnight.

Before serving, churn the sorbet for 2 hours and place back in the freezer, ready to serve.

Toasted brioche crumb

200g brioche, cut into cubes
50g ground almonds

Preheat the oven to 190°C/Fan 170°C low speed/Gas 5. Blitz the brioche in a blender to fine crumbs, then tip into a bowl. Add the ground almonds and mix together.

Spread the crumb mix out on a baking sheet and toast in the oven for about 20 minutes until dark golden, stirring a few times. Remove from the oven and set aside to cool.

Raspberry tuile

50g unsalted butter
125g icing sugar
75g raspberry purée (Boiron)
5g crimson food colouring
35g plain flour

Cream the butter and icing sugar together in a bowl until pale and smoothly combined. Stir in the raspberry purée and food colouring, then add the flour and stir to bring the mixture together.

Wrap the tuile mixture in cling film and rest in the fridge for 1 hour.

Preheat the oven to 180°C/Fan 160°C/Gas 4. Line a baking sheet with a silicone mat.

Spread the tuile mixture very thinly and evenly on the silicone mat to a 3mm thickness. Bake for 15 minutes.

Remove from the oven and, while still warm, cut the tuile sheet into strips, 8cm long and 1cm wide. Coil each strip around a thin tube to form a spiral.

Allow the tuile spirals to cool and then store in an airtight container, with silica gel to help keep them crisp and dry.

Raspberry & rose jelly

560g raspberries
30g caster sugar
2 rose flavour drops
90ml white wine
4 sheets of bronze leaf gelatine

Put 400g of the raspberries into a vacuum-pack bag with the sugar, rose flavour drops and white wine. Vacuum-seal the bag and immerse in a water-bath at 80°C for 30 minutes.

Open the bag and pour the fruit mixture into a muslin-lined chinois set over a bowl. Fold over the excess muslin and press with a weight. Place in the fridge overnight to extract the juice from the raspberries.

Then next day remove the fruit pulp from the cloth and set aside (it will be used in the trifle assembly). Measure the raspberry syrup; you should end up with 400ml.

Soak the gelatine in a dish of cold water to soften for 5–10 minutes.

Meanwhile, pour the raspberry syrup into a saucepan and bring to a simmer, then remove from the heat. Squeeze out the excess water from the gelatine, then add it to the hot syrup, stirring until fully melted.

Pass the raspberry liquid through a fine chinois into a warm jug and leave to cool slightly. Halve the remaining 160g raspberries and use to line the base of 8 individual glass serving dishes. Pour in enough raspberry jelly to just cover the berries. Chill in the fridge to set the jelly.

White chocolate cremosa

175g white chocolate, in pieces
185ml whole milk
60ml double cream
3 medium free-range egg yolks
25g caster sugar

Put the white chocolate into a large bowl and keep to one side.

Pour the milk and cream into a heavy-based saucepan and bring to the boil. Meanwhile, whisk the egg yolks and sugar together in a bowl to combine. Pour on the hot creamy milk, whisking as you do so.

Return the mixture to the saucepan and cook over a medium-low heat, stirring constantly, until the crème anglaise reaches 82°C (check the temperature with a digital probe).

Pass the cooked crème anglaise through a fine chinois onto the chocolate and stir until melted and smooth. Cover the surface closely with baking parchment to prevent a skin from forming and refrigerate overnight to firm up.

Custard

375ml double cream
1 vanilla pod
2 medium free-range eggs
15g caster sugar

Put the cream and vanilla pod into a heavy-based saucepan and bring to the boil over a medium heat. Remove from the heat and leave to infuse for 30 minutes.

In the meantime, beat the eggs and sugar together in a bowl until smoothly blended.

Bring the vanilla-infused cream back to the boil, then slowly pour onto the beaten egg mix, whisking as you do so to combine.

Pour back into the pan and cook, stirring constantly, over a medium-low heat until the custard thickens and reaches 88°C (use a digital probe to check the temperature).

Immediately remove from the heat and pass through a fine chinois into a clean bowl. Press a layer of cling film onto the surface to prevent a skin forming and leave the custard to cool for about 30 minutes until it is at room temperature.

Pour the custard into a high-powered jug blender (Vitamix) and blitz for 30 seconds; this will lighten it slightly.

To assemble & serve

400g thick crème fraîche
8 freeze-dried raspberries, crushed

Once the raspberry jelly has set in the dishes, pipe an even layer of white chocolate cremosa on top and spread evenly with a stepped palette knife. Place in the fridge to set.

Once the chocolate cremosa has firmed up, spoon a layer of the raspberry pulp on top of it and return to the fridge.

When ready to serve, scatter a layer of brioche crumb over the raspberry pulp layer and press to compact into a fairly even layer.

Pour the custard on top of the biscuit layer, leaving enough room for the final layer. Chill in the fridge until the custard is set.

Finally, pipe the crème fraîche on top of the custard, to cover it and smooth the surface using a warmed spatula.

Top with a quenelle of raspberry sorbet and a sprinkling of crushed freeze-dried raspberries. Finish with a spiral raspberry tuile and serve.

For reference

Fish stock

Makes 1 litre
1kg fish bones (turbot, brill
*   or similar)*
1 small onion, peeled and chopped
1 small leek, green tops removed,
*   washed and sliced*
½ fennel bulb, sliced
2 garlic cloves, peeled and sliced
1 bay leaf
1 sprig of thyme
6g white peppercorns
6g fennel seeds
6g coriander seeds
1 star anise

Put all of the ingredients into a stockpot or large saucepan. Cover with cold water, bring to the boil and skim off any impurities from the surface. Lower the heat and simmer for 20 minutes.

Remove from the heat and pass the stock through a fine chinois into a jug, then pass it through a sieve lined with 6 layers of muslin into a jug or bowl. Cover and chill until needed. Use within 3 days.

Chicken stock

Makes 5 litres
1.4kg chicken wings
1kg chicken carcasses
1 calf's foot, split
1 Spanish onion, peeled and chopped
1 carrot, peeled and roughly chopped
1 celery stick, chopped
1 garlic bulb, cut across in half,
*   through the equator*
600g tinned plum tomatoes

Preheat the oven to 205°C/Fan 185°C/Gas 6–7. Place the chicken wings and carcasses in a roasting tray and roast in the oven for 45 minutes–1 hour until dark brown and caramelised.

Transfer the roasted bones to a stockpot or large saucepan, add all the remaining ingredients and pour on enough cold water (about 8 litres) to cover. Bring to the boil and skim off any impurities from the surface. Lower the heat and simmer gently for 8 hours (or cook in a pressure cooker for 3 hours).

Pass the stock through a fine chinois into a jug and then through a sieve lined with 6 layers of muslin into a jug or bowl. Cover and chill until needed. Use within 3 days.

Chicken sauce

Makes 500ml
1.5kg chicken wings
5 litres chicken stock (see left)

Preheat the oven to 205°C/Fan 185°C/Gas 6–7. Put the chicken wings into a roasting tray and roast in the oven for 25–30 minutes until dark brown and caramelised.

Transfer the roasted bones to a stockpot or large saucepan, pour on the stock to cover and bring to the boil. Skim off the impurities that rise to the surface and simmer to reduce gently by half, skimming throughout.

Pass the stock through a fine chinois and then through a sieve lined with 6 layers of muslin into a bowl. Chill, to allow the fat to set on the surface, then remove the fat.

Pour the reduced stock into a clean pan. Bring to a simmer and reduce down until the sauce is thick enough to coat the back of a spoon.

Cover and chill until needed. Any sauce that is not being used within a day or so can be sealed in a vacuum-pack bag and kept in the fridge for up to a week.

Lamb sauce

Makes 500ml
3kg lamb bones, chopped
5 litres chicken stock (see opposite)

Preheat the oven to 205°C/Fan 185°C/Gas 6–7. Put the lamb bones into a large roasting tray and roast in the oven until dark brown and caramelised.

Transfer the roasted bones to a stockpot or large saucepan, pour on the stock to cover and bring to the boil. Skim off the impurities that rise to the surface and simmer to reduce gently by half, skimming throughout.

Pass the stock through a fine chinois and then through a sieve lined with 6 layers of muslin into a bowl. Chill, to allow the fat to set on the surface, then remove the fat.

Pour the reduced stock into a clean pan. Bring to a simmer and reduce down until the sauce is thick enough to coat the back of a spoon.

Cover and chill until needed. Any sauce that is not being used within a day or so can be sealed in a vacuum-pack bag and kept in the fridge for up to a week.

Pork sauce

Makes 500ml
3kg pork bones, chopped
5 litres chicken stock (see opposite)

Preheat the oven to 205°C/Fan 185°C/Gas 6–7. Put the pork bones into a large roasting tray and roast in the oven until dark brown and caramelised.

Transfer the roasted bones to a stockpot or large saucepan, pour on the stock to cover and bring to the boil. Skim off the impurities that rise to the surface and simmer to reduce gently by half, skimming throughout.

Pass the stock through a fine chinois and then through a sieve lined with 6 layers of muslin into a bowl. Chill, to allow the fat to set on the surface, then remove the fat.

Pour the reduced stock into a clean pan. Bring to a simmer and reduce down until the sauce is thick enough to coat the back of a spoon.

Cover and chill until needed. Any sauce that is not being used within a day or so can be sealed in a vacuum-pack bag and kept in the fridge for up to a week.

Venison sauce

Makes 500ml
Carcass from a saddle of venison, chopped
5 litres chicken stock (see opposite)

Preheat the oven to 205°C/Fan 185°C/Gas 6–7. Put the venison carcass into a large roasting tray and roast in the oven until dark brown and caramelised.

Transfer the roasted bones to a stockpot or large saucepan, pour on the stock to cover and bring to the boil. Skim off the impurities that rise to the surface and simmer for about an hour to reduce gently by half, skimming throughout.

Pass the stock through a fine chinois and then through a sieve lined with 3 layers of muslin into a bowl. Chill, to allow the fat to set on the surface, then remove the fat.

Pour the reduced stock into a clean pan. Bring to a simmer and reduce down until the sauce is thick enough to coat the back of a spoon.

Cover and chill until needed. Any sauce that is not being used within a day or so can be sealed in a vacuum-pack bag and kept in the fridge for up to a week.

Herb sauce

Makes 1.75 litres
(7 x 250ml batches)
A splash of vegetable oil
½ garlic bulb, cut across in half
through the equator
1 carrot, peeled and sliced
1 celery stalk, sliced
1 large banana shallot, peeled
and sliced
2 tsp fennel seeds
2 tsp dried herbes de Provence
100ml white wine
2.5 litres chicken stock (see page 400)

To finish each batch of sauce:
125g unsalted butter, diced
25ml balsamic vinegar
1 sprig of rosemary
1 sprig of thyme

Heat a splash of oil in a large saucepan over a medium-high heat. When hot, add the garlic, cut side down, and caramelise until a dark golden brown colour.

Add the carrot to the pan and cook until darkly caramelised. Remove the carrot and garlic from the pan and wipe the pan clean.

Return the caramelised garlic and carrot to the pan and add the celery, shallot, fennel seeds, dried herbs, white wine and chicken stock. Bring to the boil and reduce by one-third.

Pass through a chinois and then through a sieve lined with 3 layers of muslin into a jug or bowl. Cover and chill until needed.

Measure 250ml herb sauce base and pour into a saucepan. (You will have more sauce base than you need so freeze the rest in 250ml batches, in small vacuum-pack bags.)

Add the butter to the 250ml sauce base, along with the balsamic vinegar and herbs. Heat to melt the butter and bring to the boil. Reduce down; the sauce will resemble bubbling toffee. Once the bubbles start to slow down, remove from the heat and pass through a fine chinois into a clean pan. Keep warm until ready to serve.

Red wine sauce

Makes about 2 litres
(8 x 250ml batches)
3.5 litres chicken stock (see page 400)
75cl bottle red wine
1 tbsp redcurrant jelly
4 banana shallots, peeled and sliced
⅓ head of celery, finely sliced
170g frozen blackberries

To finish each batch of sauce:
125g unsalted butter, diced

Put the chicken stock, red wine and redcurrant jelly into a large saucepan and bring to the boil. Skim off any impurities that rise to the surface, then add the shallots, celery and blackberries. Bring back to a simmer and reduce by one-third.

Pass through a chinois and then through a sieve lined with 6 layers of muslin into a jug or bowl. Cover and chill until needed. Check the gelatine level before using to make the sauce.

Measure 250ml red wine base and pour into a saucepan. (You will have more sauce base than you need so freeze the rest in 250ml batches, in small vacuum-pack bags.)

Add the butter to the 250ml sauce base and heat to melt it. Bring to the boil and reduce down; the sauce will resemble bubbling toffee. Once the bubbles start to slow down, remove from the heat. Pass through a fine chinois into a clean pan. Keep warm until ready to serve.

If necessary, add a splash of water and heat to re-emulsify the sauce.

Hollandaise sauce

Makes 300g
250g unsalted butter
2 medium free-range egg yolks
30ml double cream
1 tbsp shallot purée (see page 404)
20ml Cabernet Sauvignon
*   red wine vinegar*
Juice of ½ lemon, or to taste
Sea salt and cayenne pepper

Place the butter in a saucepan over a low heat to melt slowly and separate. Skim off the froth from the surface.

Carefully pour the clear yellow butter into a jug, leaving the milky layer behind. Allow the clarified butter to cool slightly, until warm but not hot. Reserve the buttermilk too.

Meanwhile, put the egg yolks, cream and shallot purée into a heatproof bowl and set over a bain-marie. Whisk until pale and thickened to create a thick sabayon.

Remove from the heat and slowly ladle the warm clarified butter into the sabayon, whisking constantly as you do so. Once the hollandaise is fully emulsified, slowly add the buttermilk, whisking to incorporate (you won't come across this in a classic recipe but we have found it helps to stop the sauce splitting).

Season with the wine vinegar and salt, cayenne and lemon juice to taste. Pass through a chinois into a container and keep warm until ready to serve.

Beurre blanc

Makes 200ml
125ml white wine
60ml white wine vinegar
2 shallots, peeled and sliced
50ml double cream
185g unsalted butter, diced
A generous squeeze of lemon juice
Sea salt and freshly ground
*   white pepper*

Put the white wine, wine vinegar and shallots into a small heavy-based pan, bring to a simmer and reduce by two-thirds. Transfer to a blender and purée until smooth.

Return to the cleaned pan, add the cream and reduce by half. Over a low heat, whisk in the butter, a piece at a time. Add the lemon juice and season with salt and pepper to taste.

Pass through a fine chinois into a jug or bowl. Serve at once, or cover and keep warm in a bain-marie but serve as soon as possible.

Clarified butter

Makes 200g
250g unsalted butter

Place the butter in a saucepan over a low heat to melt slowly and separate. Skim off the froth from the surface. Carefully pour the clear yellow liquid butter into a jug, leaving the milky layer behind. It will keep, covered, in the fridge for at least a week.

Butter emulsion

Makes 200ml
200g unsalted butter
100ml water
1 tsp salt

Heat the butter, water and salt in a pan until the butter is melted and bring to the boil. Let bubble until the bubbles slow down then remove from the heat. The emulsion is now ready to use, or you can allow it to cool and reheat before using.

Beurre noisette

Makes 100g
100g unsalted butter
2 tsp lemon juice
Sea salt and freshly ground pepper

Heat the butter in a pan until melted and foaming, and you can detect a toasty smell from the caramelising butter. Add the lemon juice and season with salt and pepper to taste. Keep warm until ready to use.

Pickling liquor

Makes 800ml
500ml white wine vinegar
½ cinnamon stick
2 star anise
1 clove
¾ tsp white peppercorns
1 tsp fennel seeds
1 tsp coriander seeds
250g caster sugar

Put all of the ingredients into a saucepan, heat to dissolve the sugar and bring to the boil.

Remove from the heat and set aside to infuse with the spices until cool, then pass through a sieve into a jug. Use as required.

Lyonnaise onions

Makes about 300g
60ml vegetable oil
1kg Spanish onions, peeled and sliced
10 white peppercorns, tied in a muslin bag
12g salt

Heat the oil in a heavy-based saucepan over a medium heat. Add the onions along with the muslin bag of peppercorns. Sprinkle with the salt and cook for 30–40 minutes until softened and darkly caramelised. Remove the muslin bag.

Shallot purée

Makes 500g
500g banana shallots, peeled and sliced
75ml white wine vinegar
75ml white wine

Put the shallots, wine vinegar and white wine into a vacuum-pack bag and place in a pressure cooker. Fill the cooker with water and cook on full pressure for 1½ hours.

Remove from the cooker and open the bag when it is cool enough to handle. Strain off the liquid into a clean saucepan, and tip the cooked shallots into a blender.

Reduce the liquor until thickened to a glaze, then pour the reduction onto the shallots and purée until smooth.

Use straight away or store in small vacuum-pack bags in the fridge and use within 1 week.

Chablis shallots

Makes 80g
4 banana shallots, peeled and finely diced
150ml Chablis (or similar white wine)

Put the shallots into a saucepan, pour on the wine and bring to a simmer. Let bubble until most of the wine has evaporated. Leave to cool in the liquor until ready to serve.

Puff pastry

Makes 1.8kg
500g unsalted butter, at room
    temperature
800g plain flour
3 tsp salt
425ml cold water
80g unsalted butter, melted

Place the 500g butter in a large
vacuum-pack bag, seal the bag 3cm
from the top and roll the butter
evenly to a square, 1cm thick.

In a large bowl, mix the flour, salt,
water and melted butter together
to form a smooth dough.

Roll out the dough on a floured
surface to a square, twice the
dimensions of the butter slab.

Take the butter slab out of the bag
and place it in the middle of the
dough, on the diagonal. Fold over the
dough corners to enclose the butter
and form a parcel. Dust lightly with
flour and roll the dough out thinly to
a rectangle, 1cm thick.

Fold the top third down and the
bottom third up, then roll out again
to a rectangle. Again, fold into thirds
then wrap in cling film and place in
the fridge overnight to rest.

The next day, repeat the rolling and
folding process. Chill again overnight.

Repeat the rolling and folding
process again on day 3, then rest in
the fridge for 1 hour.

The pastry is now ready to roll out,
glaze and cook. Any excess pastry
can be frozen for another occasion.

Salt crust dough

Makes 650g
330g plain flour
100g salt
3 medium free-range egg whites
100ml water

Put the flour and salt into a mixer
fitted with the paddle attachment.
Add the egg white and water and mix
together to form a smooth dough.

Wrap the dough in cling film and
rest in the fridge for 1 hour.

The dough is now ready to roll out
and use as required.

Soda bread

Makes 2 loaves
340g wholemeal flour
340g strong white bread flour,
    plus extra for dusting
2 tsp bicarbonate of soda
1½ tsp salt
1 tsp cracked black pepper
85g unsalted butter, softened
625ml buttermilk

Preheat the oven to 200°C/Fan
180°C/Gas 6.

Using a mixer fitted with the paddle
attachment, mix all the ingredients
together to combine and form a
smooth dough.

Divide in half, shape each portion
into a round (or other required
shape) and place on a baking sheet.
Dust each loaf with flour.

Bake in the oven for 50 minutes until
the loaves are golden brown and
sound hollow when tapped on the
base, indicating that they are cooked.
Leave to cool on a wire rack. Slice
and toast as required.

Glossary

Equipment

BAIN-MARIE
A warm water bath that cooks foods gently and evenly; we use it for delicate dishes like hollandaise sauce and beetroot royale. For delicate sauces, melting chocolate etc. you can set a heatproof bowl over a pan of barely simmering water, making sure the bowl doesn't touch the water. For delicate set custards, terrines etc., an ovenproof dish (or dishes) can be set in a roasting tin and warm water added to the tin until it reaches halfway up the side of the dish(es), then carefully placed in the oven to cook.

BLAST CHILLER
An appliance that cools things rapidly by using a fan to circulate cold air. It reduces the temperature of food much faster than a refrigerator and is used in commercial kitchens for that purpose. It is great for setting mousses or gels quickly, drawing out excess moisture from food, and chilling cooked vegetables to help preserve their colour.

DEHYDRATOR
A machine that dries ingredients slowly, by circulating air around them to remove moisture. The temperature and duration can be controlled precisely, ensuring consistent results. We have an Excalibur dehydrator, which we use for drying pork skins and veal tendons, and for preparing meringues, fruit crisps and crisp, deydrated cake, among other things.

HIGH-POWERED JUG BLENDER
A powerful blender that purées food very quickly and efficiently, giving extremely smooth results. We use a Vitamix vortex blender, which has a commercial-grade motor. It is perfect for creating ultra-smooth soups, such as our brilliant green parsley and lovage soup.

HIGH-POWERED FOOD PROCESSOR
A multi-function food processor with a strong motor and a high capacity is vital for grinding, chopping and puréeing ingredients quickly and consistently. We use Robot Coupe processors in our kitchens. They are essential to a lot of our mise-en-place, such as preparing sourdough crumb and thick emulsions.

HIGH-POWERED STICK BLENDER
A powerful hand-held stick blender is convenient to use for quick blending and aerating. We use a Bamix stick blender for tasks such as blending stabilisers into ice cream bases efficiently, and frothing soups at the last minute before serving.

ISI GUN/CREAM WHIPPER

A stainless-steel dispenser pressurised with gas cartridges that whips and aerates warm or cold ingredients. This is one of the first tools we used at The Hand & Flowers, for sweet and savoury whipped preparations, such as the Guinness foam on our moules marinière starter.

PACOJET

A machine that processes frozen ingredients to produce very smooth, light-textured sauces, mousses and sorbets. We use this for churning our ice creams and sorbets, as well as savoury items such as liver parfaits, mousses and butters.

PLANCHA

A large, flat metal hotplate that can heat pans rapidly, and can also cook ingredients placed directly on it. We use an Athanor plancha, which is a fantastic cooking surface because it offers a very consistent heat that's easy to control. It's great for achieving crispy skin on meat and fish, as well as caramelising vegetables.

STEAM OVEN

A type of oven (often called a combination or combi oven) that allows you to control the temperature and humidity very precisely, for steaming, baking or roasting. We find Rational combi ovens are the best. They can be programmed for each recipe, ensuring a consistent result every time. We use the steam function on our Rational oven for the first stage of our triple-cooked chips and many other tasks. The complete temperature control achieved with this type of oven is key to consistency in our kitchen.

THERMOMIX

A machine that can blend, process and chop as well as heat ingredients to precise temperatures – perfect for cooking and blending at the same time. We use it for making purées and custards, among other things.

VACUUM SEALER

A machine that extracts all the air out of a plastic bag, creating a vacuum and tightly sealing the ingredients inside. This prevents oxidisation, moisture loss and spoilage. It can be used to store ingredients or to cook them in a water-bath.

WATER-BATH

A temperature-controlled hot water bath, sometimes called a sous-vide machine, that allows very precise cooking of ingredients which have been vacuum-sealed in a sous-vide bag. *Sous vide* means 'under vacuum' in French.

We like to champion traditional cooking methods using pans, but we also find the water-bath a useful tool for certain foods that need to be cooked exactly to the right temperature, such as loin of venison and pork tenderloins. We also use it for poaching truffles, cooking our chicken liver parfait, slow-cooking pork belly, and many other recipes through the book.

Specialist ingredients

ANTIOXIDANT GEL POWDER (SOSA)
A flavourless white powder which prevents ingredients that are inclined to discolour once peeled and/or cut and exposed to air, from oxidising and turning brown. We use it when we are preparing apples, pears and Jerusalem artichokes, for example, to ensure they retain their original colour.

BRONZE LEAF GELATINE
Gelatine is a setting agent derived from pork products, which is used for setting gels, mousses and many other preparations. Leaf gelatine produces a finer set than powdered gelatine, and is available in different grades. Bronze is the grade used in most professional kitchens.

DEHYDRATED PORK SKIN (SOSA, AIRBAG GRANET)
Small freeze-dried pieces of pork skin that puff up like mini pork scratchings when you deep-fry them in oil. We use them to add texture and crunch to dishes.

DEXTROSE
A type of powdered sugar derived from corn, which is sometimes used as a substitute for ordinary sugar. It is chemically identical to glucose and less sweet than sugar. We use it to stabilise ice creams and reduce their sweetness, and to help pastry crusts caramelise.

GELBURGER (SOSA)
A gelling agent derived from seaweed, used to help ingredients adhere in dishes such as terrines. We use it to stick melon pieces together to make the melonberg (on page 314) for our warm pistachio sponge dessert. It can only be used in cold preparations.

GELLAN GUM POWDER TYPE F
A gelling agent made from gellan gum, which can be used to thicken or set preparations. Unlike gelatine, it retains its setting properties on heating. Type F is the most commonly used kind, which sets to a clear gel. We use it to make warm savoury jellies.

GLYCERINE
A sugar alcohol in the form of a clear, syrupy liquid, which has many culinary and scientific uses. We add it to sorbets and ice creams to prevent ice crystals from forming, and to duck liver parfaits as a stabiliser.

ISOMALT SUGAR
A sugar alcohol that resembles ordinary sugar and is often used as a substitute for it. Isomalt has a lower melting temperature than sugar and we use it to make tuiles with a glass-like appearance.

PRO SORBET
A stabiliser which reduces the formation of ice crystals in sorbets. Pro Crema does the same for ice creams.

TRANSGLUTAMINASE
A naturally occurring enzyme that bonds proteins together. Often called 'meat glue' in the restaurant industry, we use it to seal stuffed lemon sole fillets and red mullet.

TRISOL
A soluble fibre derived from wheat, which comes in powder form and is added to batters to give a crispy, crunchy texture after frying.

Index

Thanks

The Team

Our team – the people who have worked for us past and present – represent, for Beth and me, our single, biggest achievement at The Hand & Flowers. Collectively, they are what we're most proud of.

We opened The Hand & Flowers with just myself and two other chefs: Chris Mackett and Luke Butcher. Beth was front of house; and Adam Peacock (my friend, who is now the personal trainer on my diet and well-being TV programmes) was behind the bar. That was it. Today, the kitchen brigade's much larger! And many of them have been with us for years, so it makes me incredibly proud.

Chris is still with us as development chef, which means we've worked together for over 17 years now, going right back to our days at Adlard's in Norwich. He is the pivot around which many parts of the business revolve, whether that's working with me on the books, TV shows, food columns, events, Pub In The Park, pop-up restaurant spaces... You name it, Chris is involved in it.

Like Chris, so many of our staff have grown with us over the years. They've taken the business and run with it as if it's their own. And that's what makes what we've achieved so special: somehow we've managed to fuse personal and professional growth with The Hand & Flowers and its offspring. And we're still on this growing and learning curve with the team.

There are so many people who I could mention who have been anchors for the business. Lourdes Dooley and Aaron Mulliss, for example. There was a period when they were restaurant manager and head chef, respectively. Aaron joined when he was 25 and did 11 years with us before leaving last year; and Lourdes has been with us for 14 years.

Then there's Katie Mulliss, our restaurant manager who's grown with us over 11 years, and Jamie May, who's been with us for nine years and heads up The Hand's kitchen. He also came up through the ranks, starting off as demi chef de partie. He understands the DNA of The Hand & Flowers and he's creating a wonderful, warm, creative, modern working environment for our next generation of chefs.

Jamie understands that a modern kitchen is not always about 18-hour days and blood and guts and swearing and fire. He's got everyone down to eight shifts a week; plus he's got a breakfast manager in. He's really looking after the well-being of the chefs, worrying about their mental as well as their physical health.

In the old days, when I was younger, the kitchen was just about cooking and being a chef; much more of an alpha-male environment, I suppose. But Jamie's evolved it into a calmer space and that actually means it's a much more creative place. There is still a buzz and an enthusiasm, but as a working space it feels warmer, more twenty-first century.

THANKS

These days, it's not just about The Hand & Flowers. We've got six other businesses. We never expected things to expand the way they have, but our growth has meant that our staff have had more opportunities. Nick Beardshaw, for example: he's been with us for 10 years and is a phenomenal chef with a wonderful understanding of human beings: hugely respectful of people and very astute. He's gone from being the senior sous chef of The Hand & Flowers to opening The Coach in 2014 and receiving a Michelin star of his own. More recently, he took on probably the biggest opening that we've done – Kerridge's Bar & Grill.

What's great is that people often come to us from different backgrounds. Someone who's worked in Michelin-starred restaurants isn't always going to be the best person for us. A CV might be fantastic for showing experience, but it's a person's attitude that counts. Tom De Keyser, who is now head chef of The Coach, follows in Nick's incredible footsteps with a matching humility and warmth, and a great understanding of hospitality. He also has a degree in forensic science, something rarely found in a kitchen!

Aaron, who ended up as head chef at The Hand & Flowers, had previously been working in a bistro and at Virgin Mobile. And Ollie Brown, who left The Hand & Flowers as a sous chef, used to probe the sausages in the café at Waitrose before Ollie's mum introduced him to us. I met her at the doctor's not long after we opened The Hand & Flowers. We had a Michelin star at that point but there were just the three of us working in the kitchen. She said: 'My son's a chef, it would be good if he could come and spend some time with you.' So Ollie came in one Friday evening, into what was then our tiny little kitchen. He loved the buzz. Saturday morning, he was there again at 8am. I had to ask, 'Shouldn't you be at Waitrose?' He replied, 'Yeah, but I'm not going back.' All I could say was, 'Well, I haven't got a job for you, we can't afford it.' He kept coming back for a week, until it got to the point when I said, 'Well, I suppose we've got to pay you then!' He was with us, off and on, for seven years.

I could tell you so many stories like that: about people who've just bought into what we're doing here. I think it's because we've built our business on wholesome ethics. There's an honesty about our approach that people like. And it's made us very good at finding people who buy into what we ourselves believe in; and at retaining staff. That's something I'm so proud of.

And because there are a lot of people who have been working with us for years, they create a great energy in the business. They all own it, really. It's not just Beth and me. They're all a little piece of the business.

The Brewery

From the moment we opened The Hand & Flowers I've treated the pub as if we owned it: looked after it, loved it. But the truth is, Beth and I are tenants of a big brewery, Greene King, as we lease the pub from them.

Now, I'll be honest, breweries don't always get lots of pats on the back from their tenants, but Greene King has been 100% supportive of us, from the word go. I think the company could see that our ambition to make the pub a destination for food had great potential and they ran with our business plan. Looking back, I'm amazed they took a chance with us. I mean, bear in mind I was only 31 years old and as a couple Beth and I had no experience of the pub trade. Very green (if you'll pardon the pun) in the business sense.

That said, you didn't need to be Bill Gates to realise that the pub, when we first saw it, 'could do better', as school reports always say. It was closed two days a week, the turnover was on the low side and although it was a beautiful, picture-postcard pub it was just outside Marlow and so not on the circuit of wet-led pubs in the town centre. To us, it was obvious that The Hand & Flowers had to become about the food.

From day one, we've taken responsibility for The Hand & Flowers as if we owned every single brick. We've never gone to Greene King for anything. If the boiler has broken, if the roof leaked, we never phoned them up, we just repaired whatever needed fixing.

We've done things our way. And I think that helped when it came to building our relationship with them. They understood early on that we were bringing a return not to them but to their pub. We were giving value to their property, to the neighbourhood, to the space. They recognised that something outside the usual was happening when, 10 months in, we won the Michelin star – because 10 months in the grand scheme of a business isn't very long.

None of this is intended as an advert for Greene King… it's just how our relationship was at the beginning, and how it still is today.

The Community

Ideally, every restaurant and pub should be busy on a Friday, Saturday and Sunday. But it isn't the nights that will make it successful. It's the Monday, Tuesday and Wednesday lunches which decide that. Those are the services that keep places alive; they fill the gaps. And for that to happen, you need to be in an area where people can access your offering.

The Hand & Flowers has that in spades in Marlow. It's a busy little town west of London, which is also in close proximity to the countryside. It's commuter belt; it's affluent; it's very pretty and it's visited by people from nearby, for shopping, and from those from further afield for a day out.

As well as that, it's got residents who are very proud of their town. They've built a fantastic community based on families, schools and sport. At Christmas time, the town has an amazing late-night shopping event where they close the high street and have a fantastic Santa Fun Run. And in the

summertime, it has a rowing regatta, and cricket in the park. There's also a brilliant food festival called Pub In The Park that is all about embracing the community and the people who live in this area.

We've been able to harness the energy from all of these things and become a part of the Marlow community. That's meant we've always felt we have got support on our doorstep, irrespective of whether we happen to be busy or not.

When we opened The Hand & Flowers, we listened to the community and we got to know as many people as possible. We've supported local businesses, charities and schools; we sponsor the football team, Marlow FC. Marlow has a great kids' team, too.

For me (and of course I'm totally biased), Marlow is the most amazing place to be. A perfect Sunday is hanging out in the park, here, with my little man Acey; or going for breakfast at The Coach. Pubs are meeting places, places to hang out in, places that locals need to feel proud of: and if they are proud of you, they'll come through the doors whether it is tipping with rain or the most brilliantly sunny day.

This Book

This is a big list of thank yous. Firstly, to everybody at Bloomsbury and Absolute, and the other people on the publishing side, for taking my vision of this book and making it a reality. Thank you so much for your continued support – Nigel Newton, Natalie Bellos, Lisa Pendreigh, Xa Shaw Stewart, Nicola Hill, Amanda Shipp, Ellen Williams, Donough Shanahan, Laura Brodie, Janet Illsley, Will Webb and Greg Heinimann. And last, but most definitely not least, my brilliant friend and Bath's favourite wine and cognac collector, Jon Croft (hero).

To the guys who have got the food and styling completely in tune with The Hand & Flowers, Lydia McPherson and the wizard that is Cristian Barnett, as well as Chris Horwood and Lisa Paige-Smith. Thank you for making everything look so beautiful. To the home ec team who worked on the photoshoot – Nicole Herft, Rosie Mackean, Becks Wilkinson, Alex James Gray and Ben Boxall – thank you for your commitment and drive, all of your work is hugely appreciated. And big thanks to Adrienne Tilzey and

Thomas Rhodes, and everybody at Twickenham Stadium for letting us use the kitchens and the restaurant on a daily basis.

A huge thank you to Borra Garson and Louise Leftwich from DML for keeping things in check!

A massive, ginormous, colossal shout out and hugs to Amanda Afiya. Her commitment, heart, soul and love for getting my words into writing have the same passion and drive as The Hand & Flowers. Amanda, you have been a great friend for many years and I cannot thank you enough for everything that you have done to make this book so special. You are a beautiful person. Thank you.

To my right-hand man, the guy who opened the doors with me on day one, who tirelessly and relentlessly, without question and with complete loyalty, has helped drive The Hand & Flowers, our associated businesses and everything that we do into the space where we are now. A man whose passion and drive for food is unparalleled, and without whom The Hand & Flowers most definitely wouldn't be where it is today. The unsung hero behind the scenes, the guy who has put all of these recipes together and who I am so proud to say is part of our family. He is a brilliant food-led chef, but most importantly a devoted friend. Christopher Mackett, this book is as much yours as mine. Love you and thank you.

To Lourdes Dooley and Aaron Mulliss, who have been my eyes and ears out front and in the kitchen through the whole transitional period, running with my vision and making it a reality. Thank you both very much.

And, of course, a massive thank you to my supersonic sidekick, Alex Reilly, who brings everything together in such a thoughtful and diligent way.

To The Hand & Flowers crew, past and present; everyone who has ever worked at The Hand & Flowers, even if you only lasted a couple of hours. You are the anecdotes, stories, talks of triumph, fun, laughter, tears, pain and graft. Every one of you is a brick in this building. You are all magical and wonderful and I cannot thank everyone enough for buying into the dream and the journey of turning this tiny little pub into something so very special. We have done this together, and you are all amazing. If I listed everybody's name, it would take another book to do it. You all know how special you are and I cannot thank you enough for turning this rough diamond into a shiny stone.

ABOUT THE AUTHOR

About the Author

Tom Kerridge worked as a chef in restaurants across Britain before deciding to set out on his own and take over a rundown pub in the quiet Buckinghamshire town of Marlow. He opened The Hand & Flowers with his wife Beth in 2005, and it went on to become the first (and only) pub in the world to acquire two Michelin stars. In 2014 he opened a second pub in Marlow, The Coach, which was followed by The Butcher's Tap. Most recently, he and his core team launched Kerridge's Bar & Grill, which is housed in Corinthia London, and The Bull & Bear in Manchester. He is the author of many best-selling books for the home cook and regularly presents primetime cookery shows on British television. Tom lives in Marlow with Beth, their son Acey and their two dogs.

BLOOMSBURY ABSOLUTE
Bloomsbury Publishing Plc
50 Bedford Square, London, WC1B 3DP, UK

BLOOMSBURY, BLOOMSBURY ABSOLUTE, the Diana logo and the Absolute Press
logo are trademarks of Bloomsbury Publishing Plc

First published in Great Britain 2020

A catalogue record for this book is available from the British Library

Library of Congress Cataloguing-in-Publication data has been applied for

ISBN: HB: 978-1-4729-3539-7; eBook: 978-1-4729-3545-8

10 9 8 7 6 5 4 3 2

Project Editor: Janet Illsley
Design and Art Direction: Will Webb Design
Photographs: Cristian Barnett
Cover Design: Greg Heinimann
Food Styling: Chris Mackett, Nicole Herft, Rosie Mackean,
    Becks Wilkinson, Alex James Gray, Ben Boxall
Prop Styling: Lydia McPherson
Index: Hilary Bird

Printed and bound in Italy by Graphicom Srl

To find out more about our authors and books visit www.bloomsbury.com
and sign up for our newsletters